NO
BORDERS

PLAYING RUGBY FOR
IRELAND

NO BORDERS

PLAYING RUGBY FOR
IRELAND

TOM ENGLISH

This paperback edition first published in 2016 by
ARENA SPORT
An imprint of Birlinn Limited
West Newington House
10 Newington Road
Edinburgh
EH9 1QS

in association with

POLARIS PUBLISHING LTD
c/o Turcan Connell
Princes Exchange
1 Earl Grey Street
Edinburgh
EH3 9EE

www.arenasportbooks.co.uk
www.polarispublishing.com

ISBN: 978-1-909715-46-2
EBOOK ISBN: 978-0-85790-844-5

British Library Cataloguing-in-Publication Data
A catalogue record for this book is available from the British Library

Designed and typeset by Polaris Publishing, Edinburgh

Printed and bound by Gutenberg Press Limited, Malta

CONTENTS

SELECTED BIBLIOGRAPHY

BOOKS

Diffley, Sean, *The Men In Green*. Pelham Books, 1973
English, Alan, *Grand Slam*. Penguin Ireland, 2009
Fallon, Ivan, *The Player: The Life of Tony O'Reilly*. Hodder & Stoughton, 1994
Fanning, Brendan, *From There To Here*. Gill & Macmillan, 2007
Foley, Anthony, *Axel: A Memoir*. Hachette Books Ireland, 2008
Hayes, John, *My Story*. Simon & Schuster, 2012
Johnson, Tony and McConnell, Lynn, *Behind the Silver Fern*, Polaris Publishing, 2016
Keane, Moss, *Rucks, Mauls & Gaelic Football*. Merlin Publishing, 2005
McBride, Willie John, *The Story Of My Life*. Portrait, 2004
McKinney, Stewart, *Voices From The Back Of The Bus*. Mainstream Publishing, 2010
O'Callaghan, Donncha, *Joking Apart*. Transworld Ireland, 2011
O'Driscoll, Brian, *The Test*. Penguin Ireland, 2014
O'Gara, Ronan, *My Autobiography*. Transworld Ireland, 2008
O'Gara, Ronan, *Unguarded*. Transworld Ireland, 2013
O'Reilly, Peter, *The Full Bag Of Chips*. The O'Brien Press, 2004
Quinlan, Alan, *Red Blooded*. Irish Sports Publishing, 2010
Reason, John (Ed.), *How to Beat the All Blacks: The 1971 Lions Speak*. Aurum Press, 2005
Robbie, John, *The Game Of My Life*. Pelham Books, 1989
Scally, John, *The Giants of Irish Rugby*. Mainstream Publishing, 1996
Sexton, Johnny, *Becoming A Lion*. Penguin Ireland, 2013
Ward, Tony, *The Good, The Bad And The Rugby*. Blackwater Press, 1993

OTHER SOURCES

'Friends Reunited', David Kelly, *Irish Independent*
'Remembering 2007 – The One That Got Away', Gerry Thornley, *Irish Times*
'My room, your room: Mike Gibson MBE and Elaina Davis chat about life in Room Q4A, Queens' College Cambridge'. alumni.cam.ac.uk
'Unassuming Simon Easterby', Gerry Thornley, *Irish Times*
'Dockland Express', Peter O'Reilly, *Sunday Times*
'The Day Warren Gatland Gambled On The Future Of Irish Rugby', The42.ie Rugby
'An All-Time Great Comfortably At Home In Any Era', David Kelly, *Irish Independent*
'All It Takes', 3.ie with Paul O'Connell
'All It Takes', 3.ie with Robbie Henshaw
Rob Kearney Interview, *Tatler Man*
'Crotty And The Try That Still Haunts Schmidt', Ruaidhri O'Connor, *Irish Independent*
Brian O'Driscoll Interview, Newstalk Off The Ball
'Brian O'Driscoll: Ireland's Rugby Ironman', Huw Richards. *New York Times*
'Brian O'Driscoll: He changed Irish rugby's mindset for good', Donald McRae. *Guardian*
'One Hand On The Dimmer Switch',Brendan Fanning, *Sunday Independent*
Joe Schmidt Interview, Newstalk Off The Ball
'From Perfect Start To Darkest Finale', Gerry Thornley, *Irish Times*
'Ginger McLoughlin: Limerick's Rugby Legend', Dave McMahon, *Politico*
Rugby Interview with Tom Kiernan. *Politico*
'Green Behind The Ears, Neil Francis', *Sunday Tribune*
'You Can't Send Me Off: Des Fitzgerald Interview', David Walsh, *Sunday Times*
'Tamer of the Aussies: Ken Goodall Interview', Peter O'Reilly, *Sunday Times*
'The Past Is Never So Easy To Forget', *Irish Independent*.
Matt Cooper Today FM interview with Paul O'Connell, November 2015

PHOTO CREDITS

InphoPhotography: I, 10, 12, 18, 68, 73, 92, 98, 101, 103, 105, 108, 110, 112, 114, 115, 117, 119, 124, 128, 131, 133, 135, 136, 138, 140, 144, 148, 158, 163, 164, 168, 172, 177, 184, 188, 193, 196, 200, 201, 204, 209, 211 (x2), 212, 213, 218, 220, 221, 226, 229, 231, 232, 233, 234, 237, 240, 243, 244, 247, 248, 249, 250, 252, 254, 255, 257, 260, 261, 264, 273, 274, 286, 288, 294, 296, 300, 304, 308, 310, 313, 314, 315, 318, 320, 325, 326, 327, 328, 329, 336, 340, 341, 345, 349, 351, 353
Getty Images: 25, 69, 209, 320, 329
Colorsport: 59, 99
Fotosport: 168, 247, 249, 254, 261, 268, 270, 272, 273, 281, 282, 285, 288, 289, 290, 304, 313, 314, 315, 317, 318, 320, 326, 333, 336, 337, 352

For Jim Beveridge – he belonged to Glasgow

ACKNOWLEDGEMENTS

How do you go about writing a post-war history of the Ireland rugby team, a 70-year stretch that begins in 1945 with Jack Kyle taking his first steps in the international game and ends in 2015 with Paul O'Connell about to take his last?

The only way to tell a story like this was for me to get the hell out of the way and let the players tell it for me. An oral history, if you like.

The starting point was Kyle. I rang him and he was precisely as everybody said he would be – humble, kind and compelling. Next: Jimmy Nelson, another of the storied 1948 Grand Slam team. Jimmy was ninety-two years old when I interviewed him and his joy at winning, and frustration at losing, was the same as it was all those years ago when he was setting the agenda in the middle of the Irish scrum. I spoke to Jim McCarthy the same week. Another Grand Slam winner in 1948, another rugby great, another gentleman.

Sadly, all three have passed away since I interviewed them. What a rugby legacy they leave behind.

I'm indebted to so many people, but I've got to start with all the players, past and present, who gave so incredibly generously of their time and spoke so honestly about their years in the Ireland jersey. I interviewed 115 players (and coaches) and gathered 140 hours of recordings. We spoke about the highs and the lows, the euphoria, the insecurity and the slapstick, but Ireland's rugby story doesn't begin and end at the whitewash on the pitch.

It veers into politics and religion and the complexities of a united Ireland team that could have buckled and broken on numerous occasions during The Troubles but didn't because of the strength of character of some remarkable men. As the Triple Crown-winning Ulster wing, Trevor Ringland, said, 'I refused to let symbols like flags and songs be hijacked by extremists – on both sides. To me, rugby was trying to build bridges while others were destroying them. We were finding a way of working together in friendship.'

On a seventy-year journey there were bound to be gaps in the narrative. Eight years as the Irish rugby correspondent for the *Sunday Times* gave me some material to draw on, but more than that, those years gave me friends that I could pester for help. And pester them I did.

I leaned on the contacts and the journalism of Brendan Fanning of the *Sunday Independent* and Peter O'Reilly of the *Sunday Times*, two of my closest colleagues and pals back in the glory days in the Brill Building. I'm thankful to them and to so many other journalists who have covered Irish rugby down through the years in all forms of media. There are too many to name here.

Thanks to everyone at the ever-excellent *Rugby World,* especially Sarah Mockford. Mark Hendry, Craig Fergusson and Mark McDougall helped me transcribe some interviews towards the end and I only wish I discovered them right at the start. I want to thank Mark Stanton who introduced me to Peter Burns at Arena Sport and Polaris Publishing. Pete's love of rugby and his passion for this project has been a massive help along the way. He understood that writers – particularly this one – have a pretty loose grasp of the meaning of the word 'deadline' and was a joy to work with it.

My brother, Alan, is a constant source of support and inspiration. *Grand Slam*, his outstanding book about Ireland's famous 2009 season, was important to me as was *Stand Up And Fight: When Munster Beat the All Blacks* and his work as ghost on *The Test* – Brian O'Driscoll's autobiography. As the brains of our family – and with, as she may have mentioned once, an A in honours English – our sister, Sinead, could write a best-seller if she put her mind to it. She's a force of positivity – the best Sis in the world.

Our parents, Tom and Anne, have given us love and encouragement and a lifetime of laughter. It's not possible to thank them enough, but we'll give it a try next time we're in Limerick. The Scotland wing of the family hope to visit a lot more often now that the book is finished.

While we're there we can catch-up with the likely lads – Cathal, Dotsy, Gliggy, Gussie, Henny, Joe, Mucky, Rob, Seamus.

The last word goes to my wife, Lynn, and our children, Eilidh and Tom. This book took a lot longer than promised. I'd have been a wreck if it wasn't for your love and encouragement. Honestly, it'll be many years before you have to hear the words 'working on the book' again. I mean it this time...

Tom English, 2016

EYES IN THE BACK OF HIS HEAD

Joe Schmidt's reputation as a Midas is hard-earned and well-deserved. From Manawatu on New Zealand's north island, to Clermont in France, to winning trophy after trophy in his years at Leinster, everything the Kiwi touches seems to turn to gold – or silver. In 2013, Schmidt wasn't so much appointed as Ireland coach as carried shoulder high into the job by players at the province that achieved greatness on his watch.

Those Leinster guys understood what he was about. The forensic eye for detail, the extraordinary work-ethic, the obsessive demand for perfection. The Brian O'Driscolls, the Johnny Sextons, the Rob Kearneys were aware of what was coming when the New Zealander began a new era in the history of the Ireland team. Others, less so.

Paul O'Connell: I knew very little about Joe. I knew from talking to the Leinster players and reading their interviews in the papers that he was very impressive and that he was on a different level, but it's hard to imagine it until you actually experience it.

Andrew Trimble: The Leinster lads knew exactly what he was like but the rest of us were playing catch-up. We'd heard a lot about him and we were all reading into everything. In his first autumn, one player was in the team-room and he was kinda slouched back on the sofa and when Joe walked in he sat up straight. Bolt upright. It was like the head teacher had walked into the room. That made me realise how aware his players were of how aware *he* was, if you know what I mean. It's a silly one, but it's a reflection of his impact.

Johnny Sexton: At times, it's almost like he's a voice in my head. When I'm analysing my own game and I spot myself doing something wrong I can hear him pointing it out to me. You'd go in on the Monday and there's a video session and nothing is said and you'd go in on the Tuesday and there's another video session and nothing is said and you think, 'Great, I got away with it,' and then it's the last

Opposite: Joe Schmidt.

clip on a Thursday and this thing comes up. And you think, 'Ah Jesus, I thought I had him for once.'

Rob Kearney: There's a touch of the obsessive about him. Rugby seems to be his love and drives him on every day, like a lot of us. There's a touch of genius as well.

Rory Best: He misses nothing. You know the one about the key card holder?

Paul O'Connell: The room key at the hotel comes in a little sleeve with your name and room number on it and somebody dropped it in the corridor of the Carton House, our training base with Ireland.

Conor Murray: It wasn't me.

Rory Best: Joe found it and brought into the team meeting. He says, 'Just to let you know that somebody on their way to their room dropped their key card holder on the floor and that sort of stuff won't be tolerated. If we're sloppy off the pitch then we'll be sloppy on it'. I was sitting there going, 'Oh my God.'

Paul O'Connell: He said it reflected badly on an Irish international player that he was almost littering in a hotel. And he had a point.

Conor Murray: I actually don't know who it was, but the story of the key card holder gave everybody a clear view of what Joe was trying to get across and what he wanted from us. He was going to run a tight ship.

Tommy Bowe: I learned pretty early on that Joe has eyes in the back of his head.

In Schmidt's first season, Ireland won four games out of five and took the Six Nations title in a dramatic denouement in Paris. It was Brian O'Driscoll's final day in the green jersey, but it was just the start of Schmidt's remarkable influence.

In the autumn of 2014, an Irish team weakened by injury walloped South Africa in Dublin and then followed it up with a thrilling victory over Australia. They rose up the world rankings and started to be spoken about as a dark horse for the World Cup in 2015.

In the spring of 2015, the Six Nations went to the wire again. On a last day, almost unimaginable in its drama, Ireland won a second successive title and sparked a debate about where this era stood in the history of the Ireland team.

Those with the longest memories took us back to another age, sixty-six years before. It was 1949 and it was the last – and only other – time that Ireland had won the Championship back-to-back. It was a period so far removed from the modern game and the cosmic preparation as typified by Schmidt; it was an innocent time, but a great time.

These were the originals. The immortals. The standard-bearers for all who followed. In the telling of the post-war story of how the Ireland team got to where it is today, via heartache, embarrassment, rancour, tragedy and isolated passages of glory, there is a natural starting point, a man who is no longer with us but whose class transcends the eras: Kyle.

ONE

PHONING THE WIFE, IS IT? AH, BALLS

Jack Kyle: Some international rugby matches were played in the late war years, a few here and there, nothing major and there were no caps given out. Ireland played the British Army at Ravenhill and I remember as a schoolboy going and watching some of those games and never imagining for a moment that I would ever play for Ireland. I loved my rugby, but I never dreamt that big.

Bertie O'Hanlon: Jack Kyle. John Wilson Kyle. Nature's gentleman.

Jack Kyle: The first time I played at Lansdowne Road was for Ulster schools against Leinster schools. My goodness, what a wonderful thrill going all the way to Dublin to play rugby. I was getting out brochures and reading about where I should go and what I should see - The Book of Kells and all these other things in my big journey south.

Bertie O'Hanlon: He had a wonderful pair of hands, you know. They were like glue. He was a brilliant player. And you couldn't help but like him.

Jim McCarthy: Nobody could touch Jack. He'd play games and he wouldn't need to have his shorts laundered afterwards.

Jack Kyle: Those of us who ever achieved anything on a rugby field were fortunate in a way to be born with a certain ability. We had the right sort of genes. As far as my own game was concerned it was at least 85% in-born. A lot of it was instinct. I never quite knew why I was doing something, but I did it anyway. The first time I wore the green jersey was mid-December, 1945. It was an Irish XV against the British Army in Belfast. I can still remember lying in bed in the morning and thinking, 'What happens if I keep dropping passes and play an absolute shambles of a game?' I was only a young lad then. God, I remember it clearly.

Crito, rugby correspondent writing in the Irish Press: *In one glorious swoop the Irish XV wiped out memories of four defeats in a row at the hands of powerful British Army*

Opposite: On the road to the 1948 Grand Slam: the Ireland players are swarmed by the crowd after their victory over England at Twickenham.

combinations with as devastating and convincing a victory as has ever been scored by
an Irish side. Kyle, a nineteen year old youth just out of school, positively sparkled on
this, his first appearance on an Irish team.

Jack Kyle: There was absolutely no planning, ever. If you saw the opportunity, you went for it. If there was no opportunity you had to come up with something else. It was totally spontaneous. In 1946, the Five Nations started. Unofficially anyway. If you look at the record books, those games don't exist. But they were real enough to us. I'm pretty sure I didn't imagine the French second-rows and back-rows running hard at me in that first game – Jean Prat and Guy Basquet, Robert Soro and Alban Moga, who went by the rather ironic nickname, Bambi. We didn't know anything about them at the time, but we knew they came from exotic-sounding places – St Vincent-de-Tyross, Brive-la-Gaillarde, Fontenay-sous-Bois. It was all very glamorous – until they hit you.

Jack Kyle.

Crito: It's thirty-three years since we gave the French rugby team a real licking, but if our strong suits turn out trumps at Lansdowne Road tomorrow when we renew international relations with the French after a break of fifteen years, not only should we beat them but we may go near repeating that glorious 24-nil victory we scored in Cork in 1913.

Jack Kyle: We met on the Friday afternoon, worked out our signals and passed the ball up and down a field a few times with the other three-quarters. Nothing too strenuous. Then we went back to the hotel, which was usually the Shelbourne, and had a team meeting which was run by the captain because there was no coach. The captain was sitting up the front and basically saying 'Has anybody got any ideas for tomorrow?'

Crito: The French team which we thought so harmless gave Irish rugby a rare shaking at Lansdowne Road on Saturday. No adequate excuses can be offered for our defeat.

Jack Kyle: It was 4-3.

Crito: I don't want to detract from the merit of the French side, but I do think that our side gave a fairly miserable exhibition.

Jack Kyle: When you were chosen to play, nobody phoned or telegrammed. We'd all listen to Radio Athlone on a Sunday evening to find out if you were on the next team or it often just appeared in the paper and then you'd get a letter from the IRFU on the Tuesday or the Wednesday which said 'You have been chosen to play for your country' and that 'your jersey will be provided at the beginning of the game but must be returned afterwards, otherwise a charge of 30 shillings shall be made.' So, we lost to France in Dublin and who did we play then? England in Twickenham, wasn't it?

Crito: Forwards like damp squibs that spluttered and died, a back division crippled by injuries, a place-kicker who couldn't kick, a full-back and a wing who couldn't carry the rest of the team on their shoulders. That was the Irish team which was licked and humbled by England.

Jack Kyle: We lost all our games in 1946. It wasn't acceptable to give interviews, which might have been just as well. The IRFU felt that we should know our place and keep our thoughts to ourselves. We were to be on the stage for eighty minutes and then we were to stay in the background and that was that. The year after,

1947, was when the games were made official again. I'd been playing for two years but it wasn't until 1947 that I was actually recognised as having won a cap. We lost to France. People didn't have high expectations.

Bertie O'Hanlon: I came into the team for the second game, against England above in Dublin. We won 22-0 and I scored two tries. 'Twas a mighty day.

The Irish Press: *Like chaff hurled far and wide by a furious whirlwind which didn't know when it had enough done, the might of England's rugby lies in thraneens in the straw-strewn pitch at Lansdowne Road where on Saturday, an Irish side hardly given a chance, whipped the opposition in a manner which almost made the spectators rub their eyes in amazement and forget that they were nearly frozen stiff from the bitterly cold conditions.*

Bertie O'Hanlon: My parents died when I was very young. I was only four when my father went and I was only fourteen when my mother died. They were fifty-five and fifty-two years of age. One went of a stroke and the other was cancer. My dad was a surgeon physician in Mallow. He worked his arse off. And he died when he was fifty-five.

The Irish Press: *An attack on the left was blunted and [winger Barney] Mullan, getting possession, attempted a drop at goal. The ball went right across the pitch and O'Hanlon getting to it before [winger David] Swarbrick, showed fine ball control in dribbling over the line for a try.*

Bertie O'Hanlon: My eldest brother worked in the bank and 'twas him who paid for my education at Rockwell College; my older brother, Cormac, a real father to me. He was a regional manager inside in the AIB in Ennis and then transferred to Cork. Went right to the top. There was about twenty years between us and he looked after me. Sent me to Rockwell as a boarder for five years. I got a wonderful Catholic education with the Holy Ghost Fathers. Mass every morning at 8 o'clock. Jeepers, you'd no choice.

The Irish Press: *Shortly afterwards came the real nail in the English coffin. O'Hanlon fielded a Hall cross-kick near the halfway line, handed off Swarbrick, left [fullback Arthur] Gray standing with a marvellous side-step and swerve and again turned on the speed to make sure.*

Bertie O'Hanlon: I was twenty-three at the time. I was Irish sprint champion. I won it in Dundalk. I did, yeah. That's why I was picked for the wing. I was playing in the centre for Munster but Ireland put me out on the wing because they had other fellas in the centre and Paddy Reid from Garryowen and Dessie McKee from the north of Ireland weren't long in coming on the scene. So I was a winger.

Before the match, you'd always be psyched-up. Playing the old enemy and all that. You'd be thinking of the Empire and the Brits dominating us for so long and you'd be mad to tear into them. I had a great debut altogether. Two good tries – a handy ol' thing from the twenty-five and one from the halfway line. Sheer speed. I went into the corner, you know.

Jack Kyle: Lansdowne Road was packed. In those days they used to put seats along the touchline and at the throw-in you were practically looking into the eyes of the people. They were more or less talking to you.

Bertie O'Hanlon: Oh God, you always loved to hammer England. It was one of the greatest hidings Ireland ever gave them. I floated off the pitch. You'd never forget that. The history of it. England? You wanted to kick the shit out of them. Us downtrodden Irish doing it for our great grandfathers. The Irish history, we all read it. If you were doing history and geography you knew what they did to us. The whole Colonial crowd, the bloody Empire, the full bit.

Jack Kyle: The IRFU gave us our train fare but there was always a little note which told us, 'You shall dine off the set menu but not a la carte. Any other orders to the room such as telephone calls or other pieces of food or drink shall be at your own expense.'

Bertie O'Hanlon: Billy Jeffares was the secretary of the union and he was a shit. Tough as nails and mean as shit. He was. In every way. He wanted receipts and all that. You couldn't cod him. He was great for the union. Everyone was trying to shove in things trying to make a few quid on the expenses, but you got away with nothing. You'd try a few tricks but he knew 'em all. No free phone calls. Not at all. A phone call me arse. You might have sent it in but you weren't paid for it. What phone call would you need to be making? Phoning the wife, is it? Ah, balls.

Jimmy Nelson: I was a work-horse in the second-row. I never pretended to be anything else. The boys had just missed out on a Triple Crown in 1947 by losing 6-0 in Wales and in the next match, against Australia, I came in at lock and we lost heavily and then I got dropped immediately. I always maintained that I was unlucky. Wherever we were staying the night before, the heat was desperate in my bedroom and I never got to sleep. I was exhausted going on to the field. I wasn't surprised they got rid of me. I was determined to come back, though.

I'll tell you a story. I was 6ft 1in tall, which was quite small for a lineout player. Somebody asked me how I leaped so high when I wasn't the biggest. I said that my old grandfather was chairman of the Opera House in Belfast and I used to get free tickets, and I was there one night and there was a ballet company on and I was watching them, not because I had any interest in ballet but because I was amazed at the height they could jump. Now, I've embellished this story a bit over the years so I've half-forgotten what was real and what wasn't. But this bit is true. I was looking at these ballet dancers and wondering how in the hell they jumped up so high. They used to have a party backstage and I went along that night. I collared the chief male dancer and I asked him how he got the height that he did when he was dancing. He took me out on the stage and showed me how to stretch your body to get the maximum jump. I was on the stage for ten minutes with this fella – and I'm sure it put about three inches on my leap at the lineout.

Karl Mullen: A lot of us were doing stuff. I was never the best player on the side but, as a hooker, I recognised that speed in the strike would be essential so I used to train, swinging between the banisters and a chair. I would swing each leg back and forwards fifty times so that I could get to the ball first in the scrum. Did it help? I don't know, but I did it anyway.

Ireland finished the 1947 Five Nations Championship in the middle of the pack, below Wales and England and above Scotland and France. Paris was the first port of call the following season – and it was an odyssey. Three days before New Year, the players went from Dublin to Holyhead by boat and Holyhead to London by train. Staying the night in London, they trained it to Dover the next morning, got the ferry to Calais and then dragged themselves on to a train to Paris. They left on Wednesday afternoon and arrived in the City of Love on Thursday evening feeling like they had left one world and entered another.

Paddy Reid: Travelling to Paris for us at the time was like going to the edge of the planet. We were as green as grass.

Jim McCarthy: Paris was such a naughty place. We saw real prostitutes in the streets. I thought I'd have to get absolution. And the Folie Bergere? That'd be three extra Hail Marys.

Jack Kyle: The excitement was unreal. The Folies Bergere was an eye-opener. A few of the guys got onto the stage. I think Bill McKay, our blindside flanker, was one of them.

Jimmy Nelson: Bill McKay was a hard man, but he and I didn't really see eye to eye about anything. He had a very different sense of humour.

Jack Kyle: McKay was a Coleraine chap. A fantastic rugby player. An immensely strong man. He had quite a war record out in Burma, fighting in the jungle. He told me once that he got malaria out there and they thought he was going to die. A priest gave him the last rites. He was a boxer and was the fittest man on our team. He was a very good miler. Word had it that he ran Roger Bannister a very close second in a race once. The journalist, Sean Diffley, once described our back-row of McKay, McCarthy and Des O'Brien as 'wisecracking bandits roaming the foothills preying on unwary travellers'. And he was right.

Des O'Brien: I hadn't been capped at that stage. I was a reserve. The game in Paris was played on New Year's Day, 1948, and I was sitting near the touchline at Stade Colombes with the rain falling on me and the team flying around in front of my eyes. We were 10-0 ahead at half-time and eventually won 13-6. Paddy Reid, Jim McCarthy and Barney Mullan scored tries and at one stage I reached into a bag and pulled out a spare jersey and held it over my head as shelter. I said, 'The way this team is going, this will be the closest I ever get to wearing one of these.'

Jack Kyle: Ernie Strathdee was our scrum-half and we had a great understanding. We played alongside each other at Queen's and we just gelled really well. He was an excellent scrum-half and he was captain in Paris. And then he was gone. Didn't matter that we won. Dropped. Hugh de Lacy came in and Karl Mullen took over as captain. It was pretty ruthless.

Karl Mullen: My father was a great friend of James Connolly and they used to walk in the hills every Sunday in the years before the Easter Rising and talk and argue. The library in our house was packed with books on Communism and free thinking and I was called Karl after Karl Marx. Dad always came to the matches, but he was very shy and physically small – about four foot ten – and would stay in the terraces.

Des O'Brien: I won my first cap against England in the second game of the '48 season. Karl asked me if I would be leader of the pack. I told him I didn't feel up to it because I didn't know any of the forwards. He said, 'We can soon fix that,' and then he took me on the bus and introduced me to them one by one.

Jimmy Nelson: Des was the greatest player I played with. He was very accomplished. He worked for Guinness in Dublin and I said to him one day, 'Des, what do you do in that job of yours?' And he says, 'I call to eight or ten publicans a day.' I said, 'What do you do when you get there?' He said, 'I have a glass of stout.' I said, 'Where can I get a job like that?'

Des was a very good tactician. He, more than Karl, directed the team. He laid out the plans. Karl was a very good player and a fine motivator. We had a good set of forwards, good handlers and we were quick. There were one or two workhorses like me, but you need workhorses. JC Daly was another one. John Christopher Daly. A prop. Oh, he was a rough diamond.

Bertie O'Hanlon: JC Daly fought in the war against Rommel and all these fellas. Some called him Jack and some called him Chris. Ah, you could call him anything you wanted. I'd call him JC. He was an iron man. He fought in the famous 8th army in the war, I think. He fought all over the bloody place, against the Japs and the rest of them.

Des O'Brien: He was an extraordinary character and one of rugby's great romantics. Before the Second World War he was playing with the thirds for London Irish. As he departed for combat he said, 'When I come back, I'll be picked for Ireland'. He was stationed in Italy and had to carry heavy wireless equipment on his back. As a result, his upper-body strength was incredible. Before internationals he did somersaults to confirm his fitness.

Jack Kyle: It's important to remember the good times but also you can't forget the times you almost made a shambles of things. In our second game in 1948 we went to Twickenham. The previous year we'd beaten them 22-0 and there we were in a nice comfortable lead again. I'd scored a try and we were looking good. I'd taken a pass from Hugh de Lacy and there was a gap and I thought, 'Maybe I'll get through it,' and I scored out on the right-hand side. As we used to say, 'We don't like the Welsh beating us, we don't like the Scots beating us, but whatever we do, we can't let the English beat us. We can stand lots of things but that's more than we can stand.'

Then, later on, I ran across the field thinking there was an opportunity for another try. I threw a pass which was intercepted by Dickie Guest, who ended up scoring under our posts. It was now 11-10 and we were hanging on for dear life.

Des O'Brien: It was a terrifying last fifteen minutes.

Jim McCarthy: It was piss-in-your-trousers stuff.

Des O'Brien: They had a scrum near our line and Karl issued the instruction: 'Drop it.' They had another scrum: 'Drop it again, boys.' It wasn't illegal and we were prepared to do anything to survive. The noise was incredible. It rose up as if coming from a well and hit such a crescendo that we could barely hear ourselves think. But we made it.

Jimmy Nelson: The forwards took charge of it. That's what we did.

Jack Kyle: The final whistle was the sweetest sound I ever heard on a rugby field. We'd won. My mistake hadn't cost us. It was relief more than anything.

Bertie O'Hanlon: We beat Scotland next and that was us three wins from three games. Not bad. So it was all down to us and Wales – March 13, 1948, above in Belfast for the Triple Crown and the Grand Slam, although no one talked about Grand Slams in those days. It was the Triple Crown we were after. It was strange going up there, the old border crossing and that. The northern boys were strictly educated in the Protestant faith and we were Catholics but there was no bigotry, none of that. We were wearing the green jersey and we were one team and that was it.

Jack Kyle: Hugh de Lacy played very well against England and Scotland and I enjoyed playing with him. He had a lovely pass. He was excellent, but when it came to the final match at Ravenhill, the selectors thought he was too light to be going up against the heavy Welsh lads. Ernie Strathdee was deemed to be more solid and so there was another change. I was really sorry for Hugh. It was nice to have Ernie back, but I felt for Hugh because to play well on two winning sides and to be dropped for the big game is very tough.

Jim McCarthy: Back then, a selector was God and a player kissed every ass he had to. It didn't even occur to you to question why they travelled first class and you were in third. You didn't question anything.

Bertie O'Hanlon: I was the youngest of nine kids and with my parents dead, my brothers and sisters went to all the matches to watch me. I used to get the tickets. I had to pay for them, of course. The rugby union wasn't a charitable institution. Free tickets? Are you joking me? No way. We got feck all.

Crito: Can Ireland beat Wales for the Triple Crown at Belfast tomorrow? For almost fifty years we have been scoring near-misses at the coveted trophy. Psychologists, star-gazers, seers, critics and even old man Euclid say we can't go on missing for ever, but Wales have proved to be our Becher's so often that it is with a certain amount of trepidation that we face this last stumbling block to our cherished ambition.

Jack Kyle: I changed next to Jack Daly before that game. He thumped one fist into another and shouted, 'I'm mad to get at 'em.' We all thought Jack was a bit mad.

Paddy Reid: The night before, we had a meeting. One of the people who had given us advice was Dave O'Loughlin who had been a star Irish forward before the Second World War. To all of us on the '48 team he was an idol. He had played against the great Welsh scrum-half, Haydn Tanner, who was still calling the shots on the Welsh team. Dave told us that Tanner was the man to watch and assured us that he would make two breaks during the game. At the meeting I suggested that Des O'Brien should be appointed as Tanner's shadow. I went so far as to suggest

Jack Kyle clears the ball against Wales in Belfast in 1948.

that if he didn't do his job properly he should be dropped. Des wasn't too happy with this part of the plan. Sure enough, as Dave had promised, Haydn broke twice. Both times, Des tackled him superbly. In fact, so frustrated was Tanner on the second occasion that he slammed the ball to the ground in frustration. These things turn a match. I'm convinced it was the difference between victory and defeat.

Jim McCarthy: It sounds a bit simplistic but we just knew we were going to win. It's nothing to do with arrogance, it was just a mood.

Jimmy Nelson: The scrums were rough. The Welsh would throw punches trying to unsettle Karl. The second-row was throwing digs when we were down in the scrum. I could see the punches coming. The referee did nothing. Jack Daly said to me, 'The next time he throws a punch you belt him one.' Did I do it? Ah, I can't remember.

Karl Mullen: I got a few cuffs on occasions all right.

Bertie O'Hanlon: They'd kick the shit out of you. The Welsh were tough as nails. Miners! What do you expect? Imagine coming out of the mines on a Saturday morning and hitting for Cardiff Arms Park. Three quarters of the team were coal miners and all belonging to them came from the mines. Rugby was the religion. None of this soccer act. Cardiff, Swansea, Newport, Pontypridd, Pontypool. You got nothing easy from those fellas.

Karl Mullen: By the end of the match I couldn't see. Both my eyes were closed from the punches. Even the referee couldn't find out who was doing it, but what was happening was that Don Hayward in the Welsh second-row would tip the guy ahead of him, who would move slightly to his right, and then he would come

Karl Mullen's 1948 immortals.

through with his fist into my face. He came clean on the Lions tour a few years later. He says, 'I was the one that did you.'

Jimmy Nelson: There was one scrum midway through the second half and we went down and when we locked horns I could hear a few groans from the other side and I thought we have them now. As soon as I heard that I said to myself, 'They'll not recover.'

Jack Kyle: Jack Daly scored the famous try at Ravenhill. You know the story about him running back to the halfway line and saying that if Wales don't score again 'they'll canonise me.' I wasn't sure about it, but apparently it's true.

Jimmy Nelson: It's definitely true because I landed on top of him as he touched the ball down and I ran back with him to the halfway line.

Bertie O'Hanlon: The wings threw the ball into the lineout and it was coming down to the end of time and I mentioned to the referee, 'How long more, ref?' I had my eye on grabbing the ball, you see. He said, 'If you ask me that question again I'll put you off'. That shut me up. A minute or two later he blew the final whistle and I so happened to have the ball in my hands at the time. And did I scamper!

Jimmy Nelson: I'll tell you another one, Daly lost his shirt after the match. The crowd came on and his shirt was gone.

Jim McCarthy: The crowd rushed on to the pitch and literally ripped the shirt off his back

Jimmy Nelson: Years afterwards I met a fella and he said to me, 'You know what happened to Daly's shirt?' I said, 'No.' He said, 'I got it.' I said, 'How?' He said, 'I was still in school at the time and a crowd of us ran on to the pitch and got it and took it away and cut it into squares and sold it for sixpence each.' And then he said when the jersey was finished he went and bought a new one and cut that one up too.

Jim McCarthy: Some of the lads went off after the dinner and got drunk and unfortunately one of them ended up in a police cell because for some reason there was a parade going on at that hour and he kicked an Orangeman's drum.

Des O'Brien: I can still see the boys with the big Lambegs, taking the drums off their shoulders and coming in around us. I was sure we were about to get done. There were blows struck. We must have been close to a police station because we were hauled out, arms twisted behind our backs, run along a pavement, through swing doors and into a police station. There was one sergeant there who chucked us into a cell. We weren't very upset as I recall. Half an hour later we were marched out into the guard room, where there were about twenty RUC men standing in two rows with their hands behind their backs. We were lectured by the sergeant, who said something along the lines of 'Try that again and there will be no more

Triple Crowns for you boys.' Then they let us go. It must have been 3.30am before we got to our beds. Not a word to anyone, of course.

Jim McCarthy: I got a letter of admonishment from Billy Jeffares after the Welsh match. I'd claimed four pounds and ten shillings in expenses for the trip to Belfast but he docked me a shilling for departing from the table d'hote. I'd had a couple of raw eggs out of the hotel kitchen and made a phone call to my parents to tell them that we'd made history by beating Wales. They charged me for it.

Bertie O'Hanlon: Mean, you see. All that sort of crack.

Jack Kyle: In 1949 the team changed but we were formidable again. George Norton came in at full-back. Noel Henderson came on the scene in the centre. Jack Daly went to England to play rugby league and Tom Clifford came in instead of him. Tom was one of the greatest characters you could ever hope to meet. A great Limerickman. He was one of these men that people instantly warmed to without him ever having to open his mouth.

Jimmy Nelson: Clifford was the biggest character. He was an extraordinary person. He was received everywhere he went as if he was the King. Everybody liked him. Even when we went on the Lions tour in New Zealand in 1950 the first person the prime minister wanted to see was Tom Clifford.

Bertie O'Hanlon: Tom was a magic man. People just wanted to be around him. The pride of Young Munster – the great Tom Clifford.

Jack Kyle: In 1949 we started off by losing to France but then we beat England 14-5. None of the dramas of the previous year, thanks be to God.

Crito: Against England on Saturday, Kyle just dominated the whole proceedings. His devastating punting, remarkable defensive covering and, above all, those superbly rhythmic and seemingly effortless bursts through the centre drew the eyes of all upon him.

Karl Mullen: We went to Scotland next and beat them 13-3. Jim McCarthy scored two tries.

Crito: Opinion will vary as to who was our star but without hesitation I plump for George Norton, who gave an inspired display. His kicking, fielding and general play went a long way towards breaking the back of the opposition, but his quite astonishing place kicking was the factor which took a lot of the steam out of the Scots. The cumulative effect of his three successful kicks at goal was tremendous and the general query after the game was – 'Who is this Norton and why wasn't he on the Irish team last year?'

Jim McCarthy: So that was us playing against Wales in the big one for a second year in a row. This time we were in St Helen's.

Des O'Brien: There was a big worry over Bill McKay, who was arriving late after doing an exam in Belfast and got caught up in traffic. Terry Davis of Trinity was put into his jersey, but McKay arrived ten minutes before kick-off and poor Terry never got a cap.

Jim McCarthy: I got the winning try. There was a lineout on the left-hand side in front of the stand and Ernie Strathdee passed it to Jack. Something told me 'He's going to have to cross-kick this,' so I took off towards the posts. I arrived on Frank Trott's chest just as the ball was coming down and it stuck in my mitts.

Crito: McCarthy crossed the line with a panther-like leap.

Jim McCarthy: And no, I wasn't offside. People said I lived offside. I was never offside in my life.

Crito: Scenes bordering on hysterical occurred in Swansea on Saturday following our second successive Triple Crown victory. Welsh followers, stunned at the defeat of their own side, stood rooted to the ground as the Irish followers, bursting all barriers and police cordons, swept on to the field waving tri-colours and chaired the victorious Irishmen off the ground to the accompaniment of boisterous back-slapping, which inflicted more damage to some than did the tough Welsh forwards. Sods of grass and even some of the iron railings round the ground were snatched away as souvenirs and it took the concerted efforts of a squad of policeman to rescue from the hands of over-enthusiastic well-wishers, Jim McCarthy, star of the game and the man who scored the try which carried us through.

Bertie O'Hanlon: I only played once more after that, against France in 1950. I tore all my ligaments in my ankle in a club match against Cork Con or Garryowen or some other crowd and that was the end of me. But, sure, didn't I have the best of it. Twelve caps. One Grand Slam and one Triple Crown. I think I have one jersey left. I'd say the moths have nearly eaten it now. It's in a drawer somewhere. I should have put the bloody thing in a plastic bag to keep it safe.

TWO

THAT WAS THE BUSINESS WITH
GOD SAVE THE QUEEN

Norman Hodgson was a film-maker with a difference. Much of what he shot, he shot in colour. Originally from Lenzie, a village near Glasgow, but exiled in Skerries in north county Dublin, he was fanatical about his home-movies.

On February 10, 1951, Hodgson went to Lansdowne Road to see what footage he could get on the day Ireland played England in the second match of the Five Nations. Karl Mullen's men had already won their first game of the Championship, against France by a solitary point, thanks to tries from Jimmy Nelson and Tom Clifford. And now the Irish players posed for Hodgson's camera, the green of their shirts, the whiteness of their shorts visible in technicolour for what may be the first and only time.

The camera scans along the back-row. There's McCarthy, pensive as you like, and Nelson and O'Brien. At the end of the line is Harry Millar, the wing making his debut and looking like he's heading for the gallows. There's Kyle crouched on the floor at the feet of John Smith, the loosehead prop, and John O'Meara, sitting in front of Clifford, who's looking down the row and laughing. There's no audio, just moving pictures. But there doesn't need to be. Everything they say about Clifford's charisma comes across in these few seconds of film; the playfulness, the devilment. Of the fifteen players, he's the one your eye is drawn to.

Jack Kyle: We won that match 3-0. Des McKibbin, our second-row, stood up and poked over a penalty and that got us the victory. We were a very good side that year. We beat France, England and Scotland and, of course, it was Wales yet again standing in our way in the last game of the Championship.

T.D.F, writing in the Irish Press: *They tell me here in Cardiff that never before has the search for tickets for a rugby match been so frantic. Local word is that black market tickets will be available in abundant numbers this morning.*

Jack Kyle: George Norton was injured and how we missed his goal-kicking. I don't know how many penalties we had and failed to put over. It must have been five or six. I scored a try and Wales scored a penalty and it ended 3-3. The ifs and

Opposite: Karl Mullen laces his boots before playing Wales in Cardiff in March, 1951. Notice the holes in the Ireland captain's socks.

whatevers stayed with me for a while. If we had George we would have won that game quite easily.

T.D.F: Oh, for a place-kicker

Jimmy Nelson: We left it behind us.

Jack Kyle: It was a long time ago.

Jimmy Nelson: It was, but I still remember it like it was last week. There was one incident which I'll never forget. A regret, if you like. We were attacking the Welsh posts and we got right underneath them and I was in a bit of space and I said to myself, 'Stand back and drop a goal,' and the thought went in and out of my head in about half a second – 'Don't be daft you've never dropped a goal in your life' – and I passed it out to Des O'Brien and Des was knocked into touch. I remember that well. And I regretted that I never took the chance. I don't know if I'd have kicked it but I regretted not trying. Why didn't I give it a go? I couldn't tell you. I said it to Jack Kyle later and he said, 'If you'd put that over you'd have been a saint.'

Jim McCarthy: We didn't win the Triple Crown or the Grand Slam, but we won the Championship. We were top dogs again for the third time in four years. That was a golden era, I suppose.

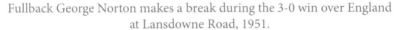

Fullback George Norton makes a break during the 3-0 win over England
at Lansdowne Road, 1951.

Ronnie Kavanagh: I came on the scene in 1952, from the Leinster back-row into the Ireland back-row. My strength was my fitness. I trained hard by the standards of the day. I spent a lot of time practicing my tackling, two or three times a week. I was pretty physical. In the summer of '52 I was invited to go on the tour of Argentina. I still have the letter from the IRFU. It finished with, 'If you want to accept this invitation then please forward a postal order for fourteen and sixpence for the cost of your visa.' Can you imagine that? Heading over there for a five-week trip and we had to pay for our own visa.

A few days after we arrived, Eva Peron died. The place was going mental. The beloved First Lady had passed away. The Spiritual Leader of the Nation, as they called her. People were crushed to death in their attempts to pay their respects. The grief was something else. The chat was that the tour was going to be cancelled, but what happened was we went to Chile for a game until the craziness eased in Buenos Aires. We beat Chile 30-0 in Santiago and then a few days after her funeral we drifted back to Argentina and got things going. I was twenty-one at the time. It was like dying and going to heaven.

Maurice Mortell: I was a winger and I made my Ireland debut against France in Belfast in January, 1953. I'll give you a laugh. I used to go to Lansdowne Road as a schoolboy and the man I'd be looking at most was Kevin Quinn, the centre from Old Belvedere. He was lethal. A fabulous player. I could never understand how the selectors could ignore him so often. Anybody playing football in those days would have put him down as the second best back in the country, behind Kyle. But he never got a look-in. There was this ol' fetish about his defence. 'Ah, his defence isn't strong.' I'd say he missed a tackle once in some war-time international against the British Army and they held it against him.

He was a kind of a hero in my mind. On the day of my debut in Belfast we were up in the pavilion in Ravenhill getting ready and Kevin's in the team and he's sitting beside me. It was his first time in the Ireland side in five years.

He leaned over and said, 'Maurice, will you keep talking to me during the match?' I said, 'I will, of course, Kevin. Why, like?' He said. 'I get very nervous when I'm playing.' Jesus, this fella was a God to me. Nervous! I was the one who was nervous. I was marking a fellow called Alain Porthault and somebody told me he had sprinted for France in the Olympic Games in Helsinki in 1952. He ran 10.7sec in the 100m. This fella was a flying machine. I was very uptight at the thought of having to deal with a guy who had that kind of speed.

Jim McCarthy: It was Jack's first time captaining the side. And Jack being Jack, he turned it on. He scored, I scored, Paddy Lawlor scored and Maurice Mortell scored. We beat them handy. Then we had a draw against England and Jack was brilliant again.

The Sunday Chronicle: *The one player who stood out head and shoulders above everyone else for ideas, imagination and innate rugby skills was Jack Kyle, a consummate artist and easily the best outside [half] now playing.*

The Observer: *The Irish forwards were terrific. And behind them Kyle at stand-off played one of the greatest games ever of his great career, brilliant in the cut-through, cool and commanding in defence.*

Ronnie Kavanagh: Jack was one of the hardest guys to handle. He was so quick. Over a short little area of twenty to thirty yards he was devastatingly fast. I played against him a lot in the Interpros and you couldn't allow yourself to get too close to him too quickly because he'd go around you. You had to try and herd him across the field rather than tear in and knock him flying because you had no chance if you tried that. He'd make a fool of you.

Cecil Pedlow: To play with Jack was terrific. Jack wandered about the place very casual. Suddenly the ball might be kicked loosely and he would pick it up and he was so quick off the mark, he went like a bomb and would score a try. But you'd have to keep talking to him to stop him looking at the clouds. He was so relaxed.

Maurice Mortell: That 1953 team scored more tries than any of the other nations before us. We scored twelve tries, you know. I scored in my first three internationals. We got four tries against France, one against England, six against Scotland and one against Wales. The Scots brought back Doug Smith, who hadn't been on the Scottish team for three years and Seamie Byrne ran around him, over him and under him, then he'd come back and do an encore. Doug is famous now for managing the 1971 Lions but Seamie scored a hat-trick and made a holy show of him. England won the title that year, but we were very close.

By the spring of 1954, Ireland's supremacy was on the wane. One by one, the Grand Slam, Triple Crown and Championship winning heroes were drifting off the scene. Karl Mullen had left the stage. So, too, had Kyle's great protectors, Bill McKay and Des O'Brien. Tom Clifford had come and gone. Jimmy Nelson also. The team was not in great shape, having lost their previous four internationals against Wales, New Zealand, France and England. The disappointment of defeat was one thing, but internal strife was quite another.

For half a century the so-called Ravenhill Strike was kept a secret among the men involved. Weighty histories of the IRFU had been written in the meantime and if there was any mention of it at all, it was cryptic. The omerta was maintained.

Maurice Mortell: That was the business with *God Save the Queen* when we played Scotland above in Belfast.

Ronnie Kavanagh: There was a row, that's true.

Maurice Mortell: Give Ronnie a ring about it, but I'm warning you, he mightn't want to talk about it.

Ronnie Kavanagh: I had played in Belfast the year before and because the game was in the north and there were Ulster boys on our team we had to stand for *God Save the Queen* as the Irish national anthem and I remember thinking at the time that I'd never do that again. For somebody from the Republic, it was terrible. Wind the clock forwards and the southern guys were going up on the train to Belfast on the Thursday and we had a discussion and we decided that we weren't going to go on to the field until after the anthems. Jim McCarthy was the captain and he had the pleasurable job of telling the selectors what we were planning. It kicked-off from there.

Cecil Pedlow: I wasn't playing that day, but I was on the Ulster team at the time and it was Ronnie Kavanagh and some others who didn't want to stand for *God Save the Queen*, which I thought was bloody foolish. When in Rome do as the Romans do. The boys from down south, about four or five of them, weren't going to go out until the anthems were over and there was a hell of a row over it. They weren't coming out.

Maurice Mortell: The debate was, 'Hold on a second lads, we're playing for Ireland and the national anthem they're going to play is *God Save the Queen*. That's not our national anthem!' On the Saturday morning, we were in the Grand Central Hotel in Belfast and two of the lads came into my room – Johnny O'Meara, the scrum-half, and Ron – and they said, 'Listen Maurice, we need to have another chat about this national anthem thing.' It came to my turn to speak and I said, 'Listen, I don't give a sugar if they play the *Red Flag*.' I was marking a fella called Weatherstone and he'd evidently being scoring a lot of tries and he was my only concern. To hell with national anthems. 'Whatever the majority says I'll go with that,' I said.

The north of Ireland lads weren't a party to this at all. We made up our minds that we'd only go on to the field after the anthems and that was that. In my innocence, I believed that this was a perfectly reasonable solution to what appeared to me to be a fairly minor problem. We never thought there would be any repercussions. We just thought we would stay off the pitch and get on with the game afterwards. Jim McCarthy was detailed to impart this to Billy Jeffares, the secretary of the union. We all got on to the bus and the next thing Billy came on and said, 'Would all the fellas from the south of Ireland come back into the hotel.'

Ronnie Kavanagh: We were summoned to room 15.

Maurice Mortell: The lads from the north were looking at each other going, 'What in the name of Jesus is going on here?' A few of the heavies from the union were waiting for us. Sarsfield Hogan was a senior IRFU man and a barrister by trade. He was alongside Cahir Davitt, the son of Michael Davitt and a former colleague of Michael Collins. It got very serious, very quickly. Cahir says, 'Look lads, most of you don't know me, but I was president of the union back in 1930-something and I understand you're having trouble with this anthem.'

He said, 'Listen, you have to understand what you're doing here. The only point of unity on this island is the rugby union. The lads in the north have been coming down to Lansdowne Road for all these years and standing to attention for *Amhran na bhFiann* and, therefore, I think we should be standing to attention for the anthem that's recognised up here. I'm telling you, fellas, if you go ahead and do what you're planning to do then it will be the end of the rugby union as we know it. And that's the last thing we want. Eamon de Valera [the Taoiseach] is a very good friend of mine and if I could get in touch with him now he'd tell you the exact same thing as I'm telling you. We want you to go out and stand for this thing and keep this unity alive.' Those, pretty much, were his words. And I tell you what, that knocked us all back.

Ronnie Kavanagh: He said, 'If you don't go on it'll split Irish rugby down the middle and it'll never recover.'

Maurice Mortell: There wasn't a dissenting voice after that. The penny dropped that we were boxing a little bit out of our depth. When we got into the bus I thought I heard somebody saying, 'Fucking Fenians.' I won't attribute it. They northern lads were aware of what was going on. Not all of them, but some of them.

Ronnie Kavanagh: When I got back to the bus I was sitting beside Fuzzy Anderson, our prop from Belfast. At the time, Pope Pius XII was reported to be ill and Fuzzy looked at me and said, 'You know, if you told us you wanted to say a prayer for the Pope we would have all gone in with you.' That's the impression Fuzzy had.

Maurice Mortell: We went out in Ravenhill and stood to attention. People said to me later that Paddy Lawlor, our second-row from Clontarf, did a bit of a jig during the anthem. Did he bollocks. He stood as straight as anything because I was standing beside him.

Ronnie Kavanagh: I'm sure a lot of the southern alickadoos didn't fancy standing for *God Save the Queen* either. Guys from Limerick or Cork wouldn't have been too keen. They wouldn't have enjoyed it any more than the rest of us, but that was the last time. The decision to play all future home matches at Lansdowne Road had already been made. It was a commercial decision. Lansdowne Road was a lot bigger than Ravenhill.

Maurice Mortell: I think Ronnie and Johnny O'Meara were unofficially marked down as being responsible for that incident because I could never understand why Ronnie was never picked for the Lions. Ronnie was a great battler.

Cecil Pedlow: The politics was mostly controlled in Dublin and we Ulstermen were polite enough not to make a row. But there was a Lions tour the following year and Jack Siggins from Belfast was the manager and I believe he said he wasn't having any of the boys involved in that thing at Ravenhill in his squad.

Ronnie Kavanagh: There might be something in that. Ah, it's impossible to say at this stage.

Maurice Mortell: A game broke out eventually and I scored two tries. One of them was a bloody peach. I threw in a couple of side-steps that I didn't even know I had. After that Scotland game and my two tries I got this communication from a paper telling me I'd been selected as sports star of the week and my award was a gold-plated cigarette lighter. In due course this thing came along with an inscription on it and I was flashing it around, very proud of myself. I was out in Bray and one of my pals says, 'Jesus, Maurice, I don't think you can keep that. You'll lose your amateur status.' I rang the famous Billy Jeffares and he said, 'No, no, no, you can't accept that. God, no. Send that back immediately.' I chewed it over for a week or two. I was playing for Bective against Lansdowne one weekend and Tommy O'Reilly from the IRFU was hanging around and I told him what was happening. 'Have you got it on you?' he says. I flashed it out at him. 'Ah, that's engraved,' he says. 'That's valueless. You can keep that, no problem.' I was delighted, but didn't I lose the fecking thing a couple of weeks later. So that was the story of the cigarette lighter.

Ronnie Kavanagh: The alickadoos and the committee men were a problem. You always got the feeling that the committee guys thought they were more important than the players. They gave you that sense. The committee were a strange kettle of fish. A lot of them wouldn't have appealed to me all that much.

Maurice Mortell: They were very strict. I went over to Wales to play a game, an international combination against Neath and there were fivers and tenners being claimed for expenses and I'd never seen that kind of thing before. I said. 'What's all this about?' One of the lads said, 'How'd you get in from the airport?' 'I got a lift from Ronnie Kavanagh's father.' He said, 'No, you didn't, you got a taxi in and you'll be getting one back as well.' I ended up with something like twenty pounds. I was afraid of my life to tell anybody.

In early January 1955, an eighteen year old red-head from Old Belvedere received a letter in the post from the IRFU inviting him to play against France at Lansdowne Road in the opening match of the Championship. Tony O'Reilly was told to bring his own 'training togs, clean white knicks, towel and soap' and was instructed to make sure that his boots are in 'playable condition.'

His debut was a sobering one. The critical score in a 5-3 win for the visitors came after Roger Martine, the French out-half, capitalised on O'Reilly's indecision and put Maurice Prat away to score. The swagger would soon come, but not yet.

Tony O'Reilly: I thought I'd turn and catch him, but God, this was a quicker game than I was used to. Against France I began to learn that international rugby wasn't quite as easy as it appeared to be. In my second game, against England, I was determined to knock Jeff Butterfield all over the ground. I must have shut my eyes because I can still see myself flying through the air and landing on the juicy grass at Lansdowne Road and doing a slalom right down the pitch as Butterfield was darting in under the posts.

Niall Brophy: Like Tony, I was a winger. And we were pals. In those days, if you let your opposite number through, you were gone from the side no matter how good you were. That was a mortal sin. If you played rugby for Ireland and your opposing number scored a try, no matter the circumstances, you were out – unless you were Tony O'Reilly. Even at that time, he was just that little bit different. He was already thinking further down the line than the rest of us students because after a match we would be in Hartigan's pub having pints and chasing the girls. But Tony wasn't one of the rugby crowd in that sense – he was ahead of us, off somewhere in a smart hotel dining with his girlfriend, whoever she happened to be at the time, or with business connections who he would be learning more from than anybody he might meet in Hartigan's.

Tony O'Reilly: I'd no interest in going to those places such as Hartigan's. In that sense I was very much a loner. Ronnie Kavanagh was my hero – the personification of controlled violence. He did most of his training up in the mountains and I used to say, 'Kav, it's not guerrilla warfare, it's rugby we're playing. We're not going to be asked to ford a stream at Lansdowne Road.' But he would have none of it and he'd say, 'We're going to run to the waterfall at Powerscourt,' and of course you'd run to the waterfall and your legs would be so seized up you'd be in bed for three days afterwards.

Ronnie Dawson: Ireland rarely saw the best of Tony. It was when he was on Lions tours when he really showed his brilliance because he was 100% at it whereas when he was at home he had so many other things going on in his life. He played very well for Ireland but when he was away he had nothing else on his mind.

Andy Mulligan: I'll tell you a story about myself and O'Reilly. It was 1955. 'Mulligan,' he explained. 'You've got to pray your way, not play your way, onto the Ireland team.' So I joined O'Reilly for 6am mass at St Theresa's. O'Reilly's unerring political instinct would serve us well. As we squeezed into the pew, there they were – the three 'Pape' Irish selectors in their dinner jackets and us two in ours. The expected surprise rippled through their ranks. What was I, a non-practicising pagan from Ulster, doing at mass?

O'Reilly was confident of the outcome. But when Radio Eireann announced the Irish team, John O'Meara was the scrum-half and Mulligan was out. O'Reilly's Jesuitical rationale rescued the moment. 'You would have made the team,' he said,

Tony O'Reilly

'if you hadn't shouted "Fire!" when the bell rang in mass.' From then on the moral was clear: play your way, don't pray your way on.

But that wasn't easy either even though we hadn't won a game in 1955 – three losses and one draw. The selectors were dominated by the legendary Ulster 'gombeen man' Ernie Crawford who was first capped shortly after the menopause and invented the immortal expression 'alickadoo' – Crawfordese for an official.

Crawford liked to tie mistletoe just above his backside when playing France in Paris so that when the crowd catcalled his goal kicks he'd turn his back on them and shout, 'Kiss me ass.'

Himself and his selectors picked me for my debut in 1956 in Paris. We lost 14-8. It was almost two years now since we had won a match. Will I ever forget our first team meeting before our next match against England at Twickenham when our captain opted for democracy rather than dictatorship? 'Right lads, let's decide how we're going to play this game. What do you think, Jack [Kyle]?'

'I think a few wee punts at the line would be dandy and maybe Andy here could have a few wee darts on his own.'

'What do you think, Tony [O'Reilly]?'

'Jaysus, I'm playing against a midget – let me have a run with the ball.'

'What about you, Cecil [Pedlow]?'

'I think a subtle combination of runnin', kickin' and breakin' would be dandy.'

Our captain summed up: 'So it's decided, lads. Jack's puntin', Andy's dartin', Tony's runnin' and Cecil's doing all three.'

Result of match: England 20 Ireland 0 and loss of confidence in democracy.

Dave Hewitt: I came into the team on January 18, 1958, when we beat Australia at Lansdowne Road. I played in the centre alongside Noel Henderson with Tony O'Reilly on one wing and Cecil Pedlow on the other. Jack and Andy Mulligan were the half-backs. A few of us made our debut on the same day.

Ronnie Dawson: I was one of them. In at hooker.

Noel Murphy: I was another. Straight into the back-row

Billy Mulcahy: Me too. Second-row

Dave Hewitt: My rugby came from my father and his brothers. He was one of a family of twelve, three girls and nine boys and of the nine boys a large number of them played rugby. It was a really traditional church-going family, a Christian family and I really bought into it. There were always more important things than rugby in my eyes. The most important thing in my life wasn't rugby, it was Bible class. I was more interested in the Bible than I was in playing rugby. But I enjoyed it all the same. And I was nervous that first day against Australia. It was Jack Kyle's last year. We over-lapped just for a short period and he was very special, not just as a player but as a person. I remember in that Australia game the ball came out and he passed it to me and I knocked it on and he came over and put his hand on my shoulder and said, 'Sorry about that pass I'll do my best the next time.' There was nothing wrong with the pass. But that was Jack. A thoughtful man even in the heat of a game like that.

Ronnie Dawson: It was the first time an Irish side had ever beaten a team from the southern hemisphere. I'm not sure we knew it at the time, but looking back now, it was a big deal. I've kept nothing from my rugby days. No jerseys or anything like that, but when my mother died I found some stuff. There was a photo company in Dublin called Lensman and they produced two books about Irish rugby in the 1950s and 1960s and as I was flicking through the pages there was a photograph of the team from 1958. I kept that one.

Jack Kyle: I finished two games later, a great old innings. I knew the end was coming, like Edith Piaf, *je ne regrette riens*. We beat Australia for the first time and it was nice to be part of that. Did I miss it when I retired? Not a bit. I knew that I wasn't playing up to the same standard that I used to play at so it was time to go. It's the guys who only get one or two caps that you feel for. I left at thirty-two and that was a long time as an Ireland player.

I've often said people's memories are very kind. They don't come up to you and say, 'I saw you play that awful game.' They say, 'Oh, I was there when you scored that try,' and you're very grateful to them for reminding you of it. There's great joy in looking back but there's often a certain sadness about old friends. When I was working in Africa back in the early 1990s, a chap stopped me in the street and said, 'Excuse me, are you Jack Kyle? I'm Bill McKay's son.' His name was Wilson. He and his girlfriend came to stay with me for a few days and he was telling me about his father, my team-mate, Bill. He emigrated to New Zealand but sadly he developed Parkinson's or Alzheimer's at the end of his days. It was sad to think that here was the fittest guy we knew and he ended up in a home and his son told me that, in a lucid interval, his father said to him, 'Oh, for God's sake would somebody just shoot me!'

You may not have heard of a man called George Stephenson who played for Ireland in the 1920s. He was the greatest centre of his time. A wonderful player. I met his son and his son said nobody has the slightest idea who his father was. So you have to remember that you have your day and you're very fortunate to have it, but there arrives others – and that's the way it ought to be.

THREE

WE WEREN'T BIG ON AURA IN MONEYGLASS

On Valentine's Day, 1959, in the minutes before Ireland ran out to play England at Lansdowne Road, Billy Jeffares stuck his head around the door of the Ireland dressing room and asked his players if everything was all right.

It was more a statement than a question, more an invitation to the players to confirm to him that all was well in their world rather than a genuine attempt to listen to a grievance. No sooner were the words out of his mouth than Jeffares was shaping to leave. He had the door three-quarters shut when a voice boomed out at him.

Syd Millar: Somebody said, 'No, everything is not okay.'

Billy Mulcahy: We all looked around and it was Tony O'Reilly. He said, 'I told you before, Billy, I need a pair of socks.' Billy says, 'You got a pair of socks last week'. Tony replies, 'They're full of holes.'

Syd Millar: The way I remember it, Billy went off in a huff and produced a pair of socks, then came back and said he was charging Tony seven shillings and six pence for the new pair.

Billy Mulcahy: And the stadium was full outside. This was twenty minutes before going out to play.

Syd Millar: There was a big stand-off. Tony says, 'Hang on, I tore the last pair while playing for Ireland, so why should I pay seven and six?' So Billy walked out with the socks in his hand and O'Reilly put the boots on his bare feet to show everyone how ludicrous it was. Jeffares came back and threw the socks at him through the door. Billy was like a hawk as far as Tony and Andy Mulligan, our scrum-half, were concerned. They were very much a double act. He'd be watching them in the hotel making sure they weren't ordering Dublin Bay prawns. Mulligan always brought his laundry with him to the hotel and, of course, you had to pay for that but Mulligan didn't pay and there was always a battle going on.

Ray McLoughlin: If you could have made a professional player out of Tony he'd

Opposite: Willie John McBride beats Wales' Delme Thomas to the ball at a lineout during the Five Nations match at Lansdowne Road, 9 March 1968.

have been one of the world's greats. You probably couldn't get him to train because
he was over in Pittsburgh running Heinz. I remember in 1959, Tony and Ronnie
Dawson were doing 100 yard sprints out in Belfield and the athletics coach was
timing them. I was watching. I didn't know Tony then. There was an argument
about the times so the coach gave me the watch. O'Reilly was 9.7 for 100 yards.
He was running in football boots, on grass and there were no starting blocks. If
you could have got him into a gym...

Tom Kiernan: Tony O'Reilly was marvellously strong and fast and while he was
renowned abroad for his attacking qualities, when playing with him I remember
him best for his defensive abilities – but that may be because his attacking
opportunities were limited when playing for Ireland. His catching, positioning
and kicking were first rate and I always felt his very stature intimidated the
opposition. It was said of O'Reilly that no other player could alone obstruct an
entire opposition back line.

  Looking back on that period, it was one of the great tragedies of Irish rugby that
Dave Hewitt played so few times for Ireland. He was part of perhaps the best three-
quarter line Ireland fielded with Kevin Flynn, Niall Brophy and Tony O'Reilly. The
pity was that they played together only on a few occasions, the last being in 1959.

In March of 1960, the African National Congress (ANC) carried out a campaign
of non-violent resistance over the South African government's laws on racial
segregation. At a demonstration in Sharpeville, near Johannesburg, police opened
fire on a peaceful crowd and killed 69 people. It became known worldwide as the
Sharpeville Massacre. Screened on television around the world, it kick-started the
anti-apartheid movement. Nine months later, the Springboks came to Dublin to
play Ireland at Lansdowne Road.

Ronnie Dawson: I was the captain and I remember the protestors outside the
Shelbourne Hotel. It was still early days in the anti-apartheid struggle but there
were protests against us playing them. Nothing like the protests we would see
in years to come, but there was discontent. People felt very strongly about it,
but there were no government embargoes or anything like that. There was no
suspension of trade with South Africa. My attitude was that the government had
to give the lead. If the politicians felt strongly enough about activity in another
country then they should cut off trade. Only then can you talk about sport. I
thought rugby was being used as a whipping boy. I stuck to that view. Don't use
sport as an excuse for not doing things at a political level.

Syd Millar: I don't remember many protestors but I won't forget the way South Africa ended up winning that match. Our front-row was myself, Ronnie and Gordon Wood. Their front-row was Fanie Kuhn, Ronnie Hill and Spiere du Toit. They were supposed to be killing every scrum they came up against but we stole four against the head that day. Then it came to the last scrum.

Ronnie Dawson: There was a very controversial try right at the end. A pushover try. Gwilym Treharne was refereeing. It was ridiculous. There was a five-yard scrum and South Africa started to push strongly as soon as they got down. So it started as a five yard scrum, then it was four yards, then three yards, then they put the bloody ball in and scored the try. That was the game. It ended up as a one yard scrum. We were raging but once it was done it was done. You couldn't complain. It was a question of good manners, my chap.

Bill Mulcahy rises to win a lineout during Ireland's historic victory over the Springboks at Lansdowne Road in 1960.

Syd Millar: When we went to South Africa for the Irish tour in the summer of 1961 the IRFU gave us a tie and that was it. There was this guy up in Coleraine who made sweaters and I got him to give us green sweaters and that was our sole identification as a team. We had no blazers. I just said to the union that I got them at a discount and I charged the boys a shilling. Adidas, in my latter days, came and said, 'We want to supply the guys with bits of gear.' I said, 'We're not allowed to, it's advertising, they'd string us up.' That was the way of it.

Ronnie Kavanagh: There was a fair bit of tension over there and you knew when you were there that there were two classes of people, the blacks and the whites.

Syd Millar: We didn't like the situation in South Africa but we didn't take much notice. It wasn't headline news then.

Ronnie Dawson: Well, apartheid was in full swing and as a group of players we talked a lot about it before we went. We were very careful when we got there not to get involved in any discussion for fear of being wrongly quoted. There was some chat about the tour and whether we should go but nothing was being said about political contact or trade. If you want to give a strong message to a country the politicians have to do it, not some amateur rugby players. Using sport as the only tool was questionable.

Ronnie Kavanagh: The tour was a bit stupid.

Ronnie Dawson: I was captain and I had a problem before we went out because the union decided that we would play the Test match first and the provincial games afterwards. The only answer I got out of the union was, 'Look, they won't see too much of us and we could spring a surprise on them.' It didn't work out.

Billy Mulcahy: Ernie Crawford was on the union and he was the Kaiser. People spoke about Ernie with a certain amount of awe. He came across as a fearsome character, a dour exterior, very grave looking features.

Syd Millar: Nobody in their right senses would have done what we did.

Ronnie Kavanagh: We flew into Cape Town and played the Test match three days after we got there. They hammered us 24-8 on a bone dry pitch. It wasn't a fair test. We won our provincial games after that and we played against Rhodesia on the way home and we beat them as well. Why was the Test match first? Don't ask me. Madness.

Ronnie Dawson: We didn't have enough time to get ourselves organised before we had to dive in and play a Test. Then we went on to win the other games reasonably well. Jerry Tormey of Terenure was new and did really well. He looked a terrific prospect. Jim Thomas, a prop from Blackrock, looked really good as well. But when we got home and the side for the first match of the 1962 Five Nations was picked, we were nearly all dropped. They brought in nine new caps to play against England at Twickenham.

Mick Hipwell: The selectors lost the run of themselves. They lost the head completely. They left out Dawson, who was the biggest miss. He was a top player. Whatever they were drinking that night, they lost the plot. Dump the experience and bring in the children. There was an almighty rush of the blood to the head.

Willie John McBride: I was one of the nine new caps. Myself, Ray McLoughlin and Mick Hipwell came into the pack. You have to have a sense of humour to choose nine new caps for any game, let alone when you go to Twickenham. I'd never been to London before. I'd never even been to an international. I was brought up in a wee farm in Moneyglass in Antrim and sport was the last thing on our mind. My father died when I was four and we had to work on the farm. I didn't play rugby until I was seventeen and the 1940s were tough. We went to school, came home and helped our mother. Sport wasn't a part of it for a long time. The first athletic thing I ever did at school was pole-vaulting. I was a pole-vaulter. Tall and skinny. I won the Ulster Schools Championships twice. Then I got too heavy and the pole broke and I was enticed out to play this game – rugby.

Johnny Quirke: I was seventeen years old at the time, the youngest scrum-half ever picked for Ireland. My house was under siege from reporters. I couldn't get in or out. There was so much hype about it. One day the IRFU smuggled me up to Belfast to practise with our out-half Gerry Gilpin. I was excited but a bit nervous too. There were dire predictions that I'd be kicked to death at Twickenham.

Billy Mulcahy: That was my first day captaining the side and it wasn't easy. I took over from Ronnie. We only got together the afternoon before the match. There wasn't a whole lot you could do. We lost 16-0. I remember the first score, we were still in the scrum when Richard Sharp went in behind us and cut us open. Ah, 'twas very dispiriting.

Ray McLoughlin: In those days, tightheads could really bring a scrum down and there was no law about collapsing the scrum or anything like that. I had a reputation for bringing scrums down and Noel Murphy came up to me before that match at Twickenham and said, 'We'll have none of this messing around today.' What I remember is that I listened to him, to a degree. I said to myself afterwards, 'I'm never listening to that again.'

Noel Turley played wing forward and it was his first and only cap. He was a Blackrock guy and a very good player, but the organisation of our back-row was inadequate and Richard Sharpe caused the damage on that day. Noel paid the price but he shouldn't have. Jimmy Dick came in for Ronnie and didn't get another cap afterwards. Larry L'Estrange didn't get another cap. Gerry Gilpin and Johnny Quirke got two more and then they were gone as well. All four were good players but they were casualties of a disorganised team.

Willie John McBride: My second cap was against France at Stade Colombes and in places like that you learned how to sort out your own problems or else you didn't survive. I played for nearly half an hour with a broken leg. The pain was something damnable. Somebody came on and gave it a rub and said 'Away you go'. I went into a scrum and I couldn't explain the pain to you, but you just didn't come off. I came home with my leg in plaster. From Dublin airport I got on a bus into Amiens Street station, hopping on one leg with my bag over my shoulder. I got on my train and came to Belfast and hopped on one leg to catch another bus. I remember as clear as today, there was a man standing there, a porter, and he had a trolley and he said, 'Here son, sit on this, you've hurt your leg.' And he wheeled me to where I needed to be. Eventually, I got back to where I was living – Ballymoney. I hopped up the hill to my flat and it took me half an hour. There was no duty of care or any of that nonsense. No health and welfare.

Ray McLoughlin: There were an awful lot of bad matches. I remember playing in Dublin against England in the muck in 1963 and the final score was 0-0. Richard Sharp, a brilliant player, was fly half for England and I was given the job of collapsing every scrum, so the ball hardly ever got to Richard Sharp. We had great fun in the muck but it must have been absolutely awful to watch.

Billy Mulcahy: My first win as a captain was in Cardiff a month after the England game. I left my boots behind me at the hotel in Porthcawl. I played in two odd boots that I used for training. We were on the bus when I realised. We were nearly in Cardiff when the penny dropped. 'Jesus, I'm after leaving my good boots behind.'

Willie John McBride: We lost an awful lot of matches. We played New Zealand at the end of 1963 and we'd won only one of our previous dozen games. There were a couple of draws in there, but we weren't exactly favourites going in against the All Blacks. Ignorance is a great thing. I knew that the All Blacks had a great name and that they normally won and that, apparently, there was a great aura about them, but I didn't care about that. Aura wasn't a big thing around Moneyglass. I remember I hit Colin Meads that day and put him down and I didn't know who the hell he was. He pushed me out of the first couple of lineouts and I warned him not to do it and then I hit him a belt. Noel Murphy says to me, 'Do you realise who you hit? Meads! We're all dead now.' Five minutes later, I got one back from him. That was the end of it. I wasn't a dirty player but I didn't take any nonsense. I always took the view that once you're selected to play for your country there's a responsibility that comes with it, so you give it everything you have and you don't allow yourself to get bullied.

Ronnie Dawson: We lost 6-5, but should have won.

Billy Mulcahy: We got a score near the very end. Eamon McGuire was our flanker and he was really fast. There was a cross-kick and Eamon was speedy out of the traps and caught it, Gaelic style, and touched it down but the referee decided that he had to be offside, but he wasn't. It was just that Eamon was a flyer off the base. We played together for Bective subsequently and for years I'd say to him, 'Well, Eamon, was it a try?' And he'd always say the same thing: 'It most certainly was.' So that was a tale of woe against the All Blacks. One of many, I suppose.

Derek Arnold, the All Black inside centre, sends Tom Kiernan off balance as he takes an inside line through the Irish defence at Lansdowne Road in December 1963.

The first half of the decade had been an unmitigated horror show. Ireland had played twenty-three Test matches and had won only three of them. They had won the Five Nations wooden spoon in 1960, 1961 and 1962 and narrowly avoided it in 1963. In that era they shipped some heavy beatings, losing to France by nineteen points and then seventeen points, losing to South Africa and England by sixteen points and to Scotland by fourteen. They were the soft touch of the Championship, easy prey to the likes of Christian Darrouy, the French winger from Stade Montois in Mont-de Marsan, who became one of Ireland's bogey men, after running in a hat-trick at Lansdowne Road in 1963.

As '63 gave way to '64 what Ireland needed was an attacker as sharp as Darrouy and all the others who were cutting them to ribbons and they found one in the shape of a quiet twenty-two year old Ulsterman called Mike Gibson.

Mick Hipwell: Mike Gibson came into the team against England at Twickenham in 1964 and from the off, he was just one of those players. He had intensity and power and was so influential. He was a marvellous footballer.

Ken Kennedy: We went to school together, from Campbell College under-11s to the Ireland international team. Mike was a thinker. He could read a game better than anybody I ever saw. He had the tactical brain to see what needed to be done and the brilliance to carry it out. He didn't drink or smoke and he didn't go out with the lads. He was the first spark of professionalism. He looked at his diet and had his own sprint coach. He was before his time.

Mick Hipwell: He was aloof. Very much reserved. A good northern Protestant. We all have our own idiosyncrasies. He kept himself to himself but he was a smashing guy. He'd do anything for anybody that needed it. And on his debut we beat England at Twickenham, which was huge, because we'd almost forgotten how to win.

Mike Gibson: When you listened to forwards talking about hitting each other in the scrum and standing on each other's toes and retaliation, it seemed to me that there was not much room left in their game for skill. It goes without saying that possession is vital in any game of rugby and nothing can be achieved without it, but I always felt that it was essential that for any team to be successful they needed to have a quality player at fly-half. The fly-half is the person who reflects the attitude and potential of his team, so the higher his quality, the richer the prospects for the team as a whole. But the fly-half also needs a positive attitude. He needs to be confident. He even needs a touch of brashness. When I was at Cambridge, I remember Dr Windsor Lewis – who had been a wonderful fly-half for Wales in the twenties and was then president of the Cambridge University rugby club and coached the Varsity team – saying to me that whenever he had gone out onto the field, he looked around to find the wing-forward in the opposing ranks and thought, 'Poor bastard. He has to mark me today.' That's the attitude a fly-half must have, but he can only develop it if he is supremely confident in the simple things of catching and passing and kicking.

I'd play games on my own where I would just kick with my left foot or just kick with my right foot and develop a strength in each area, and then concentrate on the simple things in rugby – the ability to take a pass and deliver a pass, and then the thinking bit, which is making decisions. And I think that's a facet that separates players. If you can go out and make the right decision throughout a match then your side is likely to be successful. I've always highly regarded the ability to anticipate and to read situations; I often watch players and see them drift around the field and then suddenly the action takes place close to where they are and I smile and think, 'Well done, that was class.'

Syd Millar: Gibson had this indefinable ability to read the situation and do the right thing more often than not – and that's what top class rugby is about: that the guy is in the right position at the right time and he does the right thing.

Mike Gibson: The mental side of rugby is more demanding than the physical. You can work hard and acquire the physical attributes if necessary, but mistakes are often due to a lapse in concentration, a poor decision, and that's where the mental side is extremely important. The qualities of commitment and concentration, the capacity to analyse situations and to make decisions are all very important in rugby but also in developing academically, and also developing as a person.

I think that a lack of concentration is a defect at all levels of the game. A lack of ability to devote yourself entirely to the game for eighty minutes. At international level, I only felt satisfied if I came off the field feeling mentally exhausted. I had to feel mentally shattered because I had directed all my thoughts to one objective over and over again and that was: what is going to be the best use for this particular ball?

Tom Kiernan: If I had to choose the single most outstanding player I ever came across I think I would opt for Mike Gibson, though I would also have to consider Gareth Edwards and Colin Meads. Gibson's greatest attribute was his enormous work-rate. He had all the skills of a great out-half or centre but he had a phenomenal work rate in addition to these. When he was out-half I remember he was always in the corner of my eye as I went to catch a ball or kick to touch. His presence was an enormous reassurance.

There was one particular incident in a match against Australia in Sydney which for me sums up what a great player Gibson was. He was playing out-half and ran hard into a pass and dropped it. The Australian out-half, Phil Hawthorn, snapped up the ball and made forty yards. As I tackled him he passed to his winger, John Brass, who ran in under the posts. But as he did so Gibson tackled him, twisted him and he failed to touch down. The try was disallowed. It was an incredible effort on Gibson's part and absolutely typical of him. He was a totally dedicated, generous, team-spirited player. No praise of mine is sufficient for him.

Mike Gibson: I remember, as everyone does the first time they are capped, the journey to Twickenham, putting on my jersey for the first time, but then the first fifteen minutes of the game I really have no recollection of what happened. I think I dropped the first couple of passes which came my way. But then I gradually warmed to the match.

I've always been excited about playing rugby at any level. If you can retain a freshness, if you can honestly say to yourself every time you put on the boots that you're looking forward to the match, at whatever level it may be, at international or club level, then you can make the best of your ability.

Billy Mulcahy: It meant a lot to win that game at Twickenham because I'd been captain when we were hockeyed by England with the nine new caps two years earlier. We won 18-5 and we had the famous criss-cross try. We heeled a scrum around halfway and Mike Gibson goes left and does a reverse with the late Jerry Walsh who steams off to the right corner then does another reverse with Pat Casey coming in off the right wing. Ah, 'twas a smashing try.

Gibson was an undoubted star at out-half, but he wasn't enough. That win in Twickenham was followed by three defeats, the last of them in Paris where Darrouy tormented the visitors again with two more tries in a tumultuous 27-6 victory. Ireland finished last in the Championship once again, their fourth wooden spoon in five years.

What was needed now, more than anything, was a leader who could bring organisation to the beleaguered dressing room and who could curb the influence of the IRFU. Ray McLoughlin took over the captaincy, if only for a little while, and immediately set about changing the culture of the Irish team.

Ronnie Dawson: When Ray McLoughlin became captain in 1965, he was very strong in his views and rightly so. He had a different style of leadership, but at the time people may have felt it was a bit authoritarian. I had no problem with it.

Syd Millar: Ray tried to change the philosophy and some in the union didn't like it. They didn't like the fact that he wanted the players to meet more often and to be more intense about what we were doing. They didn't regard that as being in the spirit of the game. The old heads regarded rugby as a game that you didn't take too seriously. But the players took it seriously.

Billy Mulcahy: Ray came in after me and one of the things he did was on the morning of a home match he got the team the hell out of the Shelbourne Hotel and out to Dun Laoghaire for the pre-match lunch where nobody could bother us. At the Shelbourne you had people milling about and looking for tickets and you're trying to fix them up and then you'd find the tickets for them but in the meantime they'd have already got some, so now you were stuck with these tickets and you were trying to offload them. Your mind was on either getting tickets or getting rid of tickets and a match a couple of hours down the road. Ray insisted that the team be taken out of that atmosphere and out to the Marine Hotel for the preparation. That was a good move. That first Saturday morning out in the Marine, we were having a bit of lunch and down the other end of the room the IRFU alickadoos were laughing and guffawing and the next thing Ray stood up and walked over and told them to shut up. I can still hear one of them saying, 'Certainly, Ray.' On the way in on the bus to the ground he was going around tapping fellas on the shoulder and telling them to focus. It needed to be done.

Ray McLoughlin: I had no dealings with the IRFU until I became captain – and then I had a lot of dealings with them. Before I was captain, the team would get together on a Friday, we'd have a team meeting in the Shelbourne at two o'clock and there'd five selectors and three sub-selectors and everybody would give their opinion. That always extended the time by at least forty-five minutes and so we'd have to rush out to Anglesea Road for a run. Bill Mulcahy was an excellent captain but he wasn't given the tools to work with. We'd have a couple of scrums, a couple of lineouts and then we'd go into the shower and sing *Ireland Boys Hooray*. We'd then go back to the hotel and off to the cinema that night. The following morning we'd get up and there'd be a bunch of drunks there from the night before telling you how to play the match. Ten minutes before kick-off we were brought out on to the pitch for the team photograph. We went out on the field totally under-prepared and the match could be ten minutes old before we adjusted to it.

Ken Kennedy: Irish rugby used to have a wayward approach and Ray produced discipline. He was one of the founding figures of revamping the way the team would approach a game and we had great respect for him. He was very single-minded and some of the committee people were rubbed up the wrong way because of it. It was the way of things that the committee travelled first class and we travelled third class. That was pointed out to me very forcibly on the platform at Belfast going to a trial match. I was talking to some of the selectors as the train prepared to board and they said, 'No, no, you're at the other end.' That was a reminder that they were on one level and the players were on another.

Ray McLoughlin: I went to the chairman of selectors and said, 'If you want me to be captain, I want the following things. I want us to have a room at the Shelbourne on the Thursday night so we can have a meeting. I don't want any selectors or sub-selectors to attend. On the morning of the match, I want us to go to the Marine Hotel in Dun Laoghaire at 10am. I want no selectors, sub-selectors or committee men on the bus with us. Or if they're on the bus, they cannot speak. When we eat, we want to eat alone. We don't want any committee men near us. If they are, they cannot speak. When we leave the Marine and head for Lansdowne Road, we don't want selectors, sub-selectors or committee men with us. If they are, they cannot speak. We go to the ground an hour and a quarter before kick-off. We'll have a photograph when we get there, not ten minutes before we go out to play. That's what I'm looking for.' And the IRFU said, 'Oh, we couldn't have that. The things you want to get rid of are all part of the international game.' I said, 'OK, get another captain.'

The chairman was a very courteous man. He was just saying it the way he saw it. This created a bit of a crisis. Charlie Harte was the president of the IRFU that year. Charlie was a good man. He came to me to discuss it and I said, 'Charlie, this thing is a farce. This is it, take it or leave it. If you want me as captain, it has to happen this way.' So Charlie went away and delivered the whole lot. He got it all done.

Ronnie Lamont: Ray's first match as captain was against France, which also happened to be my debut – January 23, 1965. There was an article in the *Daily Mail* saying that France were a team of thoroughbreds and Ireland were a team of circus hacks. McLoughlin used his preparation based around that article and he had me by the neck up against the wall in the dressing room. 'Are you a circus hack or a thoroughbred?!' By the time I got on the field, Lansdowne Road had no terrors for me because I was just glad to get rid of McLoughlin. We kicked off and as the ball was in the air I picked the biggest Frenchman I could find, which happened to be Walter Spanghero, and I hit him with everything I had. He didn't have the ball, but I hit him anyway. We ended up getting a 3-3 draw and in those days it counted as a victory.

Ray McLouglin: My style of captaincy wasn't every player's cup of tea. I considered it really important to focus on the game and imagine the things that might happen. Visualisation, I suppose. I wanted the players to concentrate on the match and think of situations that might arise and imagine how they would react. I wanted them to stop going to the cinema the night before and instead to think about what we would have to do in the match. Not going to the cinema probably upset some people.

Ronnie Lamont: We had a good year in 1965. We drew with France, beat England and Scotland but then lost the Triple Crown decider in Cardiff. We also beat South Africa for the first time that year. The English game at Lansdowne Road stands out. Early on, I went down on the ball and I got an awful kick on the back from a guy called Nick Silk, the England flanker. I was hurt but you couldn't go off unless you were dead. I played on and had a super match. I scored the only try. At one point, they moved the ball out wide and there was an English left winger up against me and had he beaten me on the outside he was going to go very close to a try. I smashed him into the touchline seats. There was a mention in one of the Irish papers that the 'black Protestantism of Lamont saw the situation to an end.'

After the match, the IRFU never checked whether I was injured. I remember my friend brought me home in a Mini and by the time we got back to the north I couldn't get out of the bloody car. I was so sore on the Monday night that my father took me up to hospital. There are five lumbar vertebrae and numbers two, three and four were fractured. If another one had gone I'd have had a collapsed spine. None of that had been checked down in Dublin. Once I'd got a wee rub on the field and a dose of holy water I was told to get on with it.

Ray McLoughlin: We beat South Africa in the April, so that gave us three wins and a draw from five international matches. That was a good return. Then we lost two and drew one in the first three matches of the Five Nations in 1966 and Tom Kiernan took over the captaincy.

Ronnie Lamont: Once things started to go wrong the union remembered how they had been treated by Ray and exploded a few bombs under him.

Ken Kennedy: He got the knife in the back.

Ray McLoughlin: When I came back from the Lions tour in 1966 I had a job down in Kent and it just wasn't practical to go up to London Irish, my club, a couple of times a week. I had spent eight years at university and I reckoned it was time to get a job. I wouldn't say I had my fill of rugby, but the time comes when you have to get on with life. I was twenty-seven. The following year, I was watching Ireland play France in Paris on television and Mick Molloy scored a try and I remember having no sense of missing it at all.

Ray McLoughlin returned to business life but his legacy was a more organised and more focused team that started winning more matches than they lost – four in 1967, including two victories over Australia, and three in 1968 featuring a third win over the Wallabies, sealed by a memorable try from back-row, Ken Goodall, one of the new breed of back-row forwards.

Ken Goodall: I made my debut against Australia in 1967. You loosened up and then suddenly the band started the anthem. I didn't know where the flag was. When I noticed people were facing the other way, I shuffled around and faced the south terrace. I learnt later that my grandmother, Cassie Daly, draped a cloth over the television. She was a staunch unionist. Only when the anthem was over would the cloth be removed. Mike Gibson scored our first try in that game and I was a bit full of myself as we were running back to the halfway line. It was nothing too extravagant but Noel Murphy, the captain, said to me, 'Settle yourself down, Goodall, you're not a schoolboy anymore.'

The team now had its first ever coach – the experienced former hooker and captain, Ronnie Dawson. But Dawson wasn't the only veteran who made a reappearance on the scene. Syd Millar was thirty years old when he was dropped from the Ireland team in 1964, the explanation being that the selectors wanted a younger side and that the Ulsterman was now past it. He played for his club, Ballymena, for the next four years and then the phone rang. It was 1968 and Ireland wanted him back.

Syd Millar: I was thirty-four but I was dead fit. I was in Portadown working for Shell for a while and there was a boxer who lived down the avenue and we used to go running in the morning. I'd never done that before. I was never a great man for laps, but I always held my own in a scrum and I had no worries at all that I could handle myself even though I was out of international rugby for so long.

Ronnie Dawson: I was appointed coach in 1968 but I was more a facilitator than anything else. The players were the important people. My job, as I saw it, was to assist the players to help them get the best out of themselves, to look at the strength of the opposition and the game we needed to play and how we were going to do it. I was big on detail. Before, there was never any real consideration of the opposition and how they might approach games. Was there resistance from the union? Yeah, there was. Some people thought that a coach was the thing that brought you to matches. Change takes time. In 1968 we were close to a Triple Crown and then the year after we were going for a Grand Slam against Wales in Cardiff.

It was a heady year, 1969. The fine Leinster out-half, Barry McGann, came into the team allowing Mike Gibson to move to the centre, where he excelled. So, too, did the teak-tough Ulster flanker, Jimmy Davidson. Ireland beat France, England and Scotland and fetched-up at Cardiff Arms Park on March 8 in pursuit of a Grand Slam.

Not for the last time, the boys of '48 were wheeled out for comment. Even then it seemed like an eternity since the Slam had been won.

Ken Kennedy: In the dressing room before we went out, they gave us jerseys that had been worn three times. We went out looking like the forty shades of green. This is true. My jersey had to be sewn up at the armpits. There was a big hole in it. The team doctor sewed it up with surgical silk before I went on to the pitch to play for a Grand Slam. Wales came out pristine. We were like Christian Aid Boys – second-rate stuff.

Willie John McBride: It kicked-off that day. Brian Price whacked Noisy.

Noel Murphy: Ah, don't be making a big deal out of it. No, no.

Syd Millar: We went to the Arms Park for the Grand Slam and it was an awful game. One side of the ground was razed and if you looked one way it was like playing a second XV match in a back-field and if you looked the other way the place was jam-packed and electric. It was almost unreal. It wasn't the kind of setting for a match of that importance. Murphy got smacked, a deliberate thing. We had running battles here, there and everywhere. We'd heard that they were going to smack Murphy.

Willie John McBride: Brian Price of all people. I remember playing in New Zealand with the Lions and Colin Meads clipped Price round the ear like a child. He wasn't so clever on that tour as I recall. You take players to the southern hemisphere and some of them just melt. Some guys stand up and others just fade away. In Cardiff, Noisy was in a ruck and his head was sticking out and Price belted him. He wasn't the sort of guy who would stand face-to-face and hit you a dig. I think a lot of that came from the Lions tour in New Zealand because Noisy was leading the forwards and he was always on Price's back for not putting in the work.

Ken Kennedy: I remember seeing the incident, but let me be clear. Brian Price was never a dirty player. The same could not be said of a couple of others in their team, who I won't name. I got a whack as well. I have a nice picture of me flat out on the pitch in the same game. They had a few people who were quite good at putting their fist through a scrum. There's the rules of rugby and then there's the front-row rules and you had to be aware of what was going to happen. You had to keep your eyes open. Of course, we had our enforcers as well as anybody else.

Mick Hipwell: Ah, there's always a heave in the first few minutes.

Syd Millar: There was retaliation and we lost our concentration and that was the way they wanted it.

Willie John McBride: Price's contribution to the rest of the game was very little because he kept out of the way. Unfortunately, Noisy wasn't right. He stayed on, but he wasn't right.

Noel Murphy: The thing that annoyed me was that there was an insinuation that I had done something to provoke him. I did nothing. I'll go to my maker and I'll say the same thing. That we'll all drop dead in this house in the morning, I did nothing to him. Wales had a Murphy Plan. I was to be softened up as much as possible. Mervyn Davies has the story in his book.

Mervyn Davies, *In Strength and Shadow*: The only way that any team could beat that Ireland side was to stop them from killing the ball, in particular, Noel Murphy, the flank forward. When it came to ball-killing, he was a master. Murphy was a wily character. His prime skill as a player was his ability to spoil possession and he didn't mind taking a few whacks in the process. Clive Rowlands [the Wales coach] or Brian Price or one of the senior players came up with a devastatingly simple plan. If Noel Murphy wasn't on the pitch then he wouldn't be a problem. Ireland weren't about to drop him so we had to take responsibility for his absence. The Murphy Plan was fiendishly simple. From the very first scrum, Gareth Edwards would take the ball and run straight into him. When Murphy hauled Gareth down every member of the Welsh pack would run over the Irishman and with luck put him out of the match. 'Jeez,' I thought. 'Here I am playing international rugby with the best against the best and we're planning to do this.' I went along with it because I was a new boy and unwilling to break ranks, but my heart wasn't in it.

Some of the Welsh lads had been so indoctrinated into 'Get Murphy' you could almost see the steam rising from their ears. A maul formed on the halfway line, right in front of the young Prince of Wales. Brian Price, our captain, a class act and superb player saw Murphy's head pop out of the side of the maul and went for him with a haymaker. Brian always protested that he was retaliating after someone went for his eyes but he wasn't entirely convincing. It was a poor shot but one that made contact. However, Mr Murphy must have had a plan of his own because he thought about it for a few seconds and then clutched his face and fell dramatically to the floor. Tom Kiernan, the Irish captain, came running up shouting, 'That's the Murphy Plan, that's the Murphy Plan, we've heard all about it.'

Brian Price: I think it was the French player, Benoit Dauga, who said it to us, 'You have to make the Irish quiet. If they are on the floor we go all over them and they don't talk so much.' Noel, a good friend of mine, was the main inspiration to the Ireland side, so much our discussion with Clive was about stopping him. Somehow it got out and at the Friday press conference in Bridgend. I was asked about the Murphy Plan and I said, 'I don't know what you're talking about.'

Noel Murphy: I wouldn't say he knocked me out, but I lost two teeth. I probably regret now that it took me out of the game more than it should have. I played on because there were no subs. I wasn't concussed, but I wasn't right. Concussed means you're out of your mind altogether and I wasn't that. I knew where I was, but I wasn't myself. I wouldn't have thought that Brian would have done that, but we became great pals afterwards.

Mick Hipwell: We were badly beaten on the day, 24-11. The Noisy thing has been built up into the reason why we lost, but it wasn't. We weren't in their league. We liked to think we were, but we didn't have the wherewithal to beat that Welsh team. People would want to remember who we were up against – JPR Williams, Gerald Davies, Barry John, Gareth Edwards. There was a team emerging and we didn't have the means of marking them.

Ah, I'll be shot for this. A lot of Munster people whined about that incident but I don't have much time for them. Noisy got a bang. How could Munster rugby people complain about a player getting a bang, for Christ's sake. You're into a terribly tense match and you're going to get problems in the first ten or fifteen minutes no matter what you do. Mike Gibson got a great try for us, but punch or no punch, we weren't good enough.

Noel Murphy: I was thirty-three and I knew it was my last cap. I'd had eleven years in the team and my time had come. I remember playing my very last game for Con a while later and taking my boots off and putting them away and knowing that I wouldn't play anymore. I watch a lot of horse-racing and I see jockeys over the years losing their nerve and I think I might have lost my nerve a little bit as well. It was a great ol' life, though. Forty-one caps for Ireland but, you know what, it's the people I remember, not the games. I couldn't tell you much about any of those matches. For me, it was always about the friends I made along the way. That was the special thing.

FOUR

NO BORDER IN THE IRISH DRESSING ROOM

When Dawie de Villiers' Springboks touched down in Dublin airport in January 1970 they would have known what was awaiting them – the same chaotic scenes they'd witnessed in their earlier games on tour in Leicester, Newport and Manchester, in Aberdeen, Aberavon and Aldershot and other places besides.

The Springboks had travelled the length and breadth of Britain and anti-apartheid protestors had targeted them at every turn. In London, an activist jumped behind the wheel of the South African team bus and sped off from their Park Lane hotel with half the squad on-board. A player seized the hijacker by the neck and in the pandemonium the bus ploughed into a row of cars near Green Park underground station.

Four hours later, the Springboks ran out to play England.

The disturbances in Britain were repeated in Ireland. The Springboks were supposed to play three games – against Munster in Limerick, Ulster in Belfast and Ireland at Lansdowne Road – but the Ravenhill leg was abandoned on advice from the Royal Ulster Constabulary. The following day the *Natal Mercury* in South Africa reported the cancellation saying that the game was off because the battlefield had already been booked, a reference to the growing violence in Northern Ireland.

The preamble to the Test match in Dublin was tense. President Eamon de Valera let it be known that he was declining an invite from the IRFU to attend the game. The Taoiseach, Jack Lynch, followed suit soon after.

The Irish Transport and General Workers Union (ITGWU) called on its members to refuse to deal with the visiting South Africans. Trade unions in RTE discussed taking action to stop the game being screened. Bitterness and rancour spread out in all different directions. Members of the Ulster Unionist party threatened to hold a counter picket at the game to protest at what they called the real apartheid in Irish sport – the GAA's ban on foreign games. The Ulster Volunteer Force threatened to take action if the Springboks were interfered with.

The touring party arrived on January 7, 1970 and there were scuffles at the terminal in Dublin airport. The *Irish Times* called it 'the Siege of the Springboks'. The Post Office Officials' Association cut off telephone contact to the team hotel in Bray and the local Sinn Fein organisation staged a protest. Gardai arrested a

Opposite: Mike Gibson emerges from the tunnel beneath the Arms Park as Ireland run out to face Wales in Cardiff in 1975.

man carrying an improvised explosive device near the Springboks' hotel. On the day of the game, thousands marched from Parnell Square in the city centre to Lansdowne Road to voice their anger.

Willie John McBride: They were outside the hotel, they were all over the place. I never had any problem with the protestors so long as they didn't interfere with my life. Everybody's entitled to their own opinion. Segregation is a terrible thing. It's a question of how you deal with it.

Ken Kennedy: I wasn't mature enough to say, 'Yes, we should be playing them,' or, 'No, we shouldn't.' We had our hands full in Northern Ireland and we would be wrong to criticise another country. I wasn't living in the north at the time, but my parents were there and it was a time when you looked under the car to see if there's a bomb before you drove away. We had our problems to sort out without making a big stand on somebody else's.

Ronnie Lamont: This was my comeback to the Irish side. I'd come in from nowhere. Four years I'd been out of the team and I was getting a lot of queries as to why I wasn't boycotting this match. I was fairly ignorant of the apartheid situation. I took McBride's attitude. If you can play against them and talk to them then there is a better chance of influencing them. But, to be honest, I was so delighted to get back on the team I would have gone to hell. Sportsmanship wasn't uppermost in my mind at that time.

Fergus Slattery: It was my debut and I can't really say what I'd like to say. Most Irish people hadn't a clue about South Africa or apartheid. I met an eminent surgeon around that time and he had a couple of jars on board and he was giving it to me big-time about playing against South Africa. 'You fuckers are disgrace, shame on you!' Next time I saw him was in a bar in Cape Town on a rugby tour. The hypocrisy of it. Apartheid was grotesquely wrong, there was no doubt about it. But the question was how to get rid of it. What's the best way? Marching around Dublin is grand to a point, but what does it achieve?

Ken Kennedy: You could see the security at the ground and you noticed the booing when you were on the pitch. I got hit by a bottle at a lineout, aimed at one of the Springboks. Afterwards, on the street, I was aware of people shouting at me and spitting at me.

Fergus Slattery: We were up against a great South African back-row – Piet

Greyling, Jan Ellis and Tommy Bedford – but I was playing with Ken Goodall and Ronnie Lamont, so happy days. Lamont was a number six and Ken was a number eight and I was a seven and we were a perfect match. There was definition there. But it was an odd day. You had thousands outside protesting, so the ground wasn't full. The pitch was covered in straw because of the frost and it was like we were playing in a meadow. Lansdowne Road was the place to go on the day after for farmers looking for silage. We drew 8-8. Not bad.

Ronnie Lamont: I shouldn't have come back because I did terrible damage to myself on the Lions tour four years earlier and I had to get injections in my shoulder. I was prepared to take the risk, but I should have stopped after the Five Nations in 1970. We'd won two and lost two. We hammered Wales 14-0 in our last game and I should have got out then. That was a Wales team with JPR and Dawes and Barry John and Gareth Edwards and Mervyn Davies.

Syd Millar: The 1969 match was an acrimonious affair. It was full of thuggery and violence and we lost Noel Murphy with a broken jaw after a punch from Brian Price. In 1970, the Welsh thought we were keen to avenge the events of the previous year. Well, we were. But we didn't want any nonsense. It was my last year for Ireland. I was only a month short of my thirty-sixth birthday and I had had enough. I had been on three Lions tours, being away from home for almost a year of my life, and had played twelve years of international rugby. I had a young family and a long-suffering wife and it was time to go. I couldn't have wished for a better exit.

Ronnie Lamont: The mistake I made was going to Argentina at the end of that season because that was really going into the jungle. There was no such thing as law down there. It was 'watch your back' at all times.

Mick Hipwell: It was a lovely country but we weren't aware of what was really going on in Buenos Aires at the time. We hadn't a notion that all these political activists were disappearing. They were throwing the bodies of the protestors into the fucking Atlantic. There were guys with rifles and radios on every corner. A few of us went to see a football match one day. It was Estudiantes versus Feyenoord in the Intercontinental Cup. We were outside the stadium when El Presidente's cavalcade of cops swept around the corner. Henry Murphy from UCD was standing in the wrong place at the wrong time and he vanished in the midst of all these policemen. They gave him a grilling about what he was up to, then let him go at half-time. That was Argentina for you. We'd no clue what we were dealing with.

Ronnie Lamont: We went up country for a match and I remember standing beside this guy and he wiped me with a beautiful right-hander and gave me thirteen stitches. I went off at half-time, got myself together and got back on. I tell you, I wasn't a happy bunny. In another match I got a terrible dose of concussion from a tackle. Did you ever look through a telescope the wrong way round? Well, that was what my vision was like after I woke up on the pitch and all I could see was daylight the size of a 10p coin. I didn't go off. I was running around the field looking for a ball with 10p vision. It cost me five days in hospital in Buenos Aires. And no cap, of course.

Mick Hipwell: Phil O'Callaghan got sent off against Argentina. Somebody said that it was filthy rugby but people get very uptight about things. It's like going down to Munster. It was Thomond Park hard. Whether you call it dirty or not, I don't know. The Munster lads wouldn't be saying it was dirty.

Phil O'Callaghan: The guy who was sent off with me had been put off four times that season. From the information we received we learned that getting me sent off was part of a pre-planned move.

Ronnie Dawson: I was the coach and that tour was all about our journey home. We were very hard done by. We were on a Varig flight booked through to London and the first stop from Buenos Aires was Rio and when we got to Rio the plane refuelled. There were a heck of a lot of guys in blue helmets standing around the place.

Mick Hipwell: We got off the plane while it was refuelling and there was a big ring of police around the aircraft when we were re-boarding. Special Branch came on and said we were being taken back into the terminal. We'd had a few jars but we were on our best behaviour.

Ronnie Dawson: We were accused of causing a disturbance on the plane, but that was untrue. My own opinion is that the plane was overbooked and they needed seats and we were caught. I tell you what, it was some of the toughest times I ever had. I had no Portuguese, I knew bugger all about the place.

Mick Hipwell: If we hadn't done what we were told then somebody would have got hurt. They had guns. It was heavy stuff. They needed the seats and they used the fact that we'd been drinking to get us off the plane. When we were going from the airport we didn't know where we were heading – a prison or a hotel or where the hell we were off to. We knew we'd been arrested.

Ronnie Dawson: The Irish ambassador looked after us in that we were taken to a hotel but my interest was in getting everybody home. I was back and forward to the airport every day and I found a guy who could speak English and he was helpful. It took about four or five days, but we got them all home. The IRFU issued a statement and threatened to sue Varig. They said they were looking for redress for the 'scandalous treatment and calumnies suffered' by the team. That was an interesting tour, to say the least.

The 1972 Five Nations began with a daunting trip to Stade Colombes. To say that Ireland's record in Paris was not good was an understatement. Not only had they not won there in twenty years, they'd hardly ever come close. In the ten games dating back to their previous win, in 1952, France had scored twenty-three tries to Ireland's four and 129 points to Ireland's thirty-eight.

History was made, none the less. Ray McLoughlin and Johnny Moloney scored the tries that broke the run of failure. Against all predictions, Ireland won 14-9.

Stewart McKinney: It was my debut. Ronnie Dawson, our coach, brought me in on the blindside flank and if anybody came around that left-hand side of the scrum it was my job to sort it out. Rucking and mauling was my game. I did a lot of stuff on the ground, probably illegally, but you took the kickings for it.

There was aggro in the first couple of scrums. Alain Esteve, their second-row, was kicking people and it got dirty. When I got the chance later on, I shoed him. I shoed him to hurt him. He was on the ground and he just winked at me. He should have been dead. Esteve was one of the toughest bastards around – the Beast

As France's half-scrum Richard Astre slips the ball away, Fergus Slattery goes hunting for French fly-half Jean-Louis Berot (out of picture).

of Beziers. He was one of five Beziers guys in their pack that day. They were French champions at the time. Fucking mental. Armand Vaquerin was one of them. A loosehead prop and a total looper. Years later, he blew his own brains out in a game of Russian Roulette. This is what we were dealing with.

Sean Lynch: I was scrummaging against Vaquerin and we won pulling up. Playing in France, if you were any way soft you were in trouble. I wasn't afraid of them. I could handle myself.

Johnny Moloney: That night we had, I wouldn't call it a dinner, it was a banquet. There were about twenty courses in a magnificent hotel. The whole thing was phenomenal. I thought, 'God, life doesn't get any better than this'. It was my debut, I'd scored and we'd won in France for the first time in ages. I was in heaven.

The following day, thirteen civilians were shot dead on the streets of Derry by British Army paratroopers – a fourteenth would die soon after – in an atrocity that is sometimes referred to as the Bogside Massacre but which most people know as Bloody Sunday. Three days later, more than 20,000 protestors gathered in Dublin's Merrion Square. They carried black flags while a band played the Dead March. The mood soon turned vicious. An IRA march arrived on Merrion Square and as police attempted to push them back with batons, petrol bombs were thrown over their heads and into the windows of the British Embassy. Three men broke through the cordon, hauled down the Union flags and burned them. A Tricolour was flown at half-mast instead.

The Georgian Terrace was ablaze by 5pm. The protestors stopped the fire engines getting through and when, after two and a half hours, they finally made it to the scene, the crowd tried to cut their hoses. Other buildings with British connections were also attacked. In Dun Laoghaire, a British-owned insurance office was burned down. Outside the Post Office on O'Connell Street, Sinn Fein members collected money for the IRA. Three men in black berets stood opposite a Tricolour. Anti-British feeling in the capital was at an incendiary high.

Dick Milliken: I was playing my club rugby for Queen's in Belfast and we were to go down to play UCC in the Mardyke on the first Saturday after Bloody Sunday. There was a call for a minute's silence before all rugby matches that weekend in memory of the people killed and clearly this put us lads travelling down from the north in a tight situation. It was a bit of a minefield. If we stood for the minute's silence we could upset one set of people at home and if we didn't stand we could upset another. We didn't know how to figure this one out.

When we arrived in Cork on the Friday, we were told that an old UCC guy had passed away that afternoon. I couldn't tell you if the guy existed or not. Maybe they were aware of our predicament and were giving us a way out. They asked us would we mind taking part in a minute's silence. We took it in good faith that the deceased was a great old clubman and how sad it was that he'd passed .The good Protestants from the north did their duty by this poor man. It got us off the hook. Just in case any diehards up north challenged us on it when we went home, we had an explanation ready. 'No, no, the minute's silence was for poor Seamus O'Toole, a legendary character at UCC.' We were more than happy to buy into it.

Ten days after the scenes of mayhem in Dublin, the team captained by Tom Kiernan played their second match of the Five Nations, at Twickenham, where tries from Tom Grace and Kevin Flynn put the English away. They were two from two and already mutterings about a Grand Slam could be heard.

Scotland, at Lansdowne Road, were supposed to be next. But there was a problem. Two of the Scottish squad, the wing Billy Steele and the hooker, Bobby Clark, were in the armed forces and the Scottish Rugby Union let it be known that they feared for their safety, and for the safety of others, in Dublin.

The IRFU responded by sending a seven-man delegation to Edinburgh in an attempt to reassure the Scots that there was nothing to worry about, that no paramilitary group had ever targeted the Republic and that the safety of all the Scottish players and officials could be guaranteed. The IRFU hit their counterparts with a history lesson, pointing out that that even during the horrors of the War of Independence, rugby internationals were always played in Dublin. Scotland had visited the city twice in that period. They came and went without incident back then and, they were told, the same would happen again.

In mid-February, the IRA issued a statement saying that the match should go ahead, pointing out that 'no true Irish Republican' would oppose the visit of the Scots. It wasn't enough. The SRU announced that they weren't coming. The game was off.

The response in Ireland was one of anger and indignation. 'What kind of people do they think we are?' asked the *Irish Times*. Ronnie Dawson, the Ireland coach, called it 'an extremely sad day for rugby football. The SRU have made a grave error of judgment. I would not have thought such a decision possible from a country which had such a strong affinity with Ireland.'

The *Irish Times* called it the 'worst administrative error taken by any rugby union this century.' Andy Mulligan, a former Irish captain, expressed his anger in the pages of a national newspaper. 'As an Ulster Irishman, with inevitably Scottish connections, it is hard to believe that the SRU has miscalculated the mood of

Dublin and abdicated its major responsibility which is to rugby and, in the present tragedy of Ulster, the coming together as a whole.'

Letters pages in the newspapers were crammed full of thunder, some of it coming from Scots exiled in Ireland. 'As a Scot living and working in Dublin may I say how sad and embarrassed I feel at the Scottish Rugby Football Union's decision,' wrote Jim McGowan in the *Irish Times*. 'For me to have to apologise for their decision shows how ludicrous the situation has become.'

A countryman of McGowan's wrote: 'The SRU's pathetic excuse that they are concerned for their players' safety is nonsense.' A third Scot, based in County Down, summoned up the spirit of his country's national bard, Robert Burns, to lodge his protest: 'I cannot express my disgust too harshly at the craven attitude of the SRU. What kind of 'sleekit, timorous, cowerin' beasties' are they? Scotland the Brave – a mockery.'

Stewart McKinney: It was Peter Brown who caused the whole bloody stir.

Peter Brown, Scotland captain: We wanted to play in Dublin. The players were not consulted. The interminable wait for a decision to be taken led to me being completely misquoted by the Reuters news agency. As instructed by the SRU, I stonewalled questions but, unfortunately, I closed the phone call with the Reuters journalist with the words that came back to haunt me. I said I was 'delighted that a decision had at last been reached'. The headline the next day was 'Scotland captain pleased with decision'. My name was mud in Ireland. I never forgave Reuters for that.

Ian 'Mighty Mouse' McLauchlan, Scotland prop: If they'd asked me, then I would have said I was going. Rugby is no place for politics. We made a terrible mistake. I don't know who was the driving force but there wasn't a chance I would have stayed away from Ireland had I a say in the matter. Were we in danger? No way. Christ almighty, we're a rugby team and Ireland is a united rugby nation. Nothing was ever likely to happen. Never in a million years did I see danger.

John Frame, Scotland centre: Ian is right. I don't remember being involved in a decision about whether we should go or not. I certainly don't recall being asked. You'll probably find some antediluvian selector who says the players were all asked but I don't have any memory of it.

Jim Renwick, Scotland centre: I was only a young player at the time, but nobody asked me anything. Aye, I'd have went. I'm not a political animal.

Ian Barnes, Scotland lock: It never entered my head that we shouldn't go. Were we under threat from the IRA? Total shite.

Sean Lynch: My view was that we had a good pack and we could have beaten anybody. I wasn't angry that they didn't come. It was their prerogative. But then Wales refused to come as well a few weeks later and it became a serious problem.

Ray McLoughlin: I was back on the scene and we were all disappointed that we didn't get the chance at a Grand Slam, but I had no difficulty in understanding the decision that was taken. They felt it was risky coming over because of what was going on. I can't judge whether they were justified in feeling concern about it. I didn't think that there was much risk but I could understand them thinking that there was.

Wallace McMaster: It was my first season on the team. I used to travel down to Dublin from Ballymena in the car with Willie John and Stewart McKinney because the feeling was that if you were on the train and there was a bomb on the line then that was you stuck. In the car, if there was a bomb on the road ahead, you could put the thing into reverse and go down another road and away you went.

We lived through that. We understood it. And we just got on with it. But the Scots and the Welsh were understandably shaken. On television they would have seen stories about bombs going off and it would have looked a lot worse than it actually was. So I totally got why the union guys in Edinburgh and Cardiff did what they did. They had a fear of the unknown.

Fergus Slattery: There's no doubt about it, we'd have won a Grand Slam that year. We'd already won both of our away games. We beat Scotland at home in 1970 and beat them at home again in 1974, so we would have beaten them in 1972 had they come. Wales would have been the challenge but we hammered them 14-0 at Lansdowne Road in 1970. I appreciate that it was a good Welsh side but if there was a Grand Slam up for grabs in that match, we'd have won. It's a regret. Scotland and Wales had a commitment and they didn't honour it.

Willie John McBride: I was angry about it. I was angry from two points of view. Firstly, because they didn't come and, secondly, because if they did come I think we'd have beaten them and achieved something very special. It was crazy the way they handled it. The unions in Edinburgh and Cardiff made the decision and didn't consult the players. It's the players who go on the field, not the bloody administrators.

It was always my belief that rugby people stood by each other. Throughout the murder and mayhem in Northern Ireland there wasn't a single game of rugby ever cancelled between a team from the north and a team from the south. We crossed over the border all the time to play against each other and the game was a great unifier in tough times. It kept people together. It preached tolerance. So for the Scots and the Welsh to stay away, that was disappointing.

Ken Kennedy: The team was at its peak and we'd have won a Grand Slam. We beat France and then they gave us a second game after the Scots and the Welsh refused to come and we beat them again. It was a deplorable decision by the Scottish and Welsh unions. They would have been given every protection. The Irish people would have welcomed them. I don't think the terrorists, on either side, would have dared do anything to an amateur team coming over. It would have been bad publicity for one thing. The Irish government would have made bloody sure that everybody was looked after.

A month after the truncated Five Nations ended, with Wales as champions, the French accepted an invite to come and play a friendly match in Dublin. Disregarding any thought that they might be in danger, most of their top boys made the trip – Pierre Villepreux, Jean-Pierre Lux, Alain Esteve, Jean-Claude Skrela and the captain, Walter Spanghero. Tries from Alan Duggan, Kevin Flynn and Johnny Moloney saw them beaten 24-14.

Less than three months later, Bloody Friday happened. In the space of eighty minutes on July 21 the IRA exploded twenty six car, van and parcel bombs at various locations in Belfast. Nine people died and 130 others were injured.

Willie John McBride: I was working in my rebuilt office at Royal Avenue in Belfast and we could hear the explosions going off at regular intervals. We wondered what on earth the world had come to. By three in the afternoon things had become so bad that head office sent out a directive that all staff should try to make their way home – as carefully as possible, they added. I got outside my office and saw scenes of chaos and destruction I never want to see again in my life. I heard another huge boom close by and the air was again filled with flying objects. This particular bomb was at Smithfield, somewhere behind my office building. I started to run, but almost immediately saw the extraordinary sight of an exhaust pipe flying through the air towards me. If it had hit me I would have been flattened and probably killed. The exhaust pipe flew past me and smashed into a window just where I had been standing seconds earlier. It unleashed a shower of broken glass that would have cut down a human being anywhere in its path. My great fortune was that I was sufficiently far away to dive to the ground to escape the murderous shards of glass as they flew over my head. After that, I ran.

There were a series of chilling footnotes to 1972. On the evening of November 26 a bomb went off outside a cinema on Burgh Quay in the middle of Dublin injuring forty people. Five days later, just before 8pm, a car bomb was detonated on Eden Quay on the Liffey. Twenty minutes later, a second car bomb exploded on Sackville Place, killing two people.

Thirteen days afterwards, incendiary devices were found at two locations in the city centre – in Clerys department store and in the toilet of a nearby bar. The suspicion was they were planted by the Ulster Volunteer Force.

On Saturday, January 20, as Ireland played the All Blacks at Lansdowne Road, another car bomb exploded in the middle of Dublin. There was one casualty; a twenty-two year old bus conductor called Thomas Douglas – from Scotland.

Stewart McKinney: This was happening when the All Blacks were in the country and we owe them a debt of gratitude. The team that really broke the ice in terms of saying, 'We know there's trouble going on but we're coming regardless,' were the All Blacks, who, on that tour, played Ulster in Ravenhill before they played Ireland in Dublin. The Troubles were very, very bad but these Kiwi lads would have played on the Bogside. It wouldn't have mattered to them. They were brilliant. I played against them that day and there were armoured cars around the ground and soldiers in the changing rooms with guns and all the rest of it, but nothing untoward happened.

The All Blacks played Ulster at Ravenhill on 18 November 1972 and fetched-up in Dublin in mid-January 1973 to play Ireland at Lansdowne Road. Bob Burgess was New Zealand's out-half, a player who had made his debut for his country during the epic series against Carwyn James' Lions two summers before.

Burgess had a reputation as a politically aware player. He was outspoken about the evils of apartheid and, in 1970, he had refused to make himself available for an international tour of South Africa.

Bob Burgess: I recall being nervous about going to Ulster during the Troubles but it wasn't really discussed. I don't think we really appreciated the politics of what we were getting into. The team stayed in a hotel that was about half an hour north of Belfast, at Dunadry.

We drove by bus to the game by what I understand was a rather circuitous route taking half an hour longer than we might have expected to take and I'm sure that was to do with secrecy. When we got to the ground, on the top of the stadium, there were armed soldiers. We saw them at training on the Thursday before the game. We trained at Ballymena and it was snowing. God it was cold. Snow on the

The All Blacks play Ulster under armed guard at Ravenhill.

ground and these British military forces all armed with machine-guns, which they happily showed us. The reception we got on the day of the game was huge. When we ran onto the ground there was such a roar and hand clapping that just carried on and on and on. I think we knew that our presence had been appreciated.

Before Burgess and his All Blacks reached Dublin he received a letter, dated 3 January 1973. On Sinn Fein headed notepaper the authors claimed to be speaking on behalf of the IRA and offered what they called 'advice' and 'explanation' about the level of threat that New Zealand were opening themselves up to if they fulfilled their fixture with Ireland seventeen days later.

'The Freedom fighters of the IRA are at war with Britain not with New Zealand,' it said. 'We will take steps to try and assure your safety, as we do not trust the Provos (our Black September group).

'It is unlikely that any of your members would be treated as hostages, although you play a foreign game and we know that many of you have close Ulster associations.

'No such immunity can be extended to any British team and we can assure you that it was with good reason that the Scots and Welsh teams did not come.

'By way of advice, we suggest that you should refrain from talking about politics.

'You should also refrain from making any comment on this communication. If you do, apart from other measures, we will follow our usual practice of denying all knowledge or responsibility.'

The letter was signed by two people: Mairin de Burca and Tony Heffernan.

Tony Heffernan: I was in the Official IRA for a period, from about 1969-1972. There was the Official IRA and the Provisional IRA. The Official IRA got dragged into the violence in Northern Ireland in 1970 and 1971 and, particularly, in the aftermath of Bloody Sunday in 1972.

It was a time of high emotion. The Official IRA decided to carry out a retaliation operation after Bloody Sunday. They targeted an officers' mess in Aldershot in the hope of killing senior paratroopers who had been involved in Bloody Sunday. They planted a car bomb and instead of killing senior British army figures they killed five cleaning women, a gardener and a chaplain and that caused an awful lot of people to stop and think and say, 'This simply can't go on'. A few months later, May '72, they called a ceasefire.

There would have been some activity from the Official IRA after that, but,

The letter which Bob Burgess received in advance of the All Black Test.

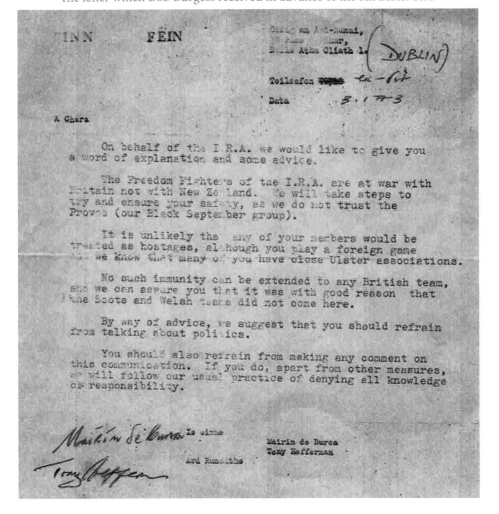

essentially, they knew at that stage that violence was not going to bring about Irish unity. It was a journey that was taking place for a lot of us. A gradual thing. After 1972 it was largely the Provos that conducted the campaign.

That's a brief take on the history. You've shown me the letter and at that time, yes, I was in Official Sinn Fein and yes, there were links with the IRA, but we didn't speak for them.

For more than forty years Bob Burgess never mentioned the letter, only revealing its existence when a New Zealand journalist, Lynn McConnell, interviewed him about that All Blacks tour for a book, *Behind the Silver Fern*. The letter was a haunting snapshot of the era and how rugby was being used as a political football in the midst of terrible times.

Burgess and the All Blacks knew they were entering an alien world in Ireland. They knew that horrific things were happening and that people were dying. They had the letter, with its undercurrent of threat masquerading as protection, as another reason to pull out as the Scots and the Welsh had done the year before, but they didn't. They came and they played despite harbouring doubts about the climate they were exposing themselves to. They were steadfast and heroic.

They didn't know at the time and will only find out now that the letter was, in fact, a fake.

Tony Heffernan: You've shown it to me and it's a hoax. When the IRA issued statements they always had false names. In the case of the Official IRA it was JJ McGarrity and in the case of the Provos it was P O'Neill. That letter would have left Mairin de Burca and myself open to a charge of membership of the IRA and various other things under the Offences Against the State Act. Nobody in their right mind would have used their real name. It would have been madness.

The New Zealand player wouldn't have known that, of course. He could only have thought that it was real and the fact that his team still came is a great tribute to them. There were a number of those letters around at the time, particularly in 1972, and for some reason they seem to have been primarily directed at the rugby community. There would have been people at the time saying that it was British intelligence doing a black operation. My view would be if that if that letter was from British intelligence the thing would be a bit more sophisticated.

The other possibility is that it was loyalist organisations circulating these things in order to hurt the economy in the south. If you had British teams pulling out and supporters worried about coming here then clearly it would have had done damage. The idea was that people would get these letters and be panicked. It didn't work in the case of the All Blacks.

Stewart McKinney: Then the English came in 1973 – and we owe them a debt, too.

Johnny Moloney: It could have been the end of the Five Nations had England not turned up in Dublin in 1973. To get it back on track, how long might that have taken?

Fergus Slattery: If England didn't come it would have fucked up rugby union and Ireland would have been bollixed because now England, Scotland and Wales wouldn't have come to Dublin and you wouldn't have known when they were coming back. There would have been no Five Nations. It would have gone down the toilet. Or we might have ended up playing our home games in Old Trafford or some place. England coming to Dublin was of profound significance because if Scotland and Wales were under pressure in 1972 then England were under ten times more pressure because, firstly, the precedent had been set and, secondly, the Troubles were worse in 1973 than they were in 1972. They could easily have pulled out. The English were up against the ropes.

Nigel Horton, England lock: The RFU said England would go to Dublin. That decision did not offend me, but the way it was done definitely did. We were told by

The forward packs battle for line-out possession in the 1973 encounter that helped save the Five Nations Championship.

the chairman of selectors that the RFU's position was that an England team would go, whether it was the first team, second team or third team. We were also told that if that we decided not to go they would respect individual decisions and it would not affect your future selection chances. We would probably have decided to go as a group, but what offended me was that we were not being asked our views at all, we were being told – even though we were out there representing our country. In the end there were five players who for various reasons didn't go to Dublin. I was one of them because, as a policeman, I was asked to attend a meeting with my chief constable and he suggested I should not go (for security reasons). I believe that none of those five, me included, played for England the following season.

Willie John McBride: I remember David Duckham phoned me. I'd been in New Zealand with Duckham on the Lions tour in 1971 and he phoned me and said, 'I don't know what to do, I've just got married and the wife is not happy that I go.' And I said, 'David, it's like this, you're the first name on that England team-sheet. If you cry-off, the thing's gone and you couldn't live with that.' He said, 'I dunno. Jean's nervous about it.' I said, 'Bring her with you. The girls will look after her.' He phoned me back and said 'Right, you're on.'

There's no doubt in my mind, had Duckham cried off then the game was gone. I remember some alickadoos saying, 'Why is Duckham bringing his wife?' Wives didn't exist in that world in those days. These guys hadn't a clue what was really going on.

David Duckham, England centre: I remember Willie John's words to this day – 'You must come, don't let the terrorists win.' That's all he said, and it sent a shiver up my spine.

John Pullin, England captain: There was another reason why I went and it was a selfish reason – and that was the fact that the English Rugby Union had said they were definitely going whether I turned up or not, and there was no way I was going to give up my England place. It meant that much to me.

David Duckham: We got off the plane, walked down the steps and straight onto a bus which looked more like an armoured personnel carrier than anything. Police outriders everywhere, high security. But the Irish Rugby Football Union, bless them, in case the IRA weren't quite sure who we were, had put a big cardboard poster thing saying 'England rugby team'.

Andy Ripley, England flanker: We concealed our apprehension beneath humour.

We played musical chairs whenever we travelled on the team bus, reasoning that the dozens of IRA snipers perched on the rooftops would find it harder to hit one of us if we were always swapping seats.

Dick Milliken: Both teams stayed at the Shelbourne Hotel before the match and there was a pretty heavy Garda presence about the place. It was a pretty grim time. Irish rugby was lucky to have people in the north like Ewart Bell and Harry McKibbin steering the whole thing through troubled waters. There would have been hotheads in the north, saying, 'Let's declare for Ulster, let's have our own team, let's not have anything to do with them down there.' All that sort of nonsense. That's the way life was. We had strong men in place who didn't entertain any thought of a break-up.

That England game was my first cap. Before I set-off for Dublin, a well-known doctor in the north, an educated man, told me: 'See when they play that *Soldier's Song* thing? You make sure you've got your back to that flag and don't be standing to attention.' This was a man I respected. He said, 'There'll be people watching you.' As a schoolboy, all I wanted to do was stand for the *Soldier's Song*, not because it was the national anthem of Ireland but because it was the thing that got played before every international – and I desperately wanted to play in an international.

David Duckham: The moment when we took the field, there was this most almighty roar. Such a moment. One or two of us were in tears. It even brings tears to my eyes talking about it now. I can't believe any of us were consciously aware of any danger but the fact was this was when we were most vulnerable. I just felt we had the comfort of 50,000 spectators and the warmth of the welcome was such I couldn't believe anything would happen.

Dick Milliken: We were going out on the pitch from the old Lansdowne Road pavilion down the far end. Tom Kiernan, our captain, was leading us out. The ovation for the English team went on and on. I remember talking to Fran Cotton subsequently. It was his first time playing at Lansdowne Road and he said before he ran out he was so fired up he was jumping on an old Ireland jersey and five minutes later, when they got that welcome, the tears were rolling down his cheeks. It was like letting the air out of a balloon.

The *Irish Times: In our thousands we stood, cheering and applauding, howling with ghoulish delight as the fifteen white-shirted Englishmen bounced onto the pitch. Left out in the cold last season by our brother Celts, this meeting of Ireland and England was an occasion to cherish. Who but the English would come to our rescue and contribute so handsomely to the wider cause of Ireland.*

Sean Lynch: Never at any stage of my career did I want to be one of the first out on the pitch but I was in a major hurry that day and Tommy Kiernan said, 'Just hold it.' He said, 'Let that applause die down and we'll go out.' Good thinking. Kiernan knew what he was at.

Wallace McMaster: We milked it a little bit for them. We let them get the ovation they were entitled to. We stayed out of sight and allowed them to savour it.

Ken Kennedy: The crowd stood to a man and woman and cheered the English team – and so they should have. It would have been the same for the Scottish and the Welsh had they come the year before. It was very emotional, even for us.

John Pullin: I don't honestly remember it that much. All I know is I didn't like standing for the national anthem and I wasn't too keen on lineouts. You were stood still too long. You felt vulnerable in the back of your mind, whether you admitted it or not.

Dick Milliken: We won 18-9 and I was extremely fortunate to score a try. There was a great photo on the front page of the *Irish Times* the following Monday of me scoring the try and I swear I dived from about fifteen yards out. In my mind's eye I can see it unfolding. The ball came across and it came to Mike Gibson and we must have had a two or three man overlap. Gibson knew that if he pinned his ears back he would get to the line. I continued to run half-expecting him to go all the way himself, but then I realised that he was going to pass me the ball. 'Why? Why are you doing this?' I got it safely into my hands and, of course, Wallace McMaster was outside me and the next thing he's screaming at me, 'Pass! Pass! Pass!' and I thought there must be somebody about to get me so I took off from miles out purely from fear that somebody was about knock me sideways.

It was a dream debut. Everything went right. Tom Kiernan came to me afterwards and said, 'You'll play many times for Ireland but you will never play better.' It was the first thing anybody said to me after the final whistle went and it was lovely. I was walking on air at that point.

David Duckham: We lost the game, but the result didn't matter in a deep way – and then JP crowned it all with his famous comment that, 'We may not be any good, but at least we turn up.'

John Pullin: I was just relieved to get out. You look back and you think 'What was the fuss about?' But you just don't know, do you?

Willie John McBride: I became captain later on in 1973. I had a guard sleeping outside my door at the Shelbourne Hotel. He was there because of threats. I said to one of them once, 'How real is this threat?' And he said, 'We don't know, but we can't take a chance.'

Syd Millar: What's Willie on about? I don't remember any policemen outside his door. That's nonsense.

Willie John McBride: Syd wasn't in the same position as me. I was captain of the team and there were people down south saying, 'What's that Protestant doing captaining Ireland?' and up here there were other people saying, for different reasons, 'Why's he captaining an Irish team?' I couldn't win with either of them. Syd was maybe not aware.

Syd Millar: The only player I know who had any sort of guard was Jim McCoy, who was an RUC constable. I don't remember any guards protecting Willie John or myself or anybody else. And I doubt that anybody gave him grief for captaining Ireland. Rugby football was not affected by The Troubles. We carried on.

Stewart McKinney: I wasn't important enough to have special branch fellas looking after me.

Dick Milliken: I don't know if there was anybody outside Willie John's door but there

Terry Moore charges off the back of the Irish scrum, supported by Johnny Moloney (right) and Fergus Slattery (left), against England at Lansdowne Road in February 1973.

was Garda presence that you'd be aware of. I didn't automatically think that it was because of paramilitaries, I just thought that it was a normal part of security. There were plain clothes guys about. For the English game it was crawling with guards.

Mick Quinn: I got on the Irish team for the first time on the day Willie John took over the captaincy, against France in Dublin, April 14, 1973. I was an out-half and so before the game I rang Mike Gibson. I'd heard that he wasn't all that friendly, but I rang anyway. I said, 'Hello, Mr Gibson, my name is Mick Quinn, I play for Lansdowne and I was wondering if I could ask you a few questions'. I asked him some stuff about the kinds of things he did in training because I knew he used to train on his own a lot. He said, 'What are you doing the weekend after next? Get a train and come to Belfast and I'll pick you up.' He picked me up from the train, took me out to his house and I stayed for the weekend. I met his wife and kids. He took me out to a running track and we trained there with some athletes. Then we did a run in a field that went downhill for the first fifty metres then fairly steeply uphill and after about fifteen or twenty of those I got sick. The first time ever, I gawked beside the pitch. I said to myself, 'This is the business!' I wanted to take in everything this guy could teach me. He was a phenomenal player, just that bit better than everybody else. But a very quiet guy. People thought he was stand-offish, but I always liked Gibbo. I heard that he was only in it for himself, a me-feiner, but I never found that. I thought it was bullshit.

Dick Milliken: In that France game I was marking Jo Maso, who was at peak of his powers. I was anxious and Gibson said to me, 'Look, just stand on his feet, hassle him, stare at him, unsettle him,' and sure enough after five minutes of messing him about in any way I could think of, you could see Maso's shoulders shrugging. He just disappeared. Gibson was a canny man.

Mick Quinn: Stewart McKinney took me aside and said, 'You just run these French lads back into me, Quinny, and I'll look after them. And he did. He was a tough bastard, an assassin, a desperate man. We won 6-4. I was so delighted to get my first Irish jersey and I wasn't giving it back or swapping it with anybody. I put it straight into my bag. I knew I'd have to pay a tenner for it. I gave Ray McLoughlin a tenner for his No 1 jersey and turned it inside out and swapped it with my opposite number, Jean-Pierre Romeu.

Ray McLoughlin: It must have been one of those magic disappearing tenners.

Mick Quinn: Now I had both No 10 jerseys. I was delighted with myself. Next thing Romeu comes into our dressing room and he says, 'Your jersey has No 1 on it'. I said, 'Yeah, yeah, it's grand, it's definitely mine, the zero fell off.'

On the first day of the 1974 Five Nations, a twenty-five year old second-row from Currow in County Kerry made his international debut. Moss Keane's mother had her rosary beads at the ready. His uncle, a canon, offered up masses. Moss had taken two days annual leave from work for the trip to Paris to play France. He bought a dress suit, black shoes and a new pair of socks for the after-match dinner. He was broke, but he was about to become famous and beloved.

Con Houlihan, a friend of Keane's, a fellow Kerryman and as fine as sportswriter as you could find, wrote of the scene at home: 'My father took a day off work to watch television. He joined many of his bosom pals in Myra McCarthy's pub in our town. There wasn't a dog to be seen in the streets. He said, "It would be a bad day for a man's cow to fall into a drain".'

Moss Keane: The French national anthem boomed out from the brass band in front of us. The sound waves seemed to thump against my chest. Their crowd joined in and sang with verve. There's something about *The Marseillaise* that stirs the heart. It got us going as much as it did the French. When the anthem finished private bands started up all over the place. I remember thinking that it was a bit like the Rose of Tralee festival back home in Kerry.

Stewart McKinney: That was a dirty ol' match.

Moss Keane: I was punched three or four times in the early stages. Even though I had been warned by the old hands the savagery of the first few minutes was something I never experienced before. I threw three or four back. There was no time to think. It was just unbelievably brutal and fast.

Stewart McKinney: The French front-row: Jean-Louis Azarete, Rene Benesis, Jean Iracabal.

Moss Keane: Twenty-five minutes into the match, Ray McLoughlin had his ankle reefed by a French forward and was shouldered off with his bad leg dangling, like an apple ready to fall off a tree.

Stewart McKinney: Second-row: Alain Esteve, Elie Cester.

Moss Keane: I found myself at the bottom of a ruck with my hands trapped in the jumble of bodies, my head sticking out on the French side. I had no way of protecting myself. I was not in an offside position, unless you could reason my head was offside, but big and all as my mouth is there is no way I could swallow the ball.

Stewart McKinney: Back-row: Olivier Saisset, Victor Bofelli, Claude Spanghero.

Moss Keane: A French forward spotted me. Probably the worst thing was I could see him coming and could do nothing about it. It was like watching a scene in slow motion. He looked to see where I was lying, looked away almost nonchalantly, as if he was looking for his mammy in the stands, and then deliberately drove his studs into the side of my head with the full force of his boot. He ran off without looking down, but he knew he was on target. He must have felt the crunch of flesh and bone under the sole of his boot.

Stewart McKinney: A couple of right ones there.

Moss Keane: The blood poured out of the gash in the side of my head between my eye and my ear. And right there in the middle of Parc des Princes, Paris, a very strange thought went through my mind. I thought it would be handy if someone had a bucket so we could have made a few black puddings. We used to kill a pig twice a year at home in Currow and the blood was mixed with bread, barley, onion and spices to make up the black puddings. I got a fit of laughing. It was a surreal thing to be thinking.

Ireland lost the match 9-6. On the full-time whistle, Keane shook hands with all but one of the French players. His assailant got the Currow stare and a vow of revenge that was uniquely Moss. 'Beidh lá eile, you French bollix,' he shouted. There'll be another day.

There was no hope of a Grand Slam and after drawing 9-9 with Wales in their second match the Triple Crown was gone, too. The only prize left was the Championship, which Ireland hadn't won outright – as opposed to shared – in twenty-three years. They had England at Twickenham and Scotland at Lansdowne Road.

Moss Keane: Willie John went ballistic in the dressing room in Twickenham. He blamed England for everything from Eve's seduction of Adam to the disappearance of the dodo, and had us champing at the bit, ready to take them on. I was astonished. I was under the impression that because Willie John was an Ulster Protestant he would in some way tone down his pre-match address to the troops. But that was the thing about playing with the northern boys: we transcended

Moss Keane peels around the front of a lineout against France in 1974.

politics. It didn't take too long for me to reconcile my Republican heritage with the diverse political and religious backgrounds of my team-mates. There was no border in the Irish dressing room.

Stewart McKinney: We beat England and played some lovely rugby. Mike Gibson got two tries. That left us and Scotland.

Mick Quinn: I used to have a bottle of holy water from Lourdes that my father gave me and I used to bless myself with it before every match. Moss saw me and he comes over and says, 'Give us a bit of that firewater.' He put some of it in the palm of his hand and next thing Mike Gibson is walking by and he splashes a bit on Gibson and he gives me a wink. Then Willie John walks by and he gives him a bit of holy water as well. And then, McKinney, the arch Ulster unionist, gets a splash. It was like sulphuric acid going on the lads. We won 9-6 and that was good enough to give us the Championship. In the dressing room afterwards, Gibson says, 'How do you think I played, Moss?' 'Like a saint, Mike.' He said, 'Well protected by Our Lady.' Winning that Championship was a big achievement. The great Wales team had won the three before it and they won the two after it, so we broke the run. McLoughlin, Gibson, McBride and Kennedy had been in the team a long time and they'd never won anything. It wasn't a Grand Slam or a Triple Crown, but it was something.

FIVE

WAS CHOLLEY DOING 200 SCRUMS A NIGHT?

Willie Duggan: My first cap was against England in 1975 and we beat them 12-9. People mightn't believe it but I was nervous every time I went out on the field. You're walking out in front of 50,000 people and if you make a cock-up you're centre stage, so you had to perform. I always felt if you weren't nervous you weren't on top of your game. Fear helped me. I always came from the negative, that I wasn't good enough to be out there and I was trying to prove that I was. I was doing reverse psychology on myself all the time. I didn't think I was any good. I didn't. But I wanted to win at all costs. It was paramount.

Fergus Slattery: Willie was hard. The D4-type forwards played rugby but they didn't beat up the opposition, which sometimes you had to do. You needed physicality and you got it from Willie. He was an instinctive rugby player. He could read the problems and deal with them whether it was a scrummaging thing or a lineout thing. His physical presence was very, very important.

Willie Duggan: Myself and Slattery – a bogman from Kilkenny and a D4 toff, who just happened to gel.

Fergus Slattery: Training was never his favourite past-time. He'd turn up at Blackrock at the beginning of a season with a doctor's cert saying he wasn't allowed to train. And he'd be smoking his fags. But he'd train on his own and he wouldn't tell too many people about it. People finding out about it might have done his image a bit of damage.

John O'Driscoll: Willie would usually come last in most of the training sessions, but he wasn't killing himself. You knew if he ever beat you, you were buggered

Willie Duggan: There's no doubt about it, I smoked and I still do. I liked my few drinks as well, but you still had to do the hard work to survive. Training was something I felt I had to do and I didn't always agree with the type of training they used to put us through. They'd take us for mile and a half runs. I won't mention

Opposite: Gerry McLoughlin

the coach, but we had a training session at Lansdowne Road one day and the coach says the next man who drops a ball is going to run five laps of the pitch. Of course I was the fella who dropped the ball and he told me to run the five laps and I told him to piss off. I told him, 'I'll tell you what I'll do for you, I'll run ninety yards because that's the most I'm ever going to run in a game at any given time.' We got back to business after that.

John O'Driscoll: There was an awful lot to Willie. On the pitch and off it. There were other tough ones, but he was as tough as any.

Willie Duggan: What did I have? Sheer thickness, I suppose. You had to be able to handle yourself. That 1975 season, we beat England and France and lost to Scotland and Wales. Two out of four. That wasn't bad. The France game stands out. Those French packs, they weren't exactly clean. I wouldn't say they were any worse than we were, but there was more of them at it.

Before that game, a great mentor of mine from Blackrock, a man by the name of Dave O'Leary, phoned me up and said 'Willie, there's this blondie lad playing for France at the weekend and the French absolutely love him.' He was talking about Jean-Pierre Rives. This was his first time playing in Dublin. Dave says, '*L'Equipe* are going to be watching every step this fella takes and there's going to be twenty-five photographs of him in their paper. If you're in eighteen of the twenty-five photographs you've had a great fecking game.'

Dave rang me a week later. 'Willie,' he says, 'I've just got *L'Equipe*. There's twenty-four photographs of Rives and you're in twenty-two of them.' That was Dave's way of measuring how well you played.

Ollie Campbell: I went to school with Karl Mullen's son, Karl Jnr, and it was young Karl's ninth or tenth birthday – a Saturday. We were sitting in his house watching Ireland play England at Twickenham – 8 February, 1964. Everyone gathered round the black and white TV. It was Mike Gibson's debut and it went like a dream. Mike Gibson became my idol that day. Twelve years later, 17 January 1976 I make my debut against Australia at Lansdowne Road. I'm twenty-one years old and I weight 11st 2lbs. And my captain is Mike Gibson. What an honour to play with the great man. I had four kicks at goal that day and had four misses. Mr Consistency. We lost 20-10 and I didn't hear from the selectors again for three and a half years.

John Robbie: I made my debut the same day. I called Mike Gibson, Mr Gibson. I was twenty, but I looked about fourteen. I was a very socially shy guy and I was

Left to right: Ollie Campbell, Phil Orr and Willie Duggan.

going through a religious phase. People thought that I was some sort of intellectual oddball, but all I really wanted to be was somebody who fitted in. I never quite cracked that. Fanatical wasn't a strong enough word to describe my love of rugby.

I wasn't big enough or fast enough to be a great rugby player, but I was clever on the field and I was a strong captain. My second cap was away to France in the first game of the 1976 Five Nations. You got two jerseys and one pair of shorts and a blazer badge, but no blazer. I bought a blazer and my granny sewed on the badge and off I went to France. The day before the game there was a reception in the Irish embassy in Paris and I went along and standing outside the embassy were Jean-Pierre Bastiat, Jean-Francois Imbernon and Michel Palmie – the No 8 and the two second-rows. They looked like gangsters. I walked past them in my little blazer, thinking to myself, 'I want to go home.' We lost 26-3 but that was the best game I had for Ireland. I tackled my guts out. I got dropped, but I gave everything for the cause.

Phil Orr: That was my debut. I'd played against Skerries the previous weekend. From Holmpatrick to Parc des Princes - it was a bit of a leap. I was scrummaging against Robert Paparemborde and I was ready for it. Get low and dig in. Playing in France was just a different experience. The stadium and the sound echoing around. A cauldron of noise. You certainly didn't go down on the ball in those days. If you were on the ball you were fair game.

Willie Duggan: There was a second-row for France, I've met him over the years. He was about 6ft 9in and every time I see him he comes over and embraces me and I don't know who he is. When he embraces me he smothers me. I stand back from him and I think, 'How in the name of Jesus did we ever go out against those lads?' The size of this fella.

At the time, though, I never worried about size. I was a great believer in the harder you go in the greater chance you have of coming out the other side. If you stand back at all, that's when you're going to get injured. Keep going forward. At the time you don't feel the punishment because you're so wound-up with what you're doing. It's only after that it really hits you – on the Monday morning. That's when the pain really clicked in.

John Robbie: Roly Meates was the coach and he was fantastic. He was way ahead of his time. I played for him at Trinity and that team was like a machine. He didn't get the results with Ireland, but it wasn't his fault.

Roly Meates: Ireland were at a very low ebb when I took over in 1976 because so many senior players had just retired – Willie John had gone, so had Ray McLoughlin, Ken Kennedy and Sean Lynch. I bought a video recorder and a video recorder back then cost a thousand pounds and video cassette tapes lasting an hour cost twenty pounds each. I used to come home from work at six o'clock and put on the tapes and study other teams, just to see what I could pick up and tell the lads. I still have the tapes. I'll never look at them again.

With six defeats in their previous seven matches, little was expected of Ireland in the 1977 Championship, which was just as well, because they lost all four games. It was the first time they'd been whitewashed in 17 years. The IRFU took their wooden spoon and promptly hit Meates over the head with it.

The lowest ebb was against Wales in Cardiff where there were routed. JPR Williams, Gerald Davies, JJ Williams, Phil Bennett and Gareth Edwards inspired the home team to a 25-9 win. The game is remembered, though, not for the rapiers in the Welsh backline but the pair of bludgeons on opposite sides in the forwards.

It wasn't a dirty game, just niggly. Ireland sought to frustrate Wales and deny them quick ball for their lethal backs and they were having some success. With thirty-eight minutes gone the score was level at 6-6. The Welsh lineout had been rendered a mess by Willie Duggan, Stewart McKinney and chums.

Geoff Wheel, the Welsh second-row, blew a gasket. He threw a punch at McKinney and down McKinney went. Duggan turned around to see his pal on the floor and in his head he was certain that Allan Martin, the other Welsh second-row, was the perpetrator. Down Martin went.

It had been ten years since any player had been sent-off in a Test match and there was only ever one dismissal before that – in 1925. Norman Sanson, the Scottish referee, doubled the tally in seconds. Duggan and Wheel walked.

Willie Duggan: McKinney was laid out after a lineout and I didn't see who did it. I looked around and I saw Allan Martin running away so I ran after Allan Martin and I hit him a poke, thinking he was running away from the scene. In fairness to the referee, he saw Geoff putting McKinney away and then he saw me boxing Martin. There wasn't a lot else he could do.

But I didn't actually get sent off, you know. The referee came over to me and asked me, 'Would you mind leaving the field?' I said, 'Not at all, Sir, I'm bollixed anyway.' There was an IRFU committee meeting the following morning. I got a week's ban and I was back for the next international. It never worried me afterwards, not for one minute.

Fergus Slattery: We finished off the season by playing France in Dublin. Another defeat.

Willie Duggan: Slattery tells a story about me. We were playing France and there was a reception the day before the match and somebody stood up and made a speech and finished by saying, 'May the best team win tomorrow,' and I'm supposed to have said, 'I hope to fuck they don't.' That's fictional. I might have thought it, but I'm sure I didn't say it.

John Robbie: Roly got shafted at the end of that season. It was terrible the way they treated him. Ludicrous. Had he been given a bit longer he would have sorted it out.

Roly Meates: There was a disappointment and disillusionment at being removed. There were certain people who just didn't want me as coach. I personally felt that I was making a useful contribution to the development of the side and I think a lot of the players did as well. Rebuilding things brick by brick takes time and I didn't have it.

Noel Murphy, the former No 8 otherwise known as Noisy, took over from Meates as Irish coach. He inherited a team that had lost ten of their previous eleven Tests, a dismal run that was reflected in the make-up of the Lions squad that headed for New Zealand that summer of 1977. Only four Irishmen made it – Mike Gibson, Willie Duggan, Moss Keane and Phil Orr. It was the smallest contingent from Ireland in 70 years.

Johnny Moloney: In 1978 the final trial was played on a Saturday and the team was announced to the players later on that night in the Shelbourne Hotel. I was sub for the trial and went home after it. There was absolutely no point in me traipsing back into the Shelbourne to find out the news. I had started one game in the previous two years. My time had gone. I said to my wife, 'Will I bother going into this meeting?' I decided I would. The team was named and I was the captain. Nobody took me aside beforehand. I nearly collapsed. It was a great honour, but it was a hell of a shock

Tony Ward: I got my first cap against Scotland in the opening match of the 1978 season. That was Johnny's first one as captain. I was nervous. Everybody goes through it. You just wonder if you're up to that standard. You question yourself. You're playing with your schoolboy heroes and people you'd watched on television. 'God, am I worthy of being in the same dressing room?' There are players who need a kick up the arse and there are people who need a slap on the back and I needed a slap on the back. I needed to be told, 'Well done, you're a great player.' But if I was told, 'You're shit, you're not living up to your reputation,' I was crap. I don't know. Maybe it was to do with my upbringing. My father died when I was very young and maybe there was an insecurity there. But I needed to be told. That day, I remember the pipe band warming up and the eerie sound of bagpipes. Once we got the anthems out of the way and the game was up and running, I got this inner confidence. It was only then that I felt like I really belonged.

Gerry McLoughlin: I was a sub in 1978 and I was due to go to on the field against Scotland. The doctor told me to go on and the coach, Noel Murphy, told me to go on and the captain, Willie Duggan, told me, 'I'll break your fucking neck if you come on.' He was down injured and he didn't want to come off. I had to bide my time.

Stewart McKinney's try and eight points from the boot of Tony Ward got Murphy's reign off to a positive start, but no sooner had the sequence of defeats ended than it started up again. They lost by one point in France and then went down to Wales and England, the small mercy being that at least they didn't finish bottom this time. Second from bottom was progress, of sorts. In the final game of 1978 the captaincy changed hands again. Once more the job was given to a player who had been out of the team. Shay Deering hadn't featured in any of Ireland's previous six Tests matches, but for the visit of the All Blacks, conquered only days before by Munster at Thomond Park, Deering was parachuted in to lead the side.

Willie Duggan: To my mind, it was unfair on him. But Shay was a great player.

Tony Ward: I worshipped Deero. He was in sixth year in St Mary's when I was in first year and I thought he was the best thing ever. He would put his body on the line for you, he was the consummate team player, a remarkable man. One of the great thrills of my life was having him as my captain against New Zealand. That was heaven to me.

Colin Patterson: I was having a few beers in the clubhouse at Instonians when word started to spread that I was going to make my debut in the match against the All Blacks. I was scared witless. I had decided that I wouldn't go, that I was going to pull a hamstring on the Tuesday because I just wasn't good enough to play against these guys. All this fear went through me. And it was a real effort to get in the car early on the Thursday morning and drive down to Dublin. The first person I met standing at reception was Fergus Slattery and he shook my hand and said, 'Well done, you richly deserve it,' and that started to calm me down.

Terry Kennedy: I came into the team the same day. They called me the Rat. It used to be Ratface, but that never caught on. I was a winger. It's a bit of a convoluted story about how the Rat thing came about, but everybody thought it was to do with me side-stepping and creating tries. I played an awful lot of Sevens rugby so I did a lot of scurrying and jinking. Throw the ball to the Rat and he'll run up his own hole but he might find his way back down again and score a try.

Colin Patterson: We went to the first training session and I was asked to go across and work with the forwards. Pa Whelan was hooker, Moss Keane and Donal Spring were four and five and the great Shay Deering, Willie Duggan and Slattery were the back-row. We were doing lineouts. They threw the ball in and Moss goes up and slaps it down and it falls exactly between the forwards and me and sticks in the muck.

So I stand with my hands on my hips looking at the ball and then I look at the forwards and I look at the ball again and Noel Murphy, the coach, runs in and says, 'Colin, Colin, what are you doing?' There was this stand-off between the forwards and me and they were no doubt thinking, 'Who does this wee bollocks think he is?'

It set me down a certain path with the forwards. They were looking at me going, 'You better know what you're doing, wee man. You're not off to the best of starts here.' Johnny Moloney was my predecessor at scrum-half and Johnny would have gone in and taken that ball, but I just refused to accept it. If you allow forwards to get away with it they'll do it all the time. I said, 'I'm not playing until I get the ball right here,' and I held up my hands. If they were allowed to, they'd slap it at you in any old direction.

Colin Patterson.

Terry Kennedy: At 10pm on the night before the match against the All Blacks I'm in the hotel room with Freddie McLennan when Mick Quinn and Johnny Moloney appear at the door. 'How're you feeling, Rat?' 'Jaysus, I dunno. Grand, I think'. They said, 'You know what you should do? Go and have an ice bath. It'll take your mind off tomorrow. You'll feel great afterwards. You won't know yourself.'

I'd never heard of an ice bath, but I thought this was a great idea. They went away and got a load of ice and threw it in on top of me in the bath. They said they'd come back when it was time for me to get out. I didn't see them again until quarter to one in the morning. I didn't thaw out until six. I hardly slept a wink, not because I was worried about the match but because my legs were so bleedin' cold.

Colin Patterson: I couldn't sleep. I couldn't eat breakfast or lunch. I might have had a nibble at a piece of toast. On the day, I went into the team meeting and I was really nervous, then I got on the bus and was less nervous, got to the ground and walked on to the pitch and I remember standing in the middle of the park and I took a deep breath, turned around and looked at the whole stadium and I said to myself, 'Right, time to make mischief.' The nerves just went. And everything was in slow motion after that. And quiet. Absolutely silent. I never heard a cheer.

Willie Duggan: There was a bit of hangover from the Lions tour the previous year. On the Lions tour we played against Manawatu and I was rucked out their side and the little scrum-half decided he'd give me a kick in the head. I went off with seven or eight stitches and I came back on with the sole purpose of doing him. I couldn't get next or near him. I had to wait until he came to Lansdowne Road. We sorted it out there.

Terry Kennedy: We lost that match 10-6, but we did well. I had a grand game, with me cold legs. Andy Dalton scored a try very late on and I always wondered if it was legit. He dived on the ball but half a second later the ball was all over the place. I don't know if he touched it down. I remember Deero sitting in the dressing room afterwards. He said, 'I wish we were playing an international next week.' He was kinda down. I said, 'Why are you saying that, Deero?' He said, 'Because we'd be picked en bloc,' and I was so naive I hadn't a clue what he was on about. He said, 'Things change.' I said, 'No, no, they'll give us all another go at the start of the Five Nations and you'll be captain again.' And he said, 'That's not the way it works, Rat.' And how right he was. He never got another cap.

On the final day of October 1978, Munster created history when beating Graham Mourie's All Blacks at Thomond Park. It was a storied result that reverberated around the world and it was the big breakthrough that Gerry McLoughlin, the Munster prop, had been desperately looking for.
Locky was once a prospective Christian Brother. He was three weeks away from taking his vows of chastity and obedience but instead turned away and chose a path that was a sight less celestial. Locky had lost his faith in one sense but was

never more sure of it in another. In his own head he was the most driven prop in Munster, Ireland and maybe even the world.

Gerry McLoughlin: Rugby became the love of my life. I was in college in Galway, but I always went home to play for Shannon. I thumbed up and down twice a week for training and matches. Playing with Shannon was the greatest thrill. You could say that playing with Shannon was fulfilment in itself. I'd have gone out on one leg for Shannon

The power was always against us in Limerick and, particularly, my club. It made you feel inferior as a person. I think we all felt that we were inferior players compared to the fellas above in Dublin, the guys at the Blackrocks and the Lansdownes. What were we only a working man's club. There was a snobbery. That made me all the more determined to get up to Dublin and prove I was something.

I was a front-row forward, a tight-head prop, right? Tight-head props have to be the most destructive, single-minded people in the team because all the pressure comes through you. You have to know the game inside out. They say props are thick. I tell you something, the tight-head has to be clever, tenacious and dominating as a person. I was in the front-row for twenty years. There's all sorts of things going on in a scrum and you have to be all one unit and somebody has to hold it together and the guy who holds it together is the guy who suffers the most and that's the tighthead prop – me.

When the IRFU asked me for my details I did all the right things; I deducted a year from my age, added a half-inch to my height and stuck seven pounds of lead down my jockstrap to make sure I was over fourteen stone. I got my big chance in January 1979 against France. Was I nervous? I was and I wasn't. I was up against Gerard Cholley – a 19st amateur boxer, but Cholley hadn't done 200 scrums a night on the back pitch at Thomond Park for the previous ten years. And that's where you learn your trade. I had tougher jobs scrummaging against the Shannon junior team than I had scrummaging against him. I'm not telling you a word of a lie. My biggest problem was holding my place in the Shannon team.

I lived down the road from Thomond Park. I had to buy a house nearby because I spent all my days there. I knew every blade of grass and every pothole. At training, I'd be insisting on fellas coming back out to do 200 scrums every night. The lads would want to go in for a pint and I'd go ape-shit if they didn't stay on for the scrummaging session. All the selectors and alickadoos in the clubhouse drinking pints. Fuck that. 'Come out here and stand on this machine while we push it around in the muck.' If we couldn't get eight people to scrummage against we'd round up twenty bodies to go on the machine with their pints in their hands.

Pa Whelan was my hooker that day against France. We took one look at Cholley and Whelan says, 'Bring him down in the scrum.' A Garryowen man telling me what to do. I said, 'He's too fucking big. I'll push him up.' I got under him and we took two balls against the head. We drew 9-9 but we should have won that match. We got a drop goal chance with a minute to go and all Wardy had to do was come back and give himself space, but he didn't come back far enough and Jean-Pierre Rives, a clever little man, stole about five yards behind the ref's back and blocked down Wardy's attempt. Other than that, we had the match won. The long and the short of it was that I stayed in the team and Cholley got dropped.

Tony Ward: In 1979 they introduced a man of the match award in the Five Nations. There were four awards in our games and I got three of them. At the end of the year there was a player of the year award and they brought all the individual men of the match to Lingfield racecourse in England to announce the overall winner. I had to contact the IRFU to get permission to attend and the reply I got was that were I to be named player of the year I was not allowed to accept or even be photographed with the trophy.

I ended up winning the thing and I went up and stood alongside the trophy but I wasn't allowed touch it or even be seen shaking hands with the sponsor. We

The shortlist for player of the year, 1979, at the award ceremony in London. *Left to right:* Tony Ward (Ireland), Gareth Edwards (Wales) and Andy Irvine (Scotland).

accepted it because we had to, but it was appalling. That fear factor was always there with the union guys. They ruled the game with an iron fist. I had a few friends on the IRFU committee at the time and they'd tell me who was bringing my name up and what they were saying about me. We went to Australia in the summer of 1979 and I was tipped-off that I might get dropped. I was playing great rugby, but the vibe in the background wasn't great.

Ciaran Fitzgerald: I roomed for the first week with Wardy and I felt for him because he was under pressure for whatever reason. Some of it was coming from the IRFU, who didn't take too kindly to the favourable press coverage of him. Through no fault of his own the guy was a pin-up and we never had that in Irish rugby before. He was very good looking, he had all the talent, he was kicking goals and was a real star and there was a lot of disgruntlement about the exposure he was getting. We were over in Edinburgh for the Scottish match and I remember a newspaper had a spread on Wardy in his swimming togs or whatever it was. Maybe he put pressure on himself, but I felt for him.

Tony Ward: There were three people centrally involved in the picking of the team in Australia. Noel Murphy, the coach. Jack Coffey, the manager, and Fergus Slattery, who was the captain. Slattery never spoke to me for that whole trip.

Ollie Campbell: Wardy had started the previous nine internationals whereas I hadn't played for Ireland since 1976. When I was picked to play against Queensland on the Tuesday before the first Test I thought that was my big moment on tour. Queensland were probably the best provincial team in the world. I thought that was my Test match and that Wardy was going to start the big one because he was European player of the year. Tony came up to me seconds before Jack Coffey announced the Test team and said, 'Ollie, congrats, you're in.' In my head, I was playing in the centre because it had been mooted as a possibility. Wardy hadn't said, 'You're in at 10,' he just said, 'You're in.' It was only when we started training as a backline that I realised what was going on. Tony had been dropped. It was an enormous surprise.

Johnny Moloney: We were aware off the fuss at home, but only to a degree. We had no mobiles or anything else. We knew there was a hullabaloo. Tony was very, very hurt. Understandably so. He went on the tour as number one, he was European player of the year and to get a kick like that was hard. There wasn't a lot you could say to him. I commiserated and left it at that.

Ollie Campbell: I don't think I fully realised what a devastating affect it was having on him

Colin Patterson: Tony was completely crestfallen, but he kept his head high and kept quiet.

Phil Orr: Sorry, but picking Ollie made perfect sense to me.

Willie Duggan: You can't just follow the ball as a back-row forward, you have to take the short-cut. You need to know where it's going to end up and then you go there. Sometimes with Wardy you looked around and he'd gone the other fucking way. You were standing there like a prick in the wrong place. He was a very good player, but with Ollie, you knew where you were. He wasn't just a goal-kicker, he was great defender and he could read a game better than anyone and he was a beautiful passer of a ball. He was a very intelligent rugby player.

Ollie Campbell and
Tony Ward

Gerry McLoughlin: The best player I ever played with in my life was Campbell. That's no reflection on Wardy, who was a fantastic player. I played with him and against him. I saw how good he was. Tremendous individual skill. A match winner. Wardy was brilliant. Campbell could do everything, though. A player's player. I'm not just comparing him to Wardy, I'm comparing him to everybody.

Tony Ward: When I look back there is no doubt that what happened in Australia did shatter me. I know I came back and played for Ireland afterwards but I was never the same player, never had the same confidence. Around that time I was a hugely confident player and I suffered on the back of the experience in Australia. It was the way it was done. There's no point in rehashing it all these years later, but it was wrong the way it was done. It was all cloak and dagger stuff. It was total political deviousness that went on in those days. Unfortunately I was a victim of that. I'm not playing a violin, but that was the reality.

Fergus Slattery: There was no doubt that Ollie should have played ahead of Tony. Both were very good kickers – as good as you could get. That was a 1-1 draw, but Ollie was a better player. Jack Coffey, Noel Murphy and myself made the decision, three man vote, 3-0. The problem with Tony's game was a lack of pace and it wasn't apparent to the intelligentsia in the media. He didn't have the pace to do the things that he tried to do. He was a great dancer, small and agile, but there was far more structure to Ollie's game. Wardy had a tendency to crab across the pitch rather than go forward and that put more pressure on the outside. It was only a bombshell to the people who didn't know what they were saying.

Gerry McLoughlin: We won both matches which was historic. Wales were over in Australia the previous year and they played the Wallabies twice and lost twice, so that'll tell you how good an achievement it was. Wales were Grand Slam champions at the time. Charlie Faulkner, Bobby Windsor, Graham Price, the whole lot. All those great players in the backline and they couldn't do what we did. There was a sad story at the end of it, though. Before I went on the tour I had hurt my back digging the garden. I had to get shots of cortisone to get through the matches. I came home and my father died ten days later. My back was still in bits and I couldn't carry his coffin. I just wasn't able. He'd wanted to go on the tour but I wouldn't let him. I'm awful sorry about that. He wasn't well enough, but he'd have loved it.

Mike Gibson: Those Test wins in Australia were my last games for Ireland, so it was a good way to go out. Looking back at my Ireland career, we would have periods when we simply did not have the class of player to deal with New Zealand or South Africa and so on, but we had fifteen people on the field who really wanted to be there and were prepared to sacrifice themselves for a victory. And if it wasn't a victory we'd cause as much difficulty as we could to the opposition. And after the match, if we won we would be delighted and if we lost we'd say, 'Well, we'll play somebody else next week.'

There are so many elements within rugby that are of use when dealing with life. The enrichment comes from the satisfaction of being the member of a successful side, but more from the fact that you were in a team which fought together – and those memories just will not leave me.

David Irwin: I was first capped in the 1980 Five Nations. I came into the midfield at Parc des Princes and we lost by a point and then I played at Lansdowne Road against Wales a fortnight later. There was no formal line-up for the anthems back then. You galloped about and when the music from the Garda band stopped you stood still and then they played the anthem. I was standing to attention and I looked around and thought, 'Why are all the other players looking at me?' and then it dawned that the Tricolour was behind me and they were all facing it and here I was a Protestant from the north standing with his back to the Irish flag. I did a fast 180 degree turn and hoped nobody noticed.

Tony Ward: Ollie kept his place and he deserved it, but I didn't want to be on the bench. You're on the bench and you're supposed to let on that you're happy, but I wasn't good at it. There'd be something wrong with you if you were. It was doubly hard because the guy who had my place happened to be the nicest guy you could ever hope to meet. I wish it had been like Seb Coe versus Steve Ovett and that there was a bit of hatred there. But you couldn't hate Ollie. It was impossible. I remember a game between Belvedere and Garryowen in Dooradoyle and the place was packed. I'd built myself up all week for this Ward versus Campbell showdown and when I saw him beforehand I deliberately didn't make eye contact with him. I wanted there to be an edge. As we were going out, Ollie comes up to me and says, 'Have a good one, Wardy,' and you absolutely knew that he meant it. He was a total gentleman.

Fergus Slattery: We kicked on into 1980 and 1981 and some of the selection was just awful. Selectors said things to me that clearly demonstrated that they didn't know what the hell they were talking about. They tried to accommodate Wardy and Ollie on the same team. Nonsense.

Ollie Campbell: The experiment began with Wardy at out-half and myself in the centre in 1981. We played three games together and lost three games and that was the end of the experiment forever. I was never happy in the centre. All of my life I was an out-half. That's what I knew. That's where I was at home. There was a world of difference between the two positions. I understood why they were doing it because since Australia there had been a lot of discussion about how both Tony and I could be fitted-in

Fergus Slattery: We lost all four games in 1981. Our problem was that our pack dominated in all of the games but we didn't have the backs to take advantage. We lost by six points against France, by one point in Cardiff, by four points against England and by one point in Edinburgh. It was a wooden spoon but it might have been a bloody Grand Slam

Ollie Campbell: Moss Keane referred to it as Ireland's greatest ever whitewash.

The 1981 Five Nations was played against a backdrop of protest over the IRFU's decision to tour South Africa later in the year. As was custom, President Patrick Hillery, was invited to Lansdowne Road to watch the games but he took the unprecedented step of declining the offer. Charles Haughey's government had earlier made clear their objection to the tour taking place, seeing it as an endorsement of apartheid.

As the weeks went on, the pressure mounted on the IRFU. Cardinal Tomas O'Fiaich issued a personal statement calling on the union to change their plans, a plea that was matched by the Church of Ireland Primate, Dr John Armstrong, and the Archbishop of Durban, Dr Denis Hurley. 'Be quite clear about it,' wrote Dr Hurley. 'Both the white South Africans and the oppressed majority of the people of South Africa clearly interpret the tour as an acceptance of the policy of apartheid.'

In February, the Third World aid organisation, Concern, voiced its objection to the tour and were soon followed by Trocaire, the Irish agency for world development. The African National Council, the Supreme Council for Sport in Africa and the South West Africa People's Organisation all condemned the IRFU. There were protests and petitions. Brian Lenihan, the minister for foreign affairs, met an IRFU delegation and asked them not to proceed with the tour 'in the interests of justice and Ireland's reputation' around the world.

His words fell on deaf ears. The union believed that sport and politics should not mix. The Ireland coach, Tom Kiernan, said: 'If you tell me my best friend is being unfaithful to his wife, should I stop meeting him? Where do you start and end with moral questions?'

In April, Donal Spring, a lawyer and a lock forward with seven international caps, the latest of them against Wales in Cardiff two months earlier, wrote an article in a legal aid magazine explaining why he was making himself unavailable for the tour on moral grounds. 'When the evil involved is so fundamental a part of society that it transcends all aspects of human life, as in South Africa, one cannot hide behind a banner labelled sport, trade or tourism.'

Spring had gone to South Africa in 1977 to see for himself what apartheid looked like. 'There seemed to be an endless supply of servants to cater for the white man's needs,' he wrote. 'The racist signposts everywhere – in stations and hotels and on buses spelt it out ... The mixture of hatred and fear that one felt among the non-whites side by side with the attempted justification and belief in the supremacy of the white man that was expressed by many of the people we met was incredible.'

The IRFU refused to buckle. The Irish Anti-Apartheid movement said their 'irresponsibility was bordering on the criminal.' In May, RTE announced that in keeping with the wishes of the Irish people they would not be covering the tour. Charles Haughey, the Taoiseach, made a personal appeal to the union to call off the tour. When they stood their ground, he called a meeting with an eight-strong delegation from Lansdowne Road to convey the 'full implications' of a situation of 'national importance.'

Nothing worked. The tour was going ahead.

Tony Ward: The IRFU were peddling a line at the time about the only way to break down apartheid was to build bridges and perhaps there was an argument in that. But I'd been there before. I'd seen it. When I was in South Africa with the Lions in 1980 we got the red carpet treatment, but myself and Colin Patterson scratched below the surface to see what was really going on. A lot of things upset me on that tour. You can call me an eejit but my conscience tells me what I should or shouldn't do and as long as my conscience is clear then that's fine. I have no doubt that I made the right decision in not going.

Ciaran Fitzgerald: I didn't go. I didn't have a choice. I was asked to declare my availability but I knew what the answer was going to be. I was based in the Second Battalion in Cathal Brugha Barracks at the time. I was captain. I put it up the channels and it went to the Department of Defence and the answer was no. That was that. It was a minor disappointment but I was conditioned to it. I knew what was coming.

Moss Keane: My decision was made easier when the government decided

Fergus Slattery, 1980.

to impose an embargo on all public servants forbidding them from travelling. This, of course, included me. I was not as influenced by the possible loss of my job as one might think. Things were bad in Ireland then – the economy was in recession and our biggest exports in those years were our emigrants – but I had been offered other jobs with different companies and knew I could find alternative employment. In the end I didn't go. I thought of the men and women who fought and died to win us freedom from the apartheid regime that existed in Ireland prior to Independence and came to my decision. But I would be a hypocrite if I said I was absolutely sure of my position, because I was not.

Tony Ward: Hugo MacNeill was a student at the time and on moral grounds Hugo made the decision not to go and I really admired him for that. Donal Spring didn't go either.

Hugo MacNeill: I listened to some of the black leaders in South Africa saying, 'Please don't come, the Afrikaners don't care about economic sanctions, but they do care about the Springboks.' The more and more I heard the stronger it resonated. It was all pointing in one direction. Ultimately, I said 'I can't go, it's just not right.'

Ollie Campbell: I was twenty-six at the time, probably quite immature in the ways of the world. Innocent, really. It's almost embarrassing to say it now, almost hollow, but all I wanted to do was play rugby. I was living and breathing it. Totally immersed in it. That's my excuse and I'm sticking to it, but I have fantastic admiration for the guys like Hugo and Wardy and the others who decided they couldn't travel.

Fergus Slattery: We slipped out of the country quietly. We decided not to go out through Dublin airport in a big group. Some left from Belfast, others from Cork and Shannon. It was heavy stuff. The government were like all governments. They had their head up their ass. They were saying you should reconsider this tour. What did they know about apartheid? Fuck all.

Willie Duggan: I got a lot of letters about going there. The view I took was that we were playing sport, we weren't politicians. What was going on out there was wrong but it wasn't down to us. About 20 years later I was on a job and a woman said to me, 'You're the rugby player who went to South Africa.' And I said, 'I am.' And she said, 'I'm not dealing with you,' and I said, 'That's fine, no problem. You're entitled to your view.'

John O'Driscoll: I'd been there with the Lions in 1980 and five years earlier I did work experience in a hospital in Cape Town for three months. The racism was there, you couldn't avoid it. I knew that the apartheid regime was a complete disgrace but I wasn't convinced that sporting isolation would make them change. I think you can get sport out of perspective sometimes. If you took away their ability to make a living that would impact them more. That's the way I explained it to myself.

Gerry McLoughlin: I was a teacher at Sexton Street, a Christian Brothers school in Limerick and I was given permission to go and the permission was withdrawn in the last week. There were protests in the school about why I was going. I could understand it. I had the height of respect for the Brothers'. Didn't I train to be a Brother myself. I wanted to go on the tour so the most honourable thing to do was to resign my job. Me and my wife decided. My blazer was measured and my gear packed.

John Robbie: I was working as a graduate trainee at Guinness, which was considered a job with a future. They had a lot of a business in West Africa – Nigeria and Ghana and places like that. They came out with a statement saying, 'We don't support the rugby tour to South Africa, but we support freedom of choice and if any employee has holiday leave we can't tell them where they can and can't go.'

That settled it. I was clear to travel. Then the Nigerian embassy came out with a statement that they weren't happy about the tour, so Guinness changed its view. One minute I could go and then the next I couldn't go. So I resigned. I guess I realised deep down that the Guinness job wasn't really for me. I look back now with some embarrassment. There's absolutely no doubt that rugby was used by the South African government to keep morale high. Symbolically, it was wrong to go. I know that now and I admit it.

To be totally honest, it was a selfish decision based on playing rugby, which my life was all about in those days. The old apartheid government got great comfort from rugby teams coming because they could say to the people, 'Look we have friends in the world.' Had the teams not toured I don't think it would have made any difference to apartheid other than the publicity. It would only have been a small, small blow to the regime. But I wish for my own soul that I had said no. And I also think what if I'd taken the correct moral decision and stayed at home. What would I be doing now? I came to South Africa and I've lived here ever since. I became a radio presenter and spoke about the evils of apartheid. The decision to come was wrong, but in many ways that decision was the defining moment of my life.

Ollie Campbell: Through his work in the South African media, John played his part in dismantling apartheid. I'm not overstating it. He was a constant voice against apartheid, a really brave campaigner.

Tony Ward: I have great time for John Robbie. Johnny really tackled the system from within. I've nothing but the highest respect for him.

Paul Dean: I was a baby on that tour. I hadn't a clue what I was doing. I went down to Soweto. I put on my blazer for the occasion. Some people I'd met took me there and they introduced me to other people in the townships and my eyes were opened as to what was really happening in the country. I was a just an innocent kid, a protected species from St Mary's College who didn't know what life was like outside my own little world.

Gerry McLoughlin: It cost me a lot financially, that tour. I had no job when I came back and I had a mortgage to pay. It wasn't easy. I was blacklisted. I couldn't get a job in a school anywhere in the country. I tried for 30 or 40 jobs – and nothing. I'd been teaching economics for 10 years before that. That's life. It was my decision to tour. I don't blame anyone for it. The memory of it is still fresh all these years later. We were taken to Soweto and I was appalled. No electricity but mansions in the middle of all this poverty. It shocked me. It was my first insight into how people in other parts of the world lived. It was a lesson for me and the images have stayed in my mind for the last 30 years of how people were treated. It had huge implications for my whole life afterwards. I sat down later and thought about it. We're part of one big universe and why should people be treated like that and not have the same opportunities as our children? I got into local government years later. I became a county councillor and then I became mayor of Limerick. What I saw in South Africa influenced the rest of my life in some ways, I'm sure of it.

SIX

TEN TICKETS! I NEEDED A HUNDRED

Fergus Slattery never had a problem in separating the rugby from the politics. When he thinks back on the tour now he talks about the significance of the matches rather than the strength of the protests. A depleted Ireland lost both Tests to the Springboks but there was a heroism in defeat that excited the captain.

The first Test ended 23-15, the second 12-10. Of all the games he ever played, for Blackrock, Leinster, Ireland and the Lions, he puts that second Test in Durban among the most memorable.

Fergus Slattery: Ollie Campbell pulled a hamstring in the first Test and that was the end of his tour and in terms of playing numbers we were on thin air at that point. Bad decisions went against us. Their captain, Wynand Claassen, came over to me after the game in Durban and said that we didn't deserve to lose. It was very gracious. We were unlucky. When we came back from South Africa we had new players and new options. We had Paul Dean, Michael Kiernan and Keith Crossan, three guys who hadn't existed before the tour. To get three like that was fantastic. We already knew we had a pack that could compete and now we had a backline, too.

Willie Duggan: When I came home I put a bet on us to win a Triple Crown and a Championship in 1982. I said, 'Jesus, we're getting this thing together at last.' I said it to Slattery.

Fergus Slattery: I had a bet as well. It was the only time I ever had a bet on rugby in my entire life.

Ciaran Fitzgerald: Fergus Slattery gave up the captaincy and I was offered it for the 1982 season and I jumped at it. The older guys – the pack, mostly – were suspicious of a guy coming in with an army background. Did I expect them to salute and jump to attention and all that stuff? I had to win their respect and I worked at it. They knew themselves that it was close to the last hurrah for some of them. They were getting hammered at home by the press and the public for losing

Opposite: Ciaran Fitzgerald

six matches in a row and the older ones didn't want to go into retirement on a low. They were lambasted as being too old. Dad's Army. It worked in my favour. I always knew what type of buttons to press and I did it one-on-one. If you can win their respect one at a time then the collective will follow soon enough. Some of them needed hyping up and some needed calming down. Some of the senior lads would have a personal battle with an opponent that I'd know about and I'd work on that, too.

Fergus Slattery: We had a fine pack with loads of experience and now we had Paul Dean, Michael Kiernan, Keith Crossan, Hugo MacNeill, Trevor Ringland. The backs were now as good as the forwards. I looked at our team and thought, 'Why wouldn't we win?'

Ciaran Fitzgerald: I was living about 300 metres from Moss Keane and I made a point of going for the odd pint with Moss and Willie Duggan. I trained with Moss every Monday and Wednesday night and I never saw a guy training as hard. This was his last stand. He was big on fitness and was more or less off the jar. I had him in my corner from the start and that was critical because if you had Moss then you had everybody, because if Moss thought I was all right then everybody else would have followed suit. They loved and trusted him too much to doubt him.

Moss Finn: Moss Keane was the greatest human being I ever met in my life.

Ollie Campbell: He was like an onion, so many layers to him. Highly intelligent and yet he spent most of his life trying to hide it.

Phil Orr: As a prop, having Mossie behind you in the scrum was like sitting on a wall. He wouldn't yield.

Ciaran Fitzgerald: The guy had such natural strength. He wasn't built in a gym. He was pure natural raw power.

Donal Lenihan: Because my father was from Kerry, Moss took me under his wing when I came into the team in 1982. Not every second-row would have been as kind to a young fella coming into his position, they'd be trying to protect themselves. But he was a rock. Looking back, I think a lot of his joviality in the beginning was for my benefit. He was putting me at ease, taking my mind off the game. He was selfless. Slattery, and a few others in that pack, were a little bit more distant to start with. With the Slatterys and the Duggans you had to bide your time and earn their respect, which was fair enough. But with Moss there was a different synergy.

I was twenty-two years old and for the first match in 1982, at home to Wales, I was the only change in the pack from the one that beat the Wallabies twice in 1979. Harry Steele had gone and I'd come in and I wouldn't say it was an armchair ride playing with those guys, but it was a privilege. Playing with Moss was an inspiration and an education. I roomed with him throughout that period. I always said that if I got through the Thursday and Friday then the international was a dawdle. The first thing he'd do is come into the hotel room and unpack the bag and he'd have six raw eggs wrapped up in 12 sheets of newspaper. He'd have two every morning for the three days to come. He'd have pollen tablets and garlic pills, all these type of things. Our room was the focal point for everybody to come in and out. It was an incredibly enjoyable place to be.

Ciaran Fitzgerald: When Moss got his hands on the ball and took off on those wild charges upfield the whole crowd at Lansdowne Road would go absolutely bananas. Starting with the first game in 1982, he got on the ball more often because he was fitter and hungrier than he'd ever been. The biggest problem we had was to stay with him and get the ball off him. When he went, it wasn't always easy to have somebody riding shotgun with him.

Gerry McLoughlin: I subbed twenty-three times for Ireland. Subbing? 'Twas four days relaxing above in a posh hotel in Dublin. It didn't eat me up being a sub. I didn't like it but I'd rather be a sub than not be involved at all. I was subbing for the last match in 1981 against Australia, but they brought me back in for Wales in 1982. Why wouldn't they?

Moss Finn: Tommy Kiernan was our coach. I used to mimic him. If Tommy made a faux pas in the team talk I'd take him off. The lads would be crackin' up. He was the greatest, though. Brutally honest. He had a ferocious insight on the game, was a great analyser of the opposition and fellas related to him. If he didn't think you were good enough he'd tell you straight out. You'd go up to Tommy with a chip on your shoulder and ask him why you weren't being picked and he'd look you dead in the eye and say, 'It's because the other fella is better than you, is that all right?' 'Jesus, grand Tommy, thanks.' Another coach might give you flannel. 'Well, I voted for you, but I could do nothing with the other four selectors.' Tommy gave it to you between the eyes – and that's the way we wanted it.

David Irwin: I was captain of Ulster and it came up every so often, 'You're a

Protestant from the north, you're captain of Ulster and yet you're playing for Ireland and you stand for their national anthem. What are you thinking about?' I'd say, 'It's sport, I live on the island of Ireland and, OK, I'm a British citizen but I've many more things in common with Ireland and the Irish than I have with the British. I'd prefer to be called Northern Irish.' These weren't good times in the north.

Trevor Ringland: My father was a policeman in the north. He came to watch me play rugby but only once did he use the free tickets we got from the IRFU. The other times he was in different places in the ground, for security reasons. He just felt it more appropriate that he kept varying where he was sitting. He was always made feel welcome, though. Always. That day against Wales – and all other days – I stood for the *Soldier's Song* and I looked up at the Tricolour, which the people who were trying to kill my father wrapped themselves in. Fortunately, they missed him, but he had to deal with the fall-out of some terrible incidents. You had to work with him as he dealt with some of the things he had to experience.

Years later, when I got into politics, I spoke to Ian Paisley. He wasn't a bad man,

Trevor Ringland.

he worked well for his constituents and he was very personable. But I said to him once, 'You know you've really blighted my life.' And he did. As did Gerry Adams. They blighted it because of what they were representing and what they inspired, the hatred they inspired. As a police family you had to deal with the consequences of that.

That day against Wales, I felt a sense of inclusion. I looked at the Tricolour and thought, 'That orange bit is about building something that includes me.' I felt a sense of belonging and I refused to let symbols like flags and songs be hijacked by extremists – on both sides. To me, rugby was trying to build bridges while others were destroying them. We were finding a way of working together in friendship.

David Irwin: I got injured in the opening game against Wales. I broke my leg. I was covering their full-back, Gwyn Evans, and it went badly wrong.

Willie Duggan: Wales were in for a try and Davie Irwin foot-tripped yer man and broke his own leg in the process. Davie was one of the hardest guys I ever played with. For a young lad, Jesus Christ, he had some will to win. He was a serious operator. He sacrificed himself that day.

David Irwin: I thought my career was over. Bob Ackerman, their wing, stood over me and shouted, 'You dirty fucking bastard!' and I thought, 'I don't really need this right now.' I was carted off on a stretcher, in underneath the old west stand and into the medical room. I got an inflatable splint put on it and I was taken out to the ambulance. We got going, for the hospital I presumed, but after about thirty seconds I realised we weren't going where I thought we were going. We drove in round behind the old east stand and parked. I was still in my kit. The back doors of the ambulance swung open and these two guards came round the corner fighting with this drunk who had fallen and cut his head. They threw this boy into the back of the ambulance alongside me and slammed the doors shut. I was sitting there looking at him. He turned to me and said: 'Are you alright there? Were you at the match?' That was a long day.

Trevor Ringland: I had a different experience from Davie. I scored a try – my first for Ireland.

Moss Finn: Tommy Kiernan had brought me back in from the wilderness. I was injured a lot, you see. My fecking hamstrings. From about 1978, I must have pulled 'em about twenty or thirty times. The selectors get shit-sick of you when you're continually getting injured, so for me to come back in 1982 was the greatest achievement of my life because I had to be twice as good as I was for them to look at me again given the suspicions they would have had about my injury record.

I scored two tries against Wales but I can't remember them. I got concussed. I got a belt on the head from Bob Ackerman when I scored the first one. This was when Campbell weaved his way up the blind side. I finished from six inches. I was deadly from six inches. I woke up in the middle of the second half. It's an amazing feeling to come out of concussion. I could hear noise again. Duggan was standing next to me. I said, 'Jesus, Willie, what's happening, boy?' He said, 'Shut up you fucking eejit.' Duggan wouldn't have had much time for small talk with a winger. I finished the match and was taken away to Vincent's hospital and I spent the night there. The highlights came on the television in the room and I sat there watching myself score two tries that I had no memory of scoring.

Moss Finn crosses to score his second try against Wales.

Trevor Ringland: I was dragged into O'Donoghue's that night by the older players, even though I wasn't sure I wanted to be there. I walked in and the place was full of rugby fans and I was so tired, but after two pints I didn't want to leave. You were arguing with a guy who said you were rubbish and agreeing with a guy who said you were brilliant. It was just magic.

Moss Finn: I missed the piss-up on the Saturday night and when I came out of hospital on the Sunday I was bursting for a couple of pints. Myself and some of the lads headed for O'Donoghue's. The second wave.

Ollie Campbell: We went into the season having lost seven and drawn one of the previous eight games – the draw coming against Romania at the tail-end of the previous season in a non-cap match. So there was sheer unadulterated relief after that Wales match. Our losing streak was over and nothing else mattered. A Triple Crown was the furthest thing from our minds.

Hugo MacNeill: We then played England at Twickenham. I scored a try but it's a forgotten try. Nobody remembers it. All they remember is Ginger.

Ciaran Fitzgerald: There was an interchange between forwards and backs and Gerry scored in the corner. He pulled us all over the line.

Gerry McLoughlin drives over the lines to score at Twickenham.

Gerry McLouglin: People ask me every day about the try, maybe twenty times a day. I have to make up a different story every time. It's gone from five yards to sixty five yards and from carrying five fellas to carrying fifteen fellas, it's gone from carrying Irishmen to carrying Irishmen holding me back. We had a scrum twenty-five yards out. I said to Fitzy that their scrum-half, Steve Smith, was a jerky scrum-half, he reacted to things. I told Fitzy what was going to happen. I said,

'I'm pulling this scrum about half a yard and Smith is going to put the ball in and the ref is going to call it as a crooked feed.' I said to Fitzy, 'Get ready to take a fast free-kick.' Away we went. Bang, bang, bang. Duggan, Slattery, Campbell, Keane, McLoughlin. I was looking for somebody to pass the ball to but there was nobody around so I decided to go myself. I could have gone another 15 yards.

Moss Finn: Ginger was an amazing player. He could be hammered in the scrum in the first twenty minutes by a fella, but he'd find a way through it and he'd have yer man done by the end of it. Ginger was never done. Another guy could buckle him but Ginger would keep going at him. What made him great? He had a bitterness in him. Hating the fellas above in the Pale was part of it.

Gerry McLoughlin: Two fellas ran on to the pitch when I scored – Timmy Boy Buckley and Cyril Guerin from St Mary's Park. Both dead now, God love them. One of them was on the sick and the other was working with Beamish and Crawford. Neither of them should have been in London. Two great rugby men. There was another guy who hopped down the touchline when we scored. A disabled man from Glin. Another character.

Hugo MacNeill: I was having breakfast the next morning in the hotel and Ginger had had a very short night's sleep and Nigel Starmer-Smith came in to do an interview and he was asking Ginger to describe the try and he wasn't getting much response. Then he said, 'Ginger, didn't you actually pull the entire team over the line with you?' and Ginger's eyes lit up and he said, 'Yeah, you're right, that's exactly what I did.' My recollection was that it was Nigel who came up with that famous line.

Ciaran Fitzgerald: The incredible part of that was the conversion by Ollie from the touchline, way over on the right-hand side. The match was still on a knife-edge. It was an incredible conversion.

Ollie Campbell: I missed a penalty that would have sewn the game up. I started it off left to allow for the breeze but it held its line. It was so irritating that on the Sunday I went straight from Dublin airport to Old Belvedere and did an hour's kicking, all from the same spot. Eventually I had to be moved along. The seconds were playing against Drogheda.

Hugo MacNeill: It was a time of depression in Ireland, twenty per cent unemployment, fifty per cent of whom had been unemployed for more than a year. It was really tough. The idea that we could go over to England and be better

Ollie Campbell's sensational touchline conversion of Gerry McLoughlin's try at Twickenham.

than them was so far removed from what was going on at the time. That's why the team has such a powerful legacy. It's because of the context in which it was set. It was a rare positive in a sea of negativity.

Moss Keane: I went down to Camden Town on the night of the England match for a few pints. I stood out a bit in my dress suit, with my nicely developing shiner, courtesy of a retaliatory strike that was much deserved. Rugby was never the game of choice of the Irish builders in England, many of whom would see it as a foreign game played by public schoolboys. I wasn't surprised when a ganger-man came up to me and said, 'Moss, it's an awful shame to see a big lump of a man like you wasted playing that ol' rugby. You'd be a great man at feedin' a cement mixer.' Then he bought me a drink. I didn't have to buy one all night. I had met emigrants from Kerry in Cricklewood when I was over before, decent, hard-working people who had to leave home because there was no work and no hope of work for them there. I always thought of them when I was up against England.

Gerry McLoughlin: Times were brutal. I was working part-time, I'd work Monday, Tuesday, Wednesday then off to Dublin on Thursday and Friday for the rugby, so I wouldn't get paid. I was struggling. Weren't we all? The country was in a fucking state.

Ollie Campbell: At lunch-times I'd get the 18 bus from Rathmines to the top of Anglesea Road, do an hour's kicking and get the bus back again. I'd be back down to Belvedere later on for training. I had come to an understanding with the caretaker, Christy Kavanagh. He wasn't happy about it but finally he agreed to let me turn the floodlights off after I'd finished my kicking routine on the back pitch. The Sunday before the Triple Crown decider against Scotland we were training at Merrion Road, home of Wanderers, and it was then we realised that something was up. We were used to training with nobody around and suddenly there was a crowd. Quite a large crowd. A crowd looking for autographs.

Ciaran Fitzgerald: There were about two thousand people there. I'd never seen anything like it.

Donal Lenihan: Tommy Kiernan was putting us through a really physical session. Duggan says, 'Look, Tommy, if you want me to gawk in front of two thousand supporters then keep going the way you are.'

Gerry McLoughlin: We were given ten tickets for the Scotland match. Ten! Mother of Jesus, Mary and Joseph, I had 100 people looking for tickets.

Fergus Slattery: There was an enormous build-up to it. This was the biggest rugby match in Ireland since 1949 – when we last won a Triple Crown.

Moss Keane: The night before the match I went up to Sean Lynch's pub in Aungier Street for a few quiet pints. I assured Kiernan I would be home early; I just wanted a sociable pint to get me off to sleep. Sean Lynch knew the score and spoke about anything and everything except rugby. I stopped at Paul Andreucetti's family chipper for a one-and-one on the way back. Paul was a fine centre for St Mary's and Leinster in his day and was part of the squad for the 1979 tour of Australia. There was no charge for the fish and chips. I signed autographs on greaseproof paper for a few fans in the chipper and was back in bed in the Shelbourne for 12 o'clock as promised. But for the first time since my first cap in Paris all those years before, I failed to get myself to sleep. I thought of the great players before me who had never won a Triple Crown. I thought of my family at home. I thought of the goodwill in the chipper and the unquestioning support of the fans. The worry of letting any of them down kept me awake for a long time that night.

Donal Lenihan: It was thirty-three years since we last won a Triple Crown and Jack Kyle and Karl Mullen and Jimmy Nelson and all these guys were on television and in the newspapers. The thing was, though, I'd never heard of any of them. I knew nothing about Kyle. I'd come from a completely different world, a GAA world. I had no connection whatsoever with rugby until I went to secondary school at Christian Brothers College in Cork. The first time I saw a video of a rugby match was the 1971 Lions. We were brought into the hall in CBC and we were shown it. The names of McBride and Gibson became familiar to me, but anything prior to that, I had no idea. I'd have spent my youth watching national league matches and Cork versus Kerry in the Munster football final. I didn't have any rugby pedigree.

Gerry McLoughlin: I was scrummaging against Jim Aitken, the Scottish captain. He was all right, but it's hard for any prop when you have four million people pushing against you.

Ciaran Fitzgerald: We were very disjointed and nervous at the start. We were hanging in and relying on Ollie slotting everything.

Michael Kiernan: Ollie was just masterful that day. The greatest pressure and yet he produced his greatest stuff. It was him who won it for us. A Triple Crown at last.

Hugo MacNeill: The greatest player I ever played with or against was Ollie Campbell. I used to say two prayers before I went to bed. God bless my mother

Ireland fans mob the players after securing the Triple Crown.

and father and thank you God for making Ollie Campbell an out-half and not a full-back.

Moss Keane: I sat in the dressing room not quite believing what had happened. The boys kept coming up to me, asking if I was alright. I shook hands with them – I couldn't talk. I was thinking of absent friends and how much I was looking forward to going back to Currow.

Ollie Campbell: My mum and dad both happened to be in Ravenhill when Ireland won the Grand Slam in 1948. They hadn't met each other yet, but they were both there. It was mum's 25th birthday. She went up with her older sister Peggy, who was the spitting image of Queen Elizabeth. I was born six years later and I was weaned on the exploits of that team. Jack Kyle was my dad's all-time sporting hero. He always said that the first word out of my mouth as a child was Jack, so to be out-half on the Triple Crown team 33 years after Jack Kyle had done it was very special.

Ciaran Fitzgerald: I never realised until afterwards what it meant to people. The whole of Dublin went bananas. We couldn't get off the bus at the Shelbourne Hotel for all the people waiting outside. I eventually got up to my room and the porter kept coming up with bottles of champagne from people I didn't know. Some of the bottles were two foot high.

Ciaran Fitzgerald's team joined Karl Mullen's immortals in the pantheon – and how they revelled in the success. The Five Nations schedule gave them a month off between defeating Scotland and going to Paris in search of a Grand Slam and for much of the time they were feted as heroes in a bewildering array of public appearances.

In the meantime, France quietly seethed. The Grand Slam winners of 1981 had been humiliated in the year that followed, playing eight Tests and losing seven of them, the only victory being a scratchy one at home to Romania.

A 10-point loss to Wales, a twelve-point defeat to England and a nine-point reverse against Scotland had piled the pressure on Jacques Fouroux, their coach, going into the final weekend of the Five Nations. In the maelstrom, Fouroux took out the axe and started chopping.

Seven players were dropped as Fouroux looked for the killer combination of flair and ferocity. A storied hardman, Pierre Dospital from Bayonne, was brought back at loosehead prop a year after his last cap. Another bruiser of renown, Jean-Francois Imbernon from Perpignan, was also parachuted into the side after a gap of twelve months.

Suddenly the French pack had a monstrous look. A front-row of Pierre Dospital, Philippe Dintrans and Robert Paparemborde; a second-row of Daniel Revailler and Jean-Francois Imbernon; a back-row of Jean-Pierre Rives, Laurent Rodriguez and Jean-Luc Joinel. This was the pack of forwards sent out to restore French pride against Ireland at the Parc des Princes.

Fergus Slattery: We fucked it up. France hadn't won a match. We made a bollocks of it.

Donal Lenihan: It was a weakness of the Irish psyche. If we'd played a fortnight after Scotland as opposed to a month we'd have won the Grand Slam. There's no doubt in my mind.

Michael Kiernan is felled at the Parc des Princes.

Michael Kiernan: A month was too long for a bunch of Paddies who had waited thirty-three years for a Triple Crown.

Fergus Slattery: I don't want to create the impression that we went on the piss for four weeks, but …

Donal Lenihan: There was so much hype and so many receptions. France had lost their first three and that didn't help either. The newspapers did wraparounds and pullouts for the Scotland game, which was unheard of, but the build-up to the

Grand Slam was not the same. It was as if the season was over.

Michael Kiernan: There were too many people within the set-up who didn't really care what happened in France.

With France having picked the most fearsome pack of forwards imaginable, Ireland needed all their warriors fit and ready for battle. During the week, they suffered the grim loss of their toughest customer, Willie Duggan. It was an injury, apparently.

Ciaran Fitzgerald: It was the Thursday, maybe the Wednesday. We heard there was a problem with him.

Ollie Campbell: I'm going to have to plead the fifth amendment here. I'll refer you to Fergus Slattery for further details.

Fergus Slattery: I know nothing.

Willie Duggan: What happened? That you won't be told. I'm going to write a book and put it in there to make up for all those expenses I didn't claim. A fella thought he was getting smart with us, that's where it all started. I'll say no more.

Ciaran Fitzgerald: Willie would have made a difference because Willie knew no bounds in terms of taking physical punishment and giving it back. We'd have been better placed to meet their grunt if we had him. They were out to redeem themselves. This game was their last shot at salvation and it was always going to be a war, but we had to fight it without Willie, for whatever reason.

Moss Finn: We were going to the match on the bus and we were going through this cauldron under the stadium. There was loads of mad French fans shouting and roaring at us – 'Fini! Fini!' Tommy had just given us the team talk and we had our big stern faces on. I turned around to the lads and said 'Jesus, hear that? Fini! Fini! It's great to be recognised, isn't it?' The whole bus burst out laughing.

Ciaran Fitzgerald: It was the biggest and strongest pack we ever came across – a street brawl from start to finish.

Fergus Slattery: They shoed their way through the game. The whole thing about the French, if you play them in Paris what you have to do is kick the shit out of them for the first five or ten minutes and that completely fucks them up because that's not supposed to happen. They're supposed to do it to you. Physically, you have to tear them apart. We had the shit kicked out of us that day, which is exactly the way the French had scripted it. Once that starts to happen there's no turning back.

Donal Lenihan: I thought there was nothing major about international rugby. I thought I was well-up for this level and then I went to France for the first time and this fucking juggernaut hit me. I was left scratching my head. 'Ah, right. Now I see what they're on about.'

Ciaran Fitzgerald: I got a going-over and for a good while I was seeing stars. I could see the first punch coming and I could see the second one coming but I was bound by two props so I couldn't respond. They were coming through from the second-row. It stunned me for a while.

Donal Lenihan: It was the first or second scrum of the match and we were defending on our 22. The scrum went down on Ginger's side and the whole French pack came over the top of us. It was like a combine harvester. You were being spat out on the other side. And to add insult to injury, Alan Welsby, the English referee, gave them the penalty.

Trevor Ringland: They were running at us with four-to-one overlaps and the crowd going mental and you're left defending it and just thinking, 'God help us!'

Moss Finn: It was extremely intimidating. I remember Ringland getting dizzy. He tried to run the ball out from behind his own line. He lost the head completely. He was reeling from the dizziness of the whole situation.

Paul Dean: They came running down my channel, peeling around lineouts, working off scrums. All day, the buses came. I still have nightmares. Once they get their dander up they are terribly hard to stop. I was like King Canute trying to hold back the tide.

Donal Lenihan: Only once in my life do I remember thinking, 'I'm going to be killed here.' I was caught at the bottom of a ruck, my hands were trapped, my head was sticking out on the French side and I saw Imbernon coming for me. It was the one and only time I felt vulnerable and scared on a rugby pitch. He came running in and by the grace of God I managed to wriggle my head out of the way in the last few seconds. Lucky escape. I met him subsequently. A grand fella.

Hugo MacNeill: We lost 22-9 and I remember being with a few punters in a bar that night and they were holding a pint in one hand and their other hand was clasped to their left breast covering up the badge that had 'Ireland Grand Slam 1982'. Some entrepreneur did these sweaters. They were all over Paris.

Paul Dean: It was a sobering end to the season, but nobody seemed to mind. The Triple Crown was more than enough for most people. To be honest, I was the smallest cog on that team. I was playing centre but I wasn't happy there. I was always an out-half and I always controlled the play and that was the fun of rugby for me. In the centre you're not part of the decision-making process. It was a fantastic achievement to win the Triple Crown, but I'd be lying if I said I was a big part of it. I wasn't.

After that season I decided that I wasn't going to play centre any more. I said, 'Ah, look, I'm not good in the centre and there's no fun and I'm not getting any better at it so I'll tell you what I'm going to do, I'm going to go back to St Mary's to play out-half and I'm going to enjoy myself again.' I went back to St Mary's and Tony Ward was the out-half so I said to them, 'I'll play for the seconds.' And I did and we had a ball. We were scoring tries from everywhere. I was only playing rugby for the love of it, so why play in a position that I didn't love? It wasn't like it was my job, it wasn't like I had to play centre because my livelihood depended on it. I mean, I was on the go at work from 8am to 6pm and then I'd go off to training. What's the point of putting yourself through the sessions and the matches if you weren't get a kick out of it?

Ollie Campbell: After the Triple Crown it was as if the Campbell-Ward debate had never existed. The silence was deafening. On the May bank holiday weekend, I was staying with friends in Westport in County Mayo and on the Monday I'm heading back to Dublin. It was a beautiful day and there's a woman on the side of the road thumbing a lift. I pull in and pick her

Donal Lenihan.

up. She hasn't a clue who I am. We get talking and she asks if I play sport and I say I do. 'Is it Gaelic you play?' she asks. 'No, it's rugby.' 'There's only one thing I don't understand about rugby,' she says. 'Why is Tony Ward not on the Irish team?' I'd no answer to that.

About ten years later I told that story on RTE Radio one Friday night. I went home and there's a message on my answering machine from a Margaret McMenamin – the woman I'd given a lift to. We stayed friends until her dying day. Despite my visits and my cards and phone calls she remained a committed Tony Ward fan until the end.

While Paul Dean was rediscovering his love of rugby in the St Mary's second team, David Irwin made his return to the Ireland midfield in 1983. Irwin's recovery from a broken leg and Willie Duggan's restoration after his Paris debacle marked the only two changes to the side that was coursed round the Parc the year before. They beat Wales in their opening game and then prepared to face the French. Jean Condom had replaced Daniel Revailler in the second-row and Dominique Erbani was in for Laurent Rodriguez in the back-row. New faces, but old memories stirred the Ireland team.

Donal Lenihan: We were ready for the fight because of what happened to us the year before. We set the ground rules that day. It was another brutal game. And this time we beat them.

Ciaran Fitzgerald: The level of intensity was very, very high because of the '82 match. We weren't going to be messed with that day. If you weren't prepared to be physically and mentally tough against France then you had no point being out there, no matter what skill you had. My mentality was that the more punishment I got, the more ferocious I became. It was a really easy team-talk to give inside in the dressing room. Lots of us had personal agendas. There were a few scores settled, that's true. The hunger was still there in 1983, but we got caught in Cardiff and it was a pity because we beat England after that, so it could have been a Grand Slam year. We just didn't turn up in Cardiff. I couldn't put my finger on it. There was just a deadness. We were joint-top with France, but it could have been better.

In the post-war years it was only the fourth time that Ireland had won three or more games in a single championship. Tom Kiernan's successful era as coach ended and in their attempt at continuity the IRFU turned to another great player and leader from its past – Willie John McBride.

Willie John McBride: I stupidly took it on. I was talked into it. It was the worst thing I ever did.

Willie Duggan: You have to remember that Willie John played with a lot of the lads, so it's hard to come back in when you have played with lads and then start coaching them. He really didn't do anything wrong. We were coming to the end of the road. Fergus was heading out the door, so was I, so was Moss. A lot of us in the pack were heading for the exit and Willie arrived into the middle of that. It was bad timing on his part.

Phil Orr: Willie John wasn't a coach. We did our best but it just didn't work. Willie knew some of the guys too well.

Willie John McBride endured a difficult tenure as Ireland coach.

Willie Duggan: We were getting some lads into the team who shouldn't have been there, who weren't up to the speed of the game. We were flying out to a match, and I won't tell you where, but I got one of the Irish players to come this way to pick me up and take me to the airport. We were on the road between Athy and Kilcullen and there was a truck parked on our side of the road up ahead of us and there was another truck coming against us. I was looking at it and thinking if we keep going at this speed we'll meet the parked truck at the same time as the moving truck – and that's not a scenario I wanted to be involved in because there wasn't enough road for all of us.

I said to yer man, 'Jesus, you're driving well within yourself.' I said, 'You better make up your mind now, speed up or slow down.' But he didn't. We were passing the parked truck at the same time as the truck coming down against us and the truck had to go up on the ditch and back down again to avoid hitting us. I arrived into Dublin airport and went over to Slattery and told him the story. I said, 'We're fucked on Saturday.' And I wasn't wrong.

McBride's final game as coach was one of the most mortifying experiences of his rugby life. Ireland trailed 22-0 at half-time against Scotland at Lansdowne Road and then panted and wheezed their way through the rest of the day, losing 32-9. 'I was hurt by that,' he said. 'I was glad to get back to my other life.'

McBride went, but he wasn't the only departing icon. It was Moss Keane's last game for Ireland. 'I made my way alone through the thousands of Scottish supporters who had invaded the Lansdowne pitch,' he wrote in his autobiography, *Rucks, Mauls & Gaelic Football*. 'One man in a kilt came over to me and said, "Thanks for the memories, Moss." I was trying to get my jersey off to give it to him but he was swept away in the rush of his compatriots. A small boy asked me for my autograph. I signed it and tried a second time to take the jersey off to give it away, but the crowd just swept us apart. I walked into the phalanx of Scots players lining the route in time-honoured fashion to clap us off the pitch. There were a few beers that night.'

It was also Willie Duggan's last game. And John O'Driscoll's. Fergus Slattery and Gerry McLoughlin had gone three games earlier. Ollie Campbell had exited two games before that. A driven prop, a beloved lock forward, an imperious back-row and one of the greatest out-halves of his generation had all left the stage in the space of six weeks. You had to go all the way back to 1969 to find an Ireland team-sheet without one of their names appearing on it.

Ciaran Fitzgerald: To lose all those great players and all that experience at once was scary, but my mind was very clear going into 1985. I had lost my place in the team and being out of it told me something about myself. It told me that there was still a little bit left in me and that being dropped was not the way I wanted to go out. Like Mossie and the boys, I realised I was coming near the end but I wanted a better ending. Mick Doyle was the new coach and I asked him if he'd any hang-ups with me. He said he didn't. He was starting with a blank sheet. He said he wanted to build a brand new team and he wanted me to captain it. I liked the sound of that.

SEVEN

DOYLER WAS OFF THE WALL

From his first days as Irish coach, Mick Doyle promised to make some noise. He was loud and bombastic, a force of energy and positivity and change. As a former international back-row forward and a long-time coach at Leinster he had the credentials to take on what was a difficult job in the wake of the dejection of 1984.

Doyle refused to buy into the pessimism. He took a look at the talent in the country and reckoned he could mould it into greatness. He said he wasn't going to play the traditional forward-dominated game but attacking play through the backs and a dynamic set of forwards.

He called up Brendan Mullin in the centre and Michael Bradley at scrum-half. He picked Willie Anderson in the second-row and brought in a whole new back-row; Philip Matthews at blindside flanker, Nigel Carr at openside and Brian Spillane at No 8. He said these were the boys who could achieve something special in the Five Nations, but outside of the four walls of the dressing room most people thought he was mad.

Ciaran Fitzgerald: In December 1984, Australia were playing Scotland at Murrayfield and Mick Doyle says to me, 'Will we go over and check out the Scots?' because we were playing them first in the Five Nations the following month. I says, 'Mick, if the IRFU give you the go-ahead for that then you're doing well.' Of course, they did. Things like that made a difference. Doyler was very creative and courageous and focused on what he wanted to do and he was encouraging of people who wanted to do the same. We were on the same page and what he was saying was invigorating for me because he wanted to play a stylish brand of rugby. The team was young and he said that we were going to play swashbuckling stuff and that was that.

Donal Lenihan: Doyler recognised the qualities within the group and devised a game that was tailor made to the players he had. He completely changed the way of playing. It was revolutionary. He'd had success with Leinster, but Leinster weren't playing the running game that he introduced with Ireland. So he was clever. That Ireland pack was very mobile. Willie Anderson had been in the back-row but

Opposite: Paul Dean takes a shot at goal against England at Landsdowne Road, 1985.

Michael Bradley clears the ball away from the Ireland scrum in December 1984, despite the close attentions of his opposite number, Wallaby Nick Farr-Jones.

Doyler put him in the second-row. Jim McCoy wasn't a renowned scrummager, but Doyler saw his positive attributes. He instilled confidence in fellas.

Des Fitzgerald: He'd been my coach for five years at Leinster and he was a guy who provided leadership in terms of motivation and commitment to the job, a guy who worked hard on the camaraderie side of it. He wasn't technically proficient. He wasn't a master strategist. But he was confident in himself and he was willing to take risks. He had lots of ideas, most of them not do-able. He talked us up. He said Ireland would run the ball and everybody was so busy laughing at him that they missed the fact that we actually did.

Brendan Mullin: Before that, playing rugby for Ireland really hadn't involved a lot of focus on back-play.

Paul Dean: Moss Keane was regularly heard to say in 1982, 'For fuck sake, don't give the ball to the backs, they'll run away with it.' He'd say it to Duggan. 'Willie, don't give them the fucking ball, hold on to the thing.' It was totally different now. Doyler liked to think laterally. He invested in me. He gave me a chance to be a running, passing out-half. I couldn't play any other way. I wasn't like Ollie and I wasn't like

Wardy. I didn't like kicking. Doyler was an ideas man. Now probably eight out of ten of his ideas were crap, but he'd come up with two good ones.

Keith Crossan: There was no backs coach then, it was just Mick. And he did devise some patterns for us which worked and others which were kind of weird. They were a bit over the top even for us. I remember us going to Deano after training once or twice and saying, 'See if you call that in the game, you're on your own.'

Paul Dean: Doyler used to say to me after matches, 'Why didn't you call that move I introduced last week?' And I'd say, 'We didn't get a proper chance, Doyler.' I was never going to call it because the move would have been absolutely ridiculous. Some of his stuff was off the wall.

Phil Orr: The team got a lot younger but I was hanging on as the elder statesman. I was the old head – the granddad.

Nigel Carr: I made my debut in the first match of the 1985 Five Nations against Scotland. Myself and Brian Spillane were new caps in the back-row. My old friend Philip Matthews had made his debut in the previous game, against Australia.

Mick Doyle.

Philip Matthews: Myself and Nigel were at school together, university together, lived together and that type of stuff breeds an understanding and Brian Spillane neatly fitted into that because you had two fairly disciplined guys on the flanks and then Brian who liked to make it up as he went along. It worked. You look back on some of those games and you're like, 'How did he know I was there?' or, 'How did I know he was there?' That back-row had a subconscious understanding. It was almost a telepathic thing.

Nigel Carr: One of the great things about rugby is that it gave me a north-south perspective that some people in the south of Ireland and a lot of people in the north of Ireland lacked. In that first match against Scotland there were six Ulster players in the team – myself, Philip, Willie Anderson, Jimmy McCoy, Keith Crossan and Trevor Ringland. There was a letter to the *Belfast Telegraph* saying that there are six Ulster people on the team so why aren't they playing both anthems? I was conscious of that. I can recall breathing very heavily during the *Soldier's Song* and worrying that somebody might think I was singing. It was tricky. All I wanted to do was play for and represent all of the people of this island.

Jim McCoy: I went into the RUC straight out of school. I had great pride in playing for Ireland and had no problem whatsoever standing for Amhrán na bhFiann. People in the police were proud that I was playing for Ireland.

Donal Lenihan: Jimmy became a target, with urban legend suggesting he actually received a bullet in the post from the IRA.

Jim McCoy: No, that did not happen. That was the rumour at the time. Information did come into Intelligence in the Special Branch. I was on a neighbourhood beat in Dungannon. People knew me from both sides of the community. I would go into the nationalist estates and, of course, they wouldn't be long telling me I played shite for Ireland the last day. It was a bit of crack. It worked the other way in that people got to know you but the week after that mortar attack in Newry (an IRA bomb on an RUC station killed nine RUC officers) they moved me as there was an IRA threat. I was guided by the authorities. I had the minders there and I was shifted from Dungannon to Bangor. I never questioned it. You were told you had to move and that was it. I never really thought about it or wondered if I was lucky to get out of it. Sometimes when we travelled down to Dublin for squad sessions we would be met by Garda special branch at Dundalk and escorted down, or at the train station in Dublin if we travelled by rail. That was the way it was.

Donal Lenihan: In those days, armed Special Branch were stationed outside the bedrooms of the army and police representatives in the Irish squad and these guys would often be brought to training in unmarked cars. In time, we all got to know the Garda lads and they almost became part of the team. It was normal to us.

Nigel Carr: They [security] were tasked with mingling with us and fitting in. If we were down the pub they had to be seen taking a pint as well. It wasn't a source of unease, but when you stood back you realised there was a very serious threat there.

Trevor Ringland: You had absolutely no doubt these guys would take a bullet for the guys they were protecting. You had guys playing in the 1970s and 1980s travelling to Dublin when there was an awful lot going on.

Hugo MacNeill: Doyler said, 'Go out and run the ball and have confidence.' We wanted to believe him, but we weren't quite sure. We won our first game against Scotland and played some fantastic rugby. Trevor Ringland got a try and everybody was involved in it. There was a fantastic loop by Deano.

Trevor Ringland: That try was the moment when we showed that this Ireland team was a different proposition. I finished it off, but it was a team try.

Des Fitzgerald: You had Mullin and Kiernan outside Deano and two strong wings in Ringland and Crossan and Hugo at full-back. That was a very good backline. Ringland scored two tries. We played the kind of stuff that Doyler had said we'd play.

Hugo MacNeill: In the dressing room afterwards nobody could sit down. We wanted to believe what Doyler was saying and suddenly it had all come off. 'Wow, we can actually do this!' Then we drew with the French and headed for Cardiff, where we hadn't won since 1967.

Willie Anderson, Brian Spillane (No 8) and Philip Matthews (right) envelop Wales No 8 Dick Moriarty in Cardiff during the 1985 Five Nations.

Phil Orr: Our record in Cardiff was shite. It was a graveyard.

Michael Bradley: You had 60,000 Welshmen roaring out their anthem and Spillane was singing his head off. I said, 'What are you singing that for?' and he said, 'I love this song.' That's the kind of free spirit that was in the team. It was just a group of fellas who wanted to go out and play ball.

Michael Kiernan: We didn't just beat Wales, we gave them a bit of a hiding; 21-9. To win in Cardiff after eighteen years was an unbelievable confidence-booster. There were an awful lot of demons banished. I look back on the Welsh game with more fondness than any other. The Arms Park was the most intimidating place to play. It even edged the Parc des Princes.

Hugo MacNeill: The economy in Ireland was probably in an even worse state in '85 than it was in '82, so again there was this feeling that what we were doing was almost bigger than rugby. The country was on its knees and here we were about to play a match for a Triple Crown, a match that would make us champions. As a country, we had no confidence. We didn't think we could be the champion of anything given the unemployment and the emigration and the despondency.

Michael Kiernan: The day of the Triple Crown game against England at Lansdowne Road, the country was up to 90 with all the excitement. It was a wet and miserable day and we didn't fancy that. We were a running team. The backs were scoring tries and the worse the weather the closer the teams became and that didn't suit us.

Brendan Mullin: As an outside back, one of the things I enjoyed doing was scoring tries. The try I scored that day turned out to be very important because it was a mucky day and there wasn't much opportunity to run the thing around. People still remind me of it. It was a slightly miscued kick from Deano and Chris Martin, the England full-back, had to take his time with the clearance kick because it was slippery out there. I charged up on him and I still remember the sensation of the ball hitting my hand. I knew it was out in front of me somewhere and it was only a question of trying to track it down. Sometimes you get lucky. We were a lucky team that year, things just went our way. The ball could have bounced anywhere. It could have gone to an English player, but it came to me.

Hugo MacNeill: With five minutes left it was 10-10 and Rob Andrew had a penalty about forty metres out and to the left of the posts. There was this awful moment when you're staring into the abyss. You're standing near the posts while Andrew has this kick and you're powerless to do anything about it. He pulled it wide and so we had one last chance.

Ciaran Fitzgerald: It was such a crucial stage of the match. I think I was out of things to say. I didn't know where to go next in the playbook, so I said, 'Where's your fucking pride?'

Nigel Carr: 'Where's your fucking pride?' I actually didn't hear Fitzy saying it. I only found out about it afterwards. Some of the other lads will tell you that that was the thing that made the difference, the thing that made them put in the final surge. What I give Fitzy huge credit for is the tactical changes in the latter stages of the match. Motivation alone wasn't going to win that game.

Michael Kiernan celebrates slotting his drop goal against England that sealed the Triple Crown for Ireland.

Ciaran Fitzgerald: We were starting to struggle badly so we needed something extra. We'd prepared a call for such situations. It was like pressing a button, a turbo charge, if you like. We used a short drop-out to Brian Spillane, one we'd practiced all season but never used, and that got us out of our own half. Spillane caught it and off we went up the pitch. It was probably the first time we'd been in the English half in about twenty-five minutes.

Michael Kiernan: There was a lineout and Donal Lenihan got his hands on the ball and took it up and presented it on a plate to Michael Bradley. Then, the famous drop goal. It's a wet day and the ball comes to you right in front of the posts and it was just a natural reaction. I wasn't taking a chance of passing it out the line and one of the lads dropping it. I stuck it over.

Ciaran Fitzgerald: It was a match we should have lost. The conditions were heavy and it was a big ol' English pack and they were ahead on most of the yardsticks you could care to mention. Our attitude was the thing that carried us through that day. Mind over matter.

Paul Dean: There was the pitch invasion at the end. Another Triple Crown. It was magic. The celebrations went on and on.

Philip Matthews: I wouldn't have seen a lot of this because I was living in the north and I was always amazed when I came down south because the hype and recognition was incredible. There was none of that in Northern Ireland. After the England match, all the Cork lads would be going home and they'd say to me, 'Come on down with us, we'll be partying for a week,' and we were going back up to Belfast where you could walk down Botanic Avenue and nobody would know who you were and nobody was aware that anything had happened. We were invited to the Coolmore Stud in Tipperary and there was a big marquee and Charlie Haughey was there and bands were playing and I was like, 'What is this all about?'

It was absolutely chalk and cheese compared to the north. You've got two very different cultures. The prevailing culture up in the north at the time revolved around The Troubles. Rugby was totally inaccessible to fifty per cent of the community – the Catholic community. It was very inaccessible to probably sixty per cent of the Protestant community, because it was all grammar schools. So you're talking about forty per cent awareness of the game within the Protestant community, only twenty per cent awareness of the game in the community as a whole, and the big thing I noticed when I went down to Dublin was that people down there were into all sports and they didn't see the cultural boundaries. Cultural and sectarian boundaries didn't really exist and they were just as likely to watch Ireland's Triple Crown as they were the All Ireland hurling. I remember Donal Lenihan talking about a Munster hurling final and thinking, 'Wow I've never heard an Ulster rugby player talking about Antrim hurling.' It was just unheard of. To be honest, it was one of the reason's I moved down to Dublin because that wider perspective of embracing everything was very appealing to me.

Nobody saw Ireland coming in 1985, but no team can remain a surprise packet two years running. 'The problem,' said Des Fitzgerald, 'is that when you become successful you need to work even harder to survive. Getting to the top is interesting, but staying there is much more difficult. Everybody is looking at you, finding your faults. Nobody is looking when you're not a contender.'

The others were waiting for Ireland and they had their revenge. All four of them. Doyle's team went from unbeaten champions to winless wooden spoonists, from a coming team to a faded force in the relative blink of an eye.

Hugo MacNeill: We needed to build on '85, we needed to move on to something else, but we went out and tried to do exactly the same things. People got wise to us.

Brendan Mullin: Teams changed their tactics and forced us to play a static forward-orientated game, which didn't suit us. The other countries didn't know the players in '85 so they couldn't plan for us. They had a plan in '86. Their approach was to slow it all down. We got bogged down in that. And when things weren't going well Doyler had a tendency to look around to apportion blame.

Des Fitzgerald: The victory in '85 became Doyler's and the losses in '86 became the players'. He blamed the players.

Hugo MacNeill: And when you blame the players that's when you lose the dressing room. We should have collectively acknowledged that we needed to improve. Doyler deserved enormous credit for 1985 but his wires got crossed after that. He was an emotional guy and it got too personal. His profile got a little bit too big and maybe influenced the way he behaved.

Philip Matthews: When you say he lost the plot, I think there was a lot of distractions and he was the kind of individual that would have enjoyed those distractions. My model of leadership wouldn't be Doyler's model. It would be one with a bit more humility, a bit more informed in helping people be the best they can be as opposed to, 'You're not playing well, this is making me look bad.' And that's how it was. When the team started to lose he became very critical. At that point, a real leader stands up and shows his strength. It's easy to be strong when things are good. Doyler said, 'Get your fucking fingers out.' It wasn't particularly sophisticated and I think it exposed his primary motivation which was, 'This is not making me look good,' as opposed to, 'You guys are not being as good as you can be, you're capable of so much more.'

Donal Lenihan: I would always have respect for Doyler for what he did in '85, but he became this massive public icon and when the pressure came on he didn't handle it. We were at a team meeting out in the Royal Marine Hotel in Dun Laoghaire and he said, 'I don't want to be remembered as the coach of a lucky Triple Crown team.' That was the day it dawned on me that Doyler, in his own mind, had almost become bigger than the team.

Trevor Ringland: We lost all our games in the 1986 Five Nations. We got a bit of a doing in Paris but the others were close enough. There was one interesting part to that season. I scored a try in the game against England and I have it on very good authority, from people who were there, that both wings of the Maze prison cheered when I scored. The joke is that I united Ireland that day.

Des Fitzgerald: In 1987, in the first match of the Five Nations, we beat England 17-0. There was lots of talk beforehand about England being on special diets and we had a right laugh at them. 'Give us over a couple more of them pints and let England stick to their nutrition.' We had great crack after the match, but we weren't laughing for long.

Donal Lenihan: I was captain in '87 and we actually did pretty well. We had that 17-0 win over England, then we lost by just four points at Murrayfield and by six points against France in Dublin, then we won in Wales.

Des Fitzgerald: I had a very unpleasant experience against Daniel Dubroca and Pascal Ondarts at Lansdowne Road, but the real nasties were in the back five that day. Laurent Rodriguez in the back-row was an animal. Francis Haget in the second-row was an absolute animal, a notorious hatchet man. You wouldn't be bringing him home to meet your granny. Dog rough.

Donal Lenihan: Before he died, I had great conversations with Doyler and any problem that existed between us was sorted out. He was a maverick, in fairness to him. He didn't give a shit what people said. But the fact is that by 1987 he'd lost his marbles. We had a good team and I was gung-ho for the first World Cup, which was just around the corner. I thought we could do well in it. But there was no backing whatsoever from the union. They sensed that professionalism was in the air and that the World Cup would hasten it. They saw it as the first step on the rocky road to the game going open. So we weren't allowed to train because that would look like we were taking it seriously. We got these letters, and Doyler was party to it, that told us that we had to rest for weeks before we headed off to New Zealand. I was raging. We organised unsupervised scrummaging sessions against Lansdowne, just to try to do something. Doyler wasn't at any of those sessions.

Michael Kiernan: There was a diktat from the union that we couldn't play for about four to six weeks before departing for the World Cup. We hadn't a clue. We thought this was the right way to do it. The union were dragged screaming and kicking into the World Cup. The IRFU didn't want it, so the preparation was never going to be any good.

Neil Francis: I was twenty-three when I came into the squad. I wasn't in awe of Doyler, but it was only a slightly diluted version of awe. That changed. The World Cup was all I wanted to do and I was devastated at the amateurish approach. I blamed Doyler. A fucking disgrace. I met Sean Fitzpatrick and he told me what the All Blacks had been doing in training and I was just embarrassed. He said, 'What have you guys been up to?' I said, 'Er...'

Philip Matthews: Wellington came over to play Ulster a year or so before the World Cup and when you tackled one of their backline it was like you were tackling a well-conditioned Irish forward. People say that the 1987 World Cup was an eye-opener in terms of us waking up to the difference between the way the southern hemisphere was preparing and the way we were doing it, but it wasn't for me. My eyes were already open. New Zealand were getting their provincial teams out of the country just to see how they were measuring-up against the rest of the world. I tackled Stu Wilson, the great winger, and I expected him to fold in front of me, but he didn't. And I thought, 'Wow, that's unusual.' We were years behind them. We weren't even playing the same game.

EIGHT

A BOMB – I THOUGHT HE WAS DEAD

Ireland eventually got around to training for the World Cup. Less than a month before their opening match, against Wales in Wellington, there was an international squad session in Dublin. Nigel Carr, David Irwin and Philip Rainey, the uncapped full-back, travelled together and hit the road early on that morning of April 27.
As the three players headed south, Lord Chief Justice Maurice Gibson and his wife, Lady Cecily, were heading north. Lord Gibson had been on an IRA hit-list for many years, ever since he acquitted a soldier who shot a twelve-year-old girl in Northern Ireland and then, some time later, acquitted three Royal Ulster Constabulary officers who had killed three unarmed IRA men after they sped through a police checkpoint.

Special Branch officers from the Republic had escorted the Gibsons to the border where they had a short unaccompanied drive through Killean in County Armagh before meeting the RUC escort that would take them home to Belfast. On the road was an abandoned Ford Cortina loaded with 400 pounds of explosives rigged to a remote control. The Gibsons and the car carrying the three rugby players drove past the Cortina at the same time and it was then that the bomb was detonated. Such was the weight of the explosion it caused a crater ten foot wide, twenty foot long and six foot deep. The Gibsons were killed instantly. Carr, Irwin and Rainey survived.

David Irwin: When you lived in the north in those days you almost wondered why you had never been caught up in something. When I was in school in the middle of town, there were bombs going off all over the place. From the age of ten, bombings were part of my life. When these things are happening all the time people get used to them. I'm not saying they didn't take them seriously but it was a case of, 'Ah, another bomb scare, OK, let's finish our pints and get out.' When it happened that day, the only weird thing was that it happened on the way to Dublin. You expected it to happen in the middle of Belfast. It's a bit like that film Sliding Doors where one thing had an impact on the whole day. Nigel was coming to my house and I was driving down. He kept missing these green lights on his way to my place, so that added another minute or two on to our departure time for Dublin.

Opposite: Donal Lenihan leads his team out to face Wales at the inaugural Rugby World Cup.

Nigel Carr: We were up and down that road a load of times, every weekend at certain times of the year. I recall that morning, after leaving David's place, we slipped through these traffic lights and everything was going in our favour and if we'd only had one red light on the way down there it would have made all the difference.

David Irwin: We were going through that area, Killean, chatting away, radio on, excited about the World Cup. There was this massive noise and what seemed like a thousand flash bulbs going off in my face. Light and heat. I remember thinking, 'My car has been blown up.' And I remember thinking, 'Why? This must be a mistake. Why would they do it to me?' Once I realised I was in one piece I looked to my right, to the lane heading north, and there was a big crater in the road. This has all happened in a matter of seconds. I scanned round and Nigel was in the front passenger seat beside me and the whole front of my car had been pushed in and pushed towards his side. And the roof had been pushed down. We were travelling towards Justice Gibson's car. His car was blown into the front of mine and that was an impact of maybe 120mph, never mind the bomb's impact.

Nigel Carr: I was unconscious or at least not compos mentis. It was David with his doctor's experience who had to deal with the immediate aftermath of all that. We were lucky David was there.

David Irwin: Nigel's legs were trapped and he had bad cuts on his head. He was semi-conscious. Through his window was a car that I assumed at that point was a police car and I thought, 'Ah, I get it, a police car has been blown up and we've been caught in the middle of this.' The other car was an inferno and I could vaguely see two shadows in the front two seats. I said, 'Look Nigel, you're fine, there's been a bomb, but you're OK, your head's cut and you're bleeding but you're all right.' I turned around and Philip was laid out on the back seat, not a mark on him, but he was motionless. I thought he was dead.

I managed to get my door open. Cars behind me drove past and at the time I thought, 'How can you drive past and not stop?' but they were in shock, they were just behind me when it happened and they drove off to get out of the way. Soon enough, the traffic 100 yards either side of us, north and south, just stopped. I went round and prised Nigel's door open and got his seat belt off. I tried to pull him out because I was afraid the car beside us was going to explode. His feet were caught under the dashboard. I pulled him so hard, I pulled him out of his shoes and carried him up the road, put him on a grass verge, took my belt off and tied his knees together as a sort of a splint. I went back and Philip was coming round.

I got him out and brought him up the road. At that point a big lorry was coming through. I said to the driver, 'Get up to the garage and phone for ambulances,' but the police were already standing up the road watching. They felt it was a booby trap. They thought if they rushed in there'd be another bomb. There was a surreal period of maybe five or ten minutes where I was running around trying to sort everything out and nobody was coming near us.

I got the two guys into the ambulance and away they went. I got a lift into the hospital in a police car and I rang my mum, who'd heard on the news that there'd been a bomb at the border and she knew immediately when I phoned that I was caught in it. She said, 'Are you OK?' And I said, 'I'm fine.' I rang Nigel's parents and Philip's wife and then I rang Wanderers to tell them we wouldn't be making training.

Nigel Carr: The first thing I remember is going in the ambulance to the hospital and hearing the hushed tones of the driver and realising that somebody had been killed. There was one other person in the ambulance with me and I didn't know who it was. At that stage I thought the person they were talking about was one of the boys.

Jim McCoy: I travelled to Dublin by train that day but I knew something was wrong when about twenty plain-clothes Garda turned up to the Irish training session at Merrion Road.

David Irwin: Trevor, Keith Crossan, Hugo MacNeill and Syd Millar were about five minutes behind us. They were diverted round through country roads because of the incident but they didn't know we were involved in it until they got to Dublin and somebody told them.

Philip Matthews: All I can remember is the good news that they were alive. Immediately we knew it was serious but it was lightened by the fact that they were OK, albeit not in good shape.

Jim McCoy: I often wondered did they [the IRA] think I was travelling down the road with the boys that day but clearly the target was Lord Justice Gibson. I don't know was it a blessing but I always thought that if they wanted to get me they could have got me.

David Irwin: The boys remember very little of the incident. There was a documentary made for television 25 years after the event and the two of them were in the dark as to the full story. As we were doing the documentary most of the stuff I was telling them they hadn't heard before. It was quite good for them in many ways.

Nigel Carr: I had broken five or six ribs, I had internal bleeding, lacerations and chipped bones and twisted joints. I had a lot of trouble with my knee. I was in quite a bit of pain and I'm not sure what they gave me – morphine or something like that – but I was only allowed one or two injections a day and I was trying to hold on for as long as I could between injections. I'd get an injection in my backside and the relief that came over me was indescribable. I was lying there thinking, 'If this is what it's like taking ecstasy then I understand why people get addicted.' It took me to a completely different place.

David Irwin: My father is a GP and his colleagues – psychologists and the like – were queuing up saying, 'Look, if David needs any help, we're here for him,' but I was OK. I had a wee scrape on my nose and the hair on my right forearm and the right side of my head was singed from the heat of the bomb and that was all that was wrong with me. Another thousandth of a second and instead of Judge Gibson's car hitting the front right corner of my car, it would probably have hit my door and that would have taken me out.

You had three Ulster Protestants coming down to play rugby for a united Ireland and the IRA – albeit we weren't the targets – had nearly killed us. There was condemnation from all quarters but nothing from the Republican movement itself. I think the guy who pressed the button up in the hills that day, I've forgotten

From left to right: Nigel Carr, Philip Matthews and David Irwin.

his name now, but he blew himself up a year or two later. The IRFU said they'd help out if I'd any expenses out of this. My car was wrecked, but I got nothing from the union. Everybody was sympathetic but there certainly wasn't any help. Now, in fairness, I didn't ask for it. I suppose I was just glad I was alive.

Trevor Ringland: The guy who pushed the button and exploded the bomb knew that other cars might get caught up in it and knew that they could be Catholic or Protestant. On both sides, they didn't care about the people, they just did not care. It could have been a bus load of kids, it could have been Catholic, Protestant, or whatever, they just didn't care. They were only focused on killing George Gibson and his wife.

Nigel Carr: I always felt fortunate that in a time in Northern Ireland when people were getting murdered and maimed I came out of that alive. I didn't want to be feeling bitter and resentful and gnarled up inside so I tried to look at it positively. It was important to me that I didn't let it eat me up. It had an effect on me that I didn't expect. Three thousand people died here during The Troubles and thousands more were injured far worse than I was. We were tremendously lucky. Not long after, a family were blown up in their 4x4 in a similar location. It was a mistaken identity. The bombers thought it was a police vehicle. Children died that day. I became a lot more sensitive after it. At that time, hardly a week went past without a shooting or a bombing or some sort of attack and you were rather blasé about it. But being involved in that incident gave me a different perspective on things. I was very keen to play again. I played an Ulster game against South of Scotland, but I didn't play more than five games. I got injured and while I was injured I injured something else. Those injuries were related to the bomb. I didn't play for Ireland again.

Trevor Ringland: We lost Nigel Carr, courtesy of the IRA. Nigel was fundamental to what we were trying to do – a world class openside flanker. We lost one of our very best players.

Three weeks later, Ireland headed for New Zealand for the inaugural World Cup and to say their journey was long and fractious would be putting it mildly. They didn't just fly economy, they flew economy with an airline that seemed to look on leg-room as an optional extra. They were poured into their seats and then embarked on a trek from hell.

They went through New York, Los Angeles and Hawaii. When they got above Auckland, the airport was fog-bound so they circled for two hours waiting for the skies to clear. No such luck. They rerouted to Christchurch. By the time they arrived at their hotel they'd been on the go for 32 hours.

Neil Francis: The flight told you everything you needed to know about the state of the game. Everybody turned right when they got on the plane – we spent 32 hours in steerage – no hydration, no stretching and a few beers to relax us and make us sleep. By the time we reached Auckland, I'd had two hours kip and felt as wooden as Hugh Grant. Never mind, I'd get a good rub-down from Joe Doran. Sorry, left behind in Dublin. Perhaps a plyometric stretching session with the squad's physical trainer. Unlikely, when one didn't exist. Perhaps a pool session to loosen up the aching limbs and gently get the elasticity back into those muscles. Nope. What about a three hour session of murderball and scrummaging thirty minutes after we get out of the airport. Good thinking Batman.

David Irwin: Doyler was lashing the drink into himself like there was no tomorrow. When we went down to the pitch we started running as a backline, a long line, left to right and then we realised that Doyler was at the end of the line. He was puffing and blowing. We stopped to do sit-ups and press-ups and the sweat was pouring out of him. His face was like a tomato. As we were running we were gradually getting quicker and quicker and he was trying to keep up.

Donal Lenihan: He was drinking at the time but he decided he was going to get fit. He was only in his 40s, so he was entitled to do a bit of running, but not with the Irish backline. He was trying to keep up with Kiernan and Mullin and they were winking at each other and putting on the pace.

Michael Kiernan: It was madness, but you couldn't stop him. You couldn't tell Doyler anything. He was his own man.

Des Fitzgerald: If you do things like that you shouldn't be surprised at the results. He was an enormously competitive man but what he forgot was that he had put on four stone since the time he was playing. He got a heart attack and, as the fella says, he was the only man who ever got a heart attack and suffered no damage.

David Irwin: At dinner, Syd Millar came over to me and said, 'David, can I have a word with you? Doyler's had a heart attack, he's away to hospital.' Because I was a doctor and a player, Syd wanted advice from me as to how we should break the news to the lads. I said, 'Look, say this and this.' The boys got on the bus after the dinner totally in the dark about Doyler and Syd stood up and said, 'Lads, unfortunately Mick Doyle has had a heart attack but as far as we know he's fairly stable.' There was dead silence. Now, Doyler had a fairly big gut on him and Brian Spillane piped up, 'It's okay lads, the child was saved.'

Mick Doyle: Before we left for that tournament my business was going down the tubes. I didn't have time to keep my eye on the ball in terms of business. I had never experienced stress until then but literally up to the last minute before going down under I was frantically trying to salvage my business. I was also hitting the bottle too hard and it wasn't doing me any favours. It was the darkest hour of my life because everything I had worked for was disappearing before my eyes. I should have been sent home after that. I was on tablets to sleep, tablets to wake up, tablets for hypertension and God knows what else. Most of the three or four weeks I was there I was edgy and irritable and in no way a suitable candidate for being a coach. The guys deserved a better coach than I was.

Donal Lenihan sits with Mick Doyle at a press conference during the 1987 World Cup.

Neil Francis: Doyler was in hospital and Syd took over the coaching of the team, which was a fucking disaster because we had to do five million scrums. It was just unbelievable. We were in Wellington when Doyler came back from hospital and there wasn't exactly a rip-roaring welcome for him. He walked in the door expecting a fawning response from the players and he didn't get it. He was in foul humour for the rest of the tour. He had already become a pantomime, but it got worse. It wasn't about Ireland, it was the Doyler Show. It was an ego trip.

Des Fitzgerald: Doyler was a likeable rogue, but if you're the coach of an international team then likeable rogue is not your function.

Paul Dean: By the time we got to the World Cup we were running the team ourselves anyway. We had fabulous players and good leaders and I'm not saying we didn't need a coach, but we knew what we needed to do.

Donal Lenihan: When we went down there it was our first glimpse of what the Kiwis were up to in terms of earning money from rugby. We saw rugby players on ads on television. You couldn't do that in Ireland. We were still having our taxi receipts queried. It was like entering another world.

Des Fitzgerald: I was rooming with Jim Glennon, our second-row. We went into the hotel, flopped down on the bed and turned on the telly. New Zealand were beating the crap out of somebody. At half-time the ads came on and there was an All Black driving around on a tractor. I said, 'Jim, he's getting paid for that.' And I said, 'Do you know another thing? I doubt some of these lads are working from eight until six like you and me and then going training.'

Donal Lenihan: We played Wales in the opening match. We'd beaten them in Cardiff only two months earlier. Deano was out-half and was at the core of our game but because we were playing in gale-force winds in Wellington we should have picked Wardy at 10. Wardy's game would have suited the conditions better. We picked Deano because, well, that's what we always did.

Des Fitzgerald: There we were, lining up against Wales in Athletic Park, Wellington, our first game in the World Cup and easily the most important in our pool. Wales stand there and belt out *Land of my Fathers* and the hairs are standing on the back of their necks – and ours. Then it's our turn and we get *The Rose of Tralee*. I mean we were going out to do battle, to die for Ireland with *The Rose of Tralee* ringing in our ears. What could you expect after that? The lads would have been better off picking Finnegan's Wake. At least that would have been a bit of crack. We could have all gone for it

Neil Francis: We lost 13-6. It was without parallel in the history of the game,

Michael Bradley spins the ball to Paul Dean as Robert Jones of Wales chases his pass.

universally chosen as the worst ever. Anybody who took part in it will pay a high price at the Webb Ellis pearly gates.

Phil Orr: We didn't know what we were getting into. We did our best. Even the logistics of the thing were badly run. We played our first pool match in Wellington, then we played Canada in Dunedin, which wasn't too bad except that there were two matches in Dunedin on the same weekend, which meant four hotels, and they didn't have four decent hotels, so we were in a fairly run-down operation.

Neil Francis: We were billeted in the two-star Travel Lodge in Dunedin. The food had been so bad that my ribs had begun to show – not good at a time when bulk or ballast of any kind was considered advantageous. The restaurant in the hotel was a time capsule; I've never been to a 1960s civil service canteen but this is what it smelled like. Henry Ford came to mind – you could have anything on the menu as long as it was lamb stew. I took three mouthfuls and gagged, then ate nine or 10 pieces of bread and butter and was just getting up to go when Syd Millar, who was so impressed with the quantity of bread and butter I'd eaten, insisted I had lamb spew seconds. 'What weight are you now, son?' 'About 16 stone.' 'You need to be heavier. Get it into you.' He almost stood over me as I committed gastronomic hara-kiri. When Syd left, I went outside, ran up to the top of the car park, leaned over the wall, stuck my fingers down my throat and puked for Ireland. I'd become the nation's first bulimic second-row.

Phill Orr: Then we flew to Brisbane for Tonga which took two days. We over-nighted in Christchurch. Then we flew to Sydney and on to Brisbane. You were talking about 36 hours to get to Brisbane.

Neil Francis: They picked me at No 8 for the Tonga game in that World Cup – that was my debut. I was fit. I wasn't carrying a pick of fat. I went up to Doyler and told him I hadn't played No 8 since I was fourteen years of age. I was expecting a master-class because he was a good back-row forward in his time. I knew how to pick and go, but what else? What do I do if the scrum wheels and their No 8 goes open or blind, who takes who and do I cover inside or outside. He said: 'If the Pope comes around the corner of that scrum on a Honda 50 fucking nail him,' – and he walked away.

The World Cup adventure, such as it was, came to an abrupt end when the Wallabies beat Ireland 33-15 in Sydney in the quarter-final. The circus surrounding Mick Doyle was also brought to a conclusion. He moved on and was replaced by Jimmy Davidson, the Ulsterman who, coincidentally, had also replaced Doyle on the blindside of the Irish scrum almost two decades earlier.

Jimmy D had achieved great things as coach of Ulster, who were the kingpins of the Interprovincial series. He was intense and technical and something of a visionary. He foresaw the coming of the professional game and how it might play out. Such was his dedication to the Irish job that some thought he was as good as made no difference to a professional coach himself.

Des Fitzgerald: To Jimmy D there was nothing more important than rugby. He was an obsessive. A forwards guy. He revolutionised Ulster rugby. The team that won all those Interprovincial titles – he was the architect of that. He was blessed with tremendous players but he also made average players very competent by having clear instructions. Rugby was his life. But he was mad. Everybody would say Jimmy was mad, even the guys who knew him well and loved him dearly.

Neil Francis: Jimmy D was a complete nutcase – and he hated my guts. All the stuff about him being a visionary and way ahead of his time is just bullshit. He had a keen rugby intellect, no question. But being able to apply it on a practical level was never going to happen.

Philip Matthews: There was an eccentricity about him. You had somebody who was actually looking at things from a different perspective and he was truly innovative and when you're innovative you can be regarded as odd. What you couldn't doubt was his honesty and the fact that he wasn't there for himself, he was there to see the team and the individuals in the team be as good as they could be.

Brendan Mullin: I was a big fan. He wasn't everybody's cup of tea, but he was the first stage of professionalism in rugby. The hours he spent preparing training sessions – a lot of coaches just pitched up on the day and hadn't prepared anything. He thought a lot about what we were trying to do. He wanted to up the skill level. He tried to take us forward. I completely bought into him.

Jimmy Davidson passes on instructions during a training session in 1988.

Philip Matthews: He was an outstanding individual who took absolute fulfilment in seeing young rugby players develop and grow. He wasn't somebody who sought the limelight for himself. He had an almost naive honesty in his desire to help us be as good as he thought we could be. He wasn't at all Machiavellian and I'm not going to say that was a weakness, because you shouldn't have to deal with the politics of the provinces, but he did have difficulty there. Some people had a problem with him because his Ulster team was very successful and he wanted Ireland to work in an Ulster-type way and that meant training much harder and looking after your diet and I don't think that everybody was ready to do that. There was cultural issues as well. In those days if you told an Ulster guy to do ten laps on Christmas morning, he'd do it. But I'm not sure everybody else would do it. When you're told to do something up in Ulster, you do it. You do it to the letter of the law. But other players were like, 'Ah, I'm not gonna do that.'

Des Fitzgerald: In the 1988 Five Nations we started with a win over Scotland. Lovely. Two weeks later we went to Paris. We couldn't play in Paris in those days. They were better players and they were also bigger and they were semi-professional. We'd be in terror of missing a kick to touch because they'd run the fucking thing back at you. Once those guys started running you couldn't keep up with them. We were in dread of Blanco and Lagisquet and we had nobody who could match them. And their back-row that day was Marc Cecillon, Alain Carminati and Laurent Rodriguez. Cecillon did time for shooting his wife. Any more questions?

John Sexton is chased down by Rob Andrew and leaving Will Carling floundering at Twickenham in 1988.

Neil Francis: We got blitzed in Paris and blitzed again in Twickenham and in between those two, we also lost to Wales, so one out of four in Jimmy D's first Five Nations. We went to France for a short tour in the summer of 1998. We played a team from the Basque region and got whacked. They had a backline that I'd never heard of and they were fucking electric and cut us to shreds. Every time they got the ball – six points. That was the first match. The second match was against a French XV in Auch.

Before the match, Jimmy D called me aside. He said, 'I don't like you, I don't want you, I know you think you're great, but I don't like your attitude and you're not my type of player, but I've got no choice, I've got to pick you.' This went on for five minutes. He said, 'Don't look at the ground when I'm talking to you, look at my eyes, look at the feeling in my eyes.' I said, 'Jimmy, are you trying to gee me up here or what?' He said, 'Everything I'm telling you is true.'

The French team we played in Auch was close to a Test team and their pack was evil. They picked a monstrous set of forwards. In fairness to Willie Anderson, he took a look at them and said, 'Right, we can die with our boots on or we can run out the gate. Which is it?' It was a match of undiluted savagery. I gave up after a while being afraid. In every ruck there was a kick or a punch. I went mad. Every time one of them went in and kicked somebody I went chasing after them. I had the best game of my life.

When the final whistle blew I started crying. I was just beaten up. Tony Ward, who had a super match, came over to me and said, 'Are you all right?' I thought we'd lost but we'd actually won by a point. With all the fighting, the scoreboard almost became irrelevant. Jimmy D sat beside me in the dressing room and stuck his hand out and said, 'Well done.' I looked at him, got up and walked away.

Five days later we played them again. I was taken out in the air at a lineout and got a punch in the face on my way down. I was knocked unconscious. I woke up by the side of the pitch and got sick all over the place. I was in hospital for a day or so with a splitting headache. About five days later we're playing the French Barbarians in La Rochelle and I'm obviously in no state to play. Jimmy D didn't think there was anything wrong with me. He said, 'I'm playing you at the weekend.' I said, 'Jimmy, my head is thumping so much that I'm even finding it difficult to write my postcards home.' Mick Molloy, our doctor, stepped in and said under no circumstances was I to play. My relationship with Jimmy D couldn't recover. I just don't do insanity.

Philip Matthews: We lost three out of four in the 1988 Five Nations and it was the same again the year after. There were a lot of issues around the other provinces adapting to the way that Jimmy felt we should be playing. Ulster played a rucking game and Munster and Leinster played a mauling game and it just didn't work when we came together with Ireland.

David Irwin: In the autumn of 1989 we played New Zealand at Lansdowne Road. Jimmy D knew Ian Kirkpatrick and Kirkpatrick told him that every team cowers when the All Blacks do the haka and what Ireland should do is challenge it somehow. Willie Anderson was the captain and I was vice-captain and we debated all week about what we ought to do. We decided we'd line up in front of it and just stand there. That was the plan. We'd stare them down. I was beside Willie when we lined-up. The crowd started to go ballistic and Willie got carried away.

Willie Anderson: It was planned with Jimmy D. We thought, 'Why does the public give the applause to the opposition first rather than the team they're purporting to support?' So we just tried to turn it around.

David Irwin: He started stamping his feet. My right arm was interlocked with his and I could feel him dragging me forward. I was trying to pull him back. I thought, 'Willie, we're going to run out of room here.' He was nose-to-nose with Buck Shelford and I was nose-to-nose with Steve McDowell and even though we were in each other's faces we couldn't hear because the crowd were making such a racket. Willie started waving his arms at the end of it and Sean Fitzpatrick was standing there, stretching his thighs and thinking, 'Who's this guy?'
    They kicked off and there was the typical Irish forward rush and Shelford got

Willie Anderson faces up to New Zealand captain Wayne 'Buck' Shelford as the All Blacks preform the Haka at Lansdowne Road.

completely cleaned on the deck. For about ten minutes we thought we were on to something, but it was 23-6 in the end. The IRFU said later that our advance on the haka was disgraceful and disrespectful. The alickadoos gave us a hard time. But I spoke to Shelford and Grant Fox and they said, 'Fair play, it's a challenge and you stood up to it.'

Brendan Mullin: The game after that was at Twickenham. The first match of the 1990 Five Nations – and we lost 23-0. Other countries were getting it together but we weren't. We knew that the game was effectively professional in France and South Africa and Australia and New Zealand, and England had got their act together as well. We heard that they had the very latest scrummaging machine in their dressing room. It just gave them an extra edge. They were getting more and more professional and I could see the gap opening up. It wasn't about getting a few quid. It was about feeling better prepared for what was going on at international level.

In 1990 we lost three out of four again and Jimmy D departed. He was unhappy towards the end. He didn't have the freedom to dictate how much time we were spending together. He had got Ulster playing like Team Ulster and wanted to build that ethos with Ireland and I got the impression that the union wasn't going to let him do it. He was too professional and they didn't want that. He spent too much time preparing. That was their fear; that it would inevitably lead to demands from the players for some sort of compensation.

Philip Matthews: I was sorry to see him go and I'm even sadder now in some respects. You know, leadership is something that I've invested a lot of my own time in and if you can convince a young person that you hold them in high esteem and that they are capable of anything then you can actually get them to surprise themselves. And that's effectively what Jimmy did for me and for others. He was ahead of his time. I look back on it and I think about what Jimmy stood for and what an influence he was on me in Ulster and I think, 'God, I was lucky to have someone like that.' Ireland never saw the best of him and that was Ireland's loss.

NINE

DRY ROT OF THE LOWER ORIFICE, AS THE MAN SAYS

Ciaran Fitzgerald: I was lined up to be coach of Connacht and then Syd Millar asked me would I take over from Jimmy D and coach Ireland and I said no. Then he asked me again and I said no again. I didn't feel I was equipped to do it. Eventually, I buckled.

Philip Matthews: You knew what you were getting with Fitzy. There was a lot of respect there.

Des Fitzgerald: He did a service to the union by taking the job. Fitzy was a great leader of men, but those were brutally tough times.

Donal Lenihan: Fitzy inherited Brian Smith from Jimmy D. He was an Australian. An out-half. He qualified to play for us on the granny rule even though he'd played against us for the Wallabies in the 1987 World Cup. He stuck around for two seasons and then fecked off just before the World Cup in 1991 and left everybody in the lurch. I never forgave him for the way he just disappeared. He played the 1990 and 1991 Five Nations when we won one match out of eight and then there was a summer tour to Namibia and he just vanished.

Brian Smith: Donal's right. I should have stuck it out. The background was that I'd just finished my studies at Oxford and I didn't have a job or any money. Everything had gone on my education. A big, fat, juicy rugby league contract had been stuck under my nose and I was told I had until the Friday to make my mind up. I took it and it was a bad decision. I did it for selfish reasons. I was always planning on going back home to play rugby league, but leaving so soon before the World Cup was something I regret.

Neil Francis: We went to Namibia in the summer of 1991. I walked around the grounds of the hotel in Windhoek with Simon Geoghegan and we nearly got killed two or three times by creatures who appeared out of bushes. We went back inside and sat down and the kitchen door was open and there were these wild cats and you'd want to see these things. There was a bit of a commotion inside and a cat comes flying out with a chicken breast in its mouth and the chef, like yer man from The Muppets, went chasing after it. The cat drops the chicken and yer man picks it up and goes back inside. Whether he used it or not, we don't know.

Brendan Mullin: The tour encapsulated where we were as a rugby nation at the time. The intent was good. Go and spend the best part of two weeks on tour and get some games in, but nobody had done the fine analysis. By going to Namibia you go to altitude, which is wonderful for the first three days because we were running around like champions, but once you go past three days the altitude starts to kick in and you have a sense of weakness. I still have a recollection of the first Test and we could hardly finish the warm-up. We were absolutely knackered before it started.

Philip Matthews: Wales had toured Namibia the summer before. They won both Tests but they were close and we couldn't believe how close. We said, 'Ah, that's Wales. Probably went out on the piss and didn't take it seriously.' We underestimated Namibia and lost the first Test 15-6. We were very naive.

Donal Lenihan: I wasn't on that tour, not to begin with anyway. I'd missed the 1991 Five Nations because of a neck injury and I was told I'd never play again, but I was making my way back slowly. The day of the first Test in Namibia I was looking out on Cork Harbour at the Tall Ships. I got back in the car and turned on the sports news on the radio and heard that the IRFU were urgently trying to contact me. I made a call and the next day I flew Cork-London-Frankfurt-Johannesburg-Windhoek, then I got into a Cessna two-seater plane and flew to a place called Keetmanshoop. I arrived on a Monday, played a game on Tuesday and played well. I was thrilled. I don't know what in the name of Jesus we were doing there in the first place, mind you.

Des Fitzgerald: We were out at a barbecue a few days before the second Test and the monkeys were climbing down from the trees and robbing the grub. It wasn't a great day out. The team got dry rot of the lower orifice, as the man says.

Ciaran Fitzgerald: They ate half a sheep that was put over a fire in the middle of the desert.

Mick Galwey: It was a pig, wasn't it?

Nick Popplewell: No, it was a kudu – a type of antelope. They had this thing up on a rack and the lads didn't hold back.

Mick Galwey: I wasn't in the squad for the second Test, so I was having my few pints at the barbecue without a care in the world. My tour was over so I was getting stuck in. I was allowed. The next thing the lads started dropping like flies. A rake of them were sick. I'd eaten all the same grub but I was absolutely grand. I don't know why. Maybe the drink killed the poison. They put me back in the squad.

Neil Francis: Everybody was dying. Keith Crossan? I've never seen a player as sick. It was like Legionnaire's disease. I went in to see Keith and he was so bad that had I said to him, 'Do you just want me to end it for you now?' he'd have probably said, 'Fire ahead.' He was in a terrible state. And he had to play in the match. We lost again. No wonder.

Gordon Hamilton: What was actually worse was that after we came back we played Gloucester at Kingsholm and we lost that one as well.

Ciaran Fitzgerald was a popular and respected coach but he was also a man under pressure. One victory in eight Five Nations matches over two seasons and back-to-back losses in Namibia was the kind of form that normally made the union reach for the revolver. And now there was the trauma of a World Cup to come.

Ireland were drawn in a group with Zimbabwe and Japan, the fodder, and Scotland, the heavyweights. The Scots had won the Grand Slam in 1990 and had beaten Ireland three games on the bounce. They also had home advantage, the match with Fitzgerald's men being played at Murrayfield where Scotland hadn't lost in three years.

Fitzgerald had enough to contend with on the rugby field, but there were things happening off it that were frying his brain. The game was inching towards professionalism and the new reality wasn't lost on the Irish players. There was a clash between the modern-thinkers in the dressing room and the old guard in the IRFU committee and it was a collision that threatened to destroy Ireland's World Cup campaign.

Roly Meates: I was on the union and we set up an amateur status sub-committee and this committee was to oversee a relaxing of regulations in relation to players earning money. They could open a shop, for instance, as long as they didn't do it in an Ireland jersey. They could write books and that kind of thing. But it got fractious. The players got very restless with the union. There was a 'them and us' situation and I was on both sides of it.

Des Fitzgerald: Roly backed the players, he was a players' man, a coach. I felt very sorry for him. I felt in some respects culpable. Roly was a smart guy. He could see all this stuff coming. He spotted it years earlier.

Ciaran Fitzgerald: The players had been promised certain things in terms of compensation and they weren't being delivered and there was a groundswell of revolt among the lads that simmered right through the World Cup. Johnny

Nick Popplewell breaks off the back of a rolling maul against Zimbabwe.

Moloney was my assistant and we both got involved. We said to the union: 'How do you expect us to get performances from these guys if mentally they're not there?' I could have done without all of that.

Simon Geoghegan: I don't know whether they thought that we wanted to be paid. We just wanted to be better players and we wanted the team to be better. But they didn't really have an idea of what we were about, which was a shame really.

Brendan Mullin: We were trying to get more professional and trying to introduce elements of player welfare that had never been considered before. A guy who was married and wanted to bring his wife to a game in London or Edinburgh, there was no assistance for that guy. It was small stuff, but it was the principle. On top of that, we needed to be more professional, we needed to prepare better. Roly Meates was on the union and he was trying to push that agenda in conjunction with Fitzy.

Des Fitzgerald: We had formed a players committee because that's the way it was going in other countries. We were allowed to advertise. These were changes that the IRB had brought in. Fellas could do sponsorships, so we were doing a little bit of work with the Insurance Corporation of Ireland, and we were due some money. We had an agent. We were starting to create that kind of environment and it was always going to end in tears because Irish rugby wasn't prepared for that. A lot of people around the union felt that we were selling our birthright down the river for money. They wouldn't have used that terminology but that's exactly what they meant. They were saying that we didn't understand professionalism and what it would do to the game in Ireland. And they were right. We didn't. I used to say to them, 'Look, nobody knows where this will lead to. I've loved the game as I've played it, but unless we go professional we will not be able to compete with other teams because, by the way lads, they're already professional, so the debate is over.'

Ciaran Fitzgerald: Our World Cup base was Finnstown House and I was getting these calls late at night from IRFU people. They were telling me that the players can't behave like this. I had to bite the tongue. 'Fuck sake, who caused it?' It should have been dealt with a year before. The game was evolving and some on the union were not. It wasn't only about fellas not being paid, it was about the players not having the same professional preparation as other nations. They could see how professional the other big countries had become and there was a gap opening. I said to the union: 'These players are not schoolboys, they're professional people and you can't treat them the way you're treating them. You made promises and they haven't been kept.'

Philip Matthews: Myself, Brenny Mullin and Dessie Fitz, as the more senior players, kept all the lads informed throughout the negotiations with the union. We wanted fairness. We wanted them to know that they couldn't go on treating us like idiots. It was insulting the way they were treating us.

Des Fitzgerald: We'd won our first two games and then lost to Scotland and it came to a head before the quarter-final with Australia in Dublin. The people who were running the IRFU were full of commitment and full of honour, but they were trying to build the future from the past. They were looking back at the way it used to be done and they wanted it to stay that way forever. As soon as they agreed to the

World Cup, it was over. That was the catalyst. Big companies were getting involved and the dynamic was changing fast. It got really tetchy between the players and the union. It was almost at the point of hatred. The main forces on the union were Ronnie Dawson, Syd Millar, Tommy Kiernan and Noel Murphy – enormous experience and bright guys. They were afraid of the collapse of the game.

Philip Matthews: The likes of Syd would always have had respect. I think there would have been respect for Tommy and a few others, but I can't say that for everybody else. There would have been a lack of respect for those in there who had an almost begrudging view of players getting x, y or z. 'Oh no, we don't want commercials; oh no, we don't want agents; we don't want this, we don't want that.'

Ciaran Fitzgerald: I absolutely empathised with the players. I was very much with them and I thought I could solve it with the union, but it got difficult. People in the union hardened their positions. 'How dare players suggest they get this or get that.' It threatened to get that serious that they wouldn't go on the field against Australia. I didn't doubt the strength of their feelings. I was advocating very strongly that they play.

Des Fitzgerald: I called Roly and said that he'd better inform the union committee that we wouldn't be taking the field against Australia.

Roly Meates: To quote Dessie, it was, 'Tell your friends on the union that Australia will run out and there'll be no Ireland to play against them.' Friends was a bit of an exaggeration.

Des Fitzgerald: I don't do bluffing. You don't threaten something without being able to deliver. The players had agreed that we would not play Australia because the union had reneged on the deal we had. You're talking about £1,500 a man. Now, I had a good job and £1,500 wasn't going to save my life, but it was the principle. It was our sponsorship money that was paid into the union and they were supposed to pay it back out to us. The union said, 'We'll just get a new team.' We told them that the rules say that new teams have to be announced twenty days before the competition starts, so they were a bit late on that one. It was huge drama. I'm not sure we'd thought about the possible backlash had we not gone on the field, but they released the money to us. The issue, really, was about loss of control. The union had been directing things successfully for 100 years and suddenly you have these guys appearing out of nowhere trying to change the world. But what we were doing was recognising that the world had changed. We were only the messengers.

The Wallabies were hotly tipped to win the World Cup having beaten England and New Zealand in the summer. They had the dream midfield of Jason Little and Tim Horan, the world's best half-backs in Michael Lynagh and Nick Farr-Jones, the great David Campese on the wing and a gnarled pack of forwards that was made even better by the arrival on the world stage of a twenty-one year old second-row phenomenon from Brisbane by the name of John Eales.

Neil Francis: The Australia match was on a Sunday and we had a team meeting on the Friday; a bit of video and a chat about our gameplan. At the end I said, 'Hang on, I want to say something. What we're proposing to do here is fundamentally wrong.' The success of the Australians was purely down to dominating the lineout and territory. We were planning to kick and just give them the throw. That was playing into their hands. I said, 'We can't kick to touch because this fucker Eales is untouchable. That's how they win these games. If we kick for touch, we're dead.' I kept them there for an hour and we altered our tactics. I wasn't looking for recognition, I just wanted to make sure I wasn't going to get skinned alive by this fucking freakish beanpole.

With five minutes left at Lansdowne Road, David Campese's two tries had put Australia in a 15-12 lead. Rob Saunders fed a scrum inside Ireland's own half and let a pass out to his out-half, Ralph Keyes who found Dave Curtis in the midfield. Jim Staples hit the line from full-back and kicked ahead. All of a sudden, the Wallabies were in trouble.

Gordon Hamilton: Jim Staples put through the grubber that was no more than speculative and good old Campo fiddled about with it. Jack Clarke was in very quickly on him and the temptation must have been to fly-hack. I'm pretty sure nine out of ten players would have fly-hacked that ball but he picked it up. We wouldn't have scored otherwise. I'd about forty metres to go when I got the ball from Jack. I literally fell over as I got to the line and Rob Egerton tackled me. I couldn't have run another yard. I just knew I had to keep the ball off the ground initially – the law then was that if you kept it off the ground, you could then place it over the line. I'd barely the strength to get up after.

In that moment, Lansdowne Road erupted. Supporters spilled on to the pitch, one of them standing over the prone Egerton and offering words that may not have been wholly sympathetic. Hamilton was swamped. When his captain, Philip Matthews, retrieved him from the ruck of bodies, Matthews momentarily got swallowed up as well. The scenes were deafening and chaotic. When things calmed down, Ralph Keyes curled over the conversion from wide on the left and the craziness began all over again.

Behind the Australia goal-posts, John Eales remembered that he'd handed in his dry-cleaning at the Westbury hotel that morning on the presumption that he was going to be sticking around Dublin for a while yet. Now that confidence looked thoroughly misplaced.

Donal Lenihan: I can still feel the excitement of running back after the try and imploring the lads that whatever we did from the restart, just find touch.

Gordon Hamilton scores to put Ireland into a 16-15 lead in the quarter-final.

Des Fitzgerald: We talked about it before they restarted. 'We need to win this ball and we need to put it up in the stand.' We were clear about what needed to be done and we didn't execute and the rest is history.

Neil Francis: There was no time on the clock. Then Rob Saunders misses touch – and I like Rob, but every time I see him now I say, 'You're a fucking twat.' The Aussies get the ball back and they have one more chance to win the game. Campo pops up and Jack Clarke misses the crucial tackle and Lynagh is over in the corner. Jesus, it was sickening.

Jack Clarke: I took a hammering. There were a lot of comments in the media and there were a lot of comments on the street. I was only young (twenty-three) and it affected me for a couple of years and, confidence-wise, I was never the same player after. By the time I'd come through it, my representative career was over. There was no support for players in those days, no sports psychologists to show you how to deal with these challenges.

Gordon Hamilton: I'm quite sure Rob meant the kick to go into touch and, in Jack's case, the defence in total was crap. It's very scary to look at the video and see how poor our defence was. The Australians just ran through us at will. We had drift and we had man-on-man but we didn't really have a system. Meanwhile, Campo and Lynagh knew exactly what they were doing.

Des Fitzgerald: They took their opportunity really well. We made the mistake but they executed brilliantly, so you had to take your hat off to them.

Philip Matthews: I still, to this day, play the last few minutes over in my mind. If only. All it would have taken is one little thing like the ball going into the 12th row of the stand. Could you imagine the energy in Ireland for a World Cup semi-final against New Zealand at Lansdowne Road? I'm not saying we would have won, but can you imagine the atmosphere?

Neil Francis: In the dressing room, half of the guys were elated because we hadn't been hockeyed, Saunders included. The other half were devastated. I cried bitter salty tears for half an hour. I was inconsolable. Geoghegan came over to me and we were both in a right state. It was there for us to do something special and we weren't good enough.

Donal Lenihan: It was the worst feeling ever. The likes of myself and Des Fitz knew we'd never have another chance like that, but the young lads hadn't a clue. Some of them wanted Australian jerseys and tracksuits and that really pissed me off. We had a chance to do something historic and we blew it and one of the fellas who couldn't wait to get a Wallaby tracksuit was Saunders, who'd missed the fucking kick, which drove me bananas. I was about to explode and Fitzy grabbed me and told me to sit down.

Brendan Mullin: It was a poor New Zealand side and that made it even worse. I think we could have beaten them in the semi-final.

Des Fitzgerald: I never wanted to play another rugby match after that. People didn't realise what we missed out on. I was thirty-four years old, so the end was in sight. I was sickened. It was a shattering experience. I still wake up some nights in a cold sweat thinking about it. No other match has ever had that impact on me. The one that got away.

Ciaran Fitzgerald: It was the highlight and the lowlight of my coaching career. Afterwards there was just a numbness.

Nick Popplewell: Same shit, different day. My blazer was nicked that night. I wasn't too happy about that either.

Normal business resumed in the wake of the glorious failure at Lansdowne Road. The 1992 Five Nations started with a 38-9 drubbing at Twickenham followed by two more defeats against the Scots and the Welsh. Zero from three was familiar territory. What lay ahead was a horror trilogy – a trip to Paris to avoid a whitewash and then a two-Test tour of New Zealand.

Nick Popplewell: It was my first time playing at Parc des Princes and in the first scrum I got driven back about ten yards. No disrespect, but we had holes all over our team. They ran us left and right, left and right and we were knackered and there'd be a forty foot gap in our defence and they'd walk straight through it. They won 44-12

Mick Galwey: They beat us out the door and they beat us up physically as well. There's no worse place in the world to get a hammering than the Parc des Princes. I got a few boots in the head. I got gouged as well, which was horrible. It was in a ruck. I was trying to figure out who it was, but I couldn't nail him. Everybody got a touch of it that day. We were giving back as good as we got, without gouging them, but it wasn't working. So that was four defeats from four and the wooden spoon, and next thing we were off to Dunedin and Wellington.

Nick Popplewell: Miserable bloody country.

Ciaran Fitzgerald: In Paris, I was told emphatically by the union that Johnny Moloney, my assistant, couldn't be on the ticket to New Zealand and that bugged me. I was close to pulling out at that stage. I stayed because I felt I had a duty to the team, but that was a nail in my coffin. I'd asked Johnny to help me in the first place, he was a friend of mine, a club-mate of mine and it was a very difficult thing to have to do to tell him that it was over for him and my first instinct was that if he's not going then I'm not going either. I've often thought about that in the years since. Should I have gone to New Zealand or should I have told them to stick it? I didn't want to be seen as jumping ship but I didn't want to be forced to do what I did either. My number was up at that stage.

The union replaced Moloney with Gerry Murphy, the Ireland U-21s coach, but if losing a friend hadn't unsettled Fitzgerald enough then a worse fate would soon befall him. As the countdown to the tour began in earnest, his phone started hopping. One player withdrawal followed another.

Of the team that almost beat the Wallabies eight months earlier, Simon Geoghegan, Brendan Mullin and Ralph Keyes were now unavailable, for various reasons. So, too, Des Fitzgerald, Donal Lenihan, Neil Francis and Philip Matthews.

By the time the squad boarded the plane Fitzgerald was short of seventeen front-liners. He brought in ten uncapped players plus a couple more who had only ever been capped once. And then he prayed like hell. By the time the first Test came around Ireland had already suffered two ferocious hidings – 62-7 against Auckland and 58-24 against Manawatu.

And then waiting for them in Dunedin in the opening Test were the All Blacks of John Kirwan and Frank Bunce, Inga Tuigamala and Walter Little, Sean Fitzpatrick and Ian Jones and Richard Loe. And Ireland almost won. It was a stratospherically brave performance and an agonising 24-21 defeat.

Nick Popplewell: I would say that first Test performance came from sheer fright. People were telling us it would be 100-0, but we had a moment and the All Blacks didn't take us too seriously and we could have beaten them.

Mick Galwey: We should have beaten them.

Ciaran Fitzgerald: The first Test was above and beyond the call of duty. It was everything the players had in them. Jesus, when I think about it. Ronnie Carey, the wing from Dungannon, nearly got an intercept try at the end. It would have been history. One of the greatest upsets of all-time. We caught them on the hop, but we'd nothing left in the tank for the second Test. It was an absolute hammering.

Mick Galwey: We should have finished them off when we had the chance because you don't get a second crack at it against those lads. They got eleven tries. What was it, 59-6? By fuck, there was no let-up. That was hard to take. It was just wave after wave. The days you lose are the days you learn about yourself and we were getting to know ourselves pretty fucking well by then, I can tell you.

Ciaran Fitzgerald: After that I knew I couldn't go on. I couldn't give it what was needed. I never called a press conference because there were all sorts of rumours that I was disgruntled and I didn't really want to talk about it. I had a new career that was placing a lot of demands on me and at that stage the relationship with the union was fractured. I couldn't be a puppet. I had to go.

Irish rugby was in an advanced state of crisis and one of the men who might have been able to plot a way out of it was next to go. For having the temerity to break ranks with his fellow committee members on the IRFU and show empathy with the players in those fractious times before the World Cup quarter-final against Australia, Roly Meates, the hugely respected coach and administrator, became a marked man among his colleagues.

Later, he gave an interview to Mick Doyle, now a Rottweiler columnist in the *Sunday Independent*, in which he explained the need for change in the IRFU. It was, in the eyes of the committee, an act of betrayal that demanded action. Meates was summoned to Lansdowne Road and thunderously rebuked.

Roly Meates: In the interview with Mick Doyle, I was quite outspoken about the issues that faced Irish rugby. I said we needed to move with the times. We were getting left behind and we needed to talk about these things. I talked about flexibility within the union and coaching structures and where we needed to be. A lot of the old traditional thinking would no longer suffice. The committee called me in and I apologised if I had caused any offence but they kept on and on and on. They said if I would publicly withdraw everything that I had said in the newspaper then I could stay on the union. I said I wouldn't. I said, 'I'm going for dinner with my wife and if you fellas change your mind then give me a ring.' That was the end of that.

Heading into the 1993 Five Nations, with Gerry Murphy becoming the third head coach of the decade, Ireland had lost nine Test matches in a row, which became ten in a row after they put in an insipid performance at Murrayfield in their opening game and lost 15-3. Simon Geoghegan was on the right wing that day. He waited and waited for some ball to come his way, but it never did. He would have been as well sitting in Row Z for all the action he saw.

Geoghegan was a thoroughbred rugby player; dynamic and free-spirited and utterly fed up. After the loss to Scotland he whipped off his jersey and flung it to the floor. When Noel Murphy, the Irish manager, tried to soothe his players' frustrations by saying that positives could be drawn from the defeat, Geoghegan shot back at him: 'Name them.'

The following week the winger was interviewed by the *Sunday Independent* and some of his annoyance spilled out on to the page. 'I never ever thought we had a chance of winning,' he said.

'I have read stories on other players where they say things like, "One win would turn things round" or "One victory is all this team needs." I can't say that because I don't believe it. Actually, I think it's nonsense.'

He said that his club, London Irish, put more effort into organisation than Ireland and that London Irish's players were fitter. His international record showed that he had thirteen caps and only one win. 'And the match we won, that was against Zimbabwe. I scored four tries. Two things can happen; we can go on losing. Or we can organise more games against Zimbabwe.'

When the IRFU, most notably Noel Murphy, read Geoghegan's words they went apoplectic. Some of his own team-mates weren't best pleased either. As with Meates a year earlier, this was too much truth for some people to handle.

Simon Geoghegan: It went down badly. Should have kept my mouth shut. I didn't slag any individuals, it was more an attack on the system. Naivety really – I was young, wanted to lash out. I think it highlighted the truth of what was going on but some of the lads probably resented me saying it. And I shouldn't have said it, in retrospect. Your team-mates are your team-mates.

Nick Popplewell: Simon was caught in a very bad moment after a match and was fed up. He should have been wiser. He said he was sick and tired of everybody going on the lash and not taking things as seriously as he did. It got very heated. There was a meeting among the players and a few of the lads wanted Geoghegan kicked out of the squad and in fairness to Jim Staples, he said, 'You're all being very emotional, take a deep breath and stew on it and think about it tomorrow.' And they did and the result was he got banned for a training session or something like that.

Neil Francis: Simon was a mad fucker. I was great friends with him. He got into trouble after the Scotland game and it was pathetic and stage-managed and it split the team for a while. Simon said we should play Zimbabwe more often. On the Sunday morning, before training, he was told to stay at the hotel and not turn up for training. We had this meeting and somebody read out some of his quotes and one or two guys stuck the knife into him. This was our best player. I stood up and I said, 'Hold on a second, lads. I don't know what's going on here, but this is a crock of shit. He's made a mistake.' There was talk of banning him for the Five Nations. I said, 'You must be fucking joking. I can't believe I'm hearing his team-mates saying this. You're a disgrace. I'm not standing for this witch hunt. What we do is we get him to apologise and we bring him back and if people in this team had half the attitude that Geoghegan has we'd be winning championships.' If they banned him they would have had to ban me as well. Simon was devastated that so few of us were standing up for him.

Mick Galwey: We lost to Scotland and then lost to France and that was eleven defeats in a row now. Eleven! This was February 1993 and we hadn't won a match since October 1991 – against Japan. We hadn't won in the Five Nations in nearly three years. I mean, we must have been breaking all records at this stage.

The record books were, indeed, smashed. No Irish side had ever lost eleven games in succession. Between 1875-1881 Ireland lost ten in a row and lost another ten on the spin between 1882-1886. Eleven was a new low.

Nick Popplewell: We played Wales next and managed to get a win at last and then we played England in our final game and we won again. Dean Richards wasn't playing. Injured or dropped, I don't know. But he wasn't there. And when Richards wasn't there then you always felt you had a small chance. He was the talisman. He'd dictate any game. He'd slow it down to his own pace. He could swallow the ball, a superb player. Deano was more influential than a Jerry Guscott or a Will Carling. He had that capacity to able to do the right thing at the right time.

Mick Galwey: The England win was one of those great moments. When I was young I'd have watched Ireland winning big games at Lansdowne Road and players being chaired off the pitch. It was the same that day. Some poor misfortune lifted me up on his shoulders. It was like a dream. It was worth all the hidings and it changed the course of my life because I scored our try. All of a sudden, everybody knew me. They still come up to me now. 'Remember the day you scored against England!' And you tell them how long ago it was and they can't believe it. They think it was yesterday.

Nick Popplewell: There was a Lions tour that summer. I made it but Simon Geoghegan didn't and one of my biggest regrets in rugby was that I wasn't on a

Lions tour with Geoghegan. It was very, very political. It summed up the times. He did that interview and the union didn't like it and the price he paid was that his name wasn't put forward for that Lions tour in New Zealand. And when they needed to fly out a replacement wing they sent for Richie Wallace, which was a fucking joke. Richie was a good player, but Simon was in the prime of his career.

The reaction in the media to the win over England was euphoric, not just because it was a fine performance, at last, but because it was the first time since the Triple Crown in 1985 that Ireland had managed back-to-back victories in the Five Nations.

In the *Sunday Independent*, guest columnist Willie John McBride, wrote about how the defeat of the English was sure to spark a revival in fortunes. 'I walked out of Lansdowne Road ten feet tall. The commitment, the passion, the control and, above all, the breath-taking excitement – that was my sort of game and, by God, I loved every minute of it. What we witnessed on Saturday was the rebirth of our rugby identity.'

Only it wasn't.

Neil Francis: We played in Paris in the first match of the Five Nations in 1994 and got our usual horsing; 30-15. One of their all-time hard cases was playing. If I was drawing up a list of French assassins I'd have Laurent Rodriguez out on his own as number one. Eric Champ would be number two and Olivier Merle would probably be number three. Merle was playing against us in '94.

Mick Galwey: Merle was an animal. I'm telling you, an animal. He took me out at a lineout and nearly broke my ribs. He came across me and I still blame Claw [Peter Clohessy] for it because Claw was supposed to be protecting me but he left me wide open. I was heaving from this blow and Claw ran away laughing at me.

Neil Francis: Merle was an axe murderer. He was about nine feet wide, a circus strongman, a savage beast who went around kicking people. In Paris, you either front-up or you die. They were kicking us and I'm not a dirty player, but yer man Philippe Benetton came in and killed the ball and I went and gave him a good kicking. Abdel Benazzi took exception and there was a fight. Jim Fleming was reffing and he gave the penalty to France. 'Any more of that and you're off,' he says to me. I says, 'They're doing it to us.' He says, 'Back you go.'

Mick Galwey: The game in Paris was the start of the Claw's beautiful relationship with the French.

Neil Francis: He was eaten alive. It was a disgrace.

Peter Clohessy: I never liked them. On the field, they'd be gouging, punching and catching you by the stones. If there's anything worse than having some fucker sticking his finger in your eye, it's having his buddy trying to rip the bollocks off you at the same time. That's the way it was.

Neil Francis: From the first whistle to the moment he was forced off injured sixteen minutes into the second half, Clohessy was attacked in the scrum by the twin forces of Armary and his hooker, Gonzalez. It was two against one and they really worked him. Their weight was bearing down on him the whole match and at the break-up of a lot of the scrums, Armary's head would come up and belt Claw right in the face. Everyone picked on him. If he was on the ground he'd get stood on. He was seeing stars by the time he came off.

Peter Clohessy: My abiding memory was standing on the sideline, with blood gushing down my head and the doctor trying to stitch me, and Noisy Murphy, who was the manager, running over to me and saying: 'They're going to kill you, they're going to kill you, you're not going back on that field.' And I said, 'Noisy, you're dead fucking right I'm not.' They tormented me that day. My body was ripped to bits, my head got opened a few times and the dressing room afterwards was like the casualty room of the Regional Hospital. I could have complained but what was the point? Anyway, complaining wouldn't have done a lot for my image. After a few pints we were all laughing about it and showing each other our scars. That's what the French matches did to you.

Gary Halpin: Peter played in my position and when he came into the side I felt hard done by, but when I saw him play two or three games I just had to accept that the guy was better than me. He blew his contemporaries out of the water. People talk about Phil Orr but Orr could never do the things Clohessy could. If you're making comparisons you should make them with Ray McLoughlin, because the Claw is up there with the legends.

Conor O'Shea: It was my second cap and I loved it. I loved the atmosphere at the Parc des Princes. As a kid it was the place that fascinated me most. They ran away with it in the end but the whole occasion was why I wanted to play rugby. It was a graveyard for us, but I enjoyed it.

Neil Francis: None of these French guys worked, or if they did, they worked part-time. They just trained and did weights and got paid. Their best guys were always going to be better than our best guys, but they were always fitter as well. You see Serge Blanco running riot in the last ten minutes and you say, 'Where are our guys? Why are they not making a tackle? How many French players are on this fucking pitch?' They were just fitter.

At Twickenham, Simon Geoghegan showed what he could do when given the ball in a yard of space. The wing scored a mesmeric try in the defeat of England, an unforgettable 13-12 victory that lifted spirits, if only for a little while. It was followed by a miserable 6-6 draw at home to Scotland, a game in which Geoghegan returned to his earlier status as interested, but under-utilised, observer. Soon, Ireland would be heading on a summer tour to Australia and some of the most unforgiving terrain in world rugby.

Keith Wood: That was my first ever rugby tour. I'd never been away with the club or anybody else before that and it was just one great adventure. I was working in the Irish Permanent bank on O'Connell Street in Limerick and it was unbelievably difficult for me to get time off to go away for a month. There were rumblings of professionalism but those rumblings had been there for a while, so was turning pro an incentive in my mind? Not at all. I was twenty-two years of age and I wanted to play for Ireland. That was the size of it.

Jeremy Davidson: The first place we stayed was Fremantle, a one-horse town in Western Australia. We arrived at the Esplanade Hotel and myself and David Corkery put our bags in our room and then about five minutes later we went downstairs and there was literally nobody there. We were going, 'Where have all the boys gone?' We took a walk down the street and the place was empty. Then we heard this awful ruckus coming from a pub and we looked in the door and there was the whole touring party in the bar, lashing the drink into them. Professional rugby was on its way, but amateur rugby had a bit of life left in it yet.

Victor Costello: Somebody called it the last of the great drinking tours.

Shane Byrne: I was a dirt-tracker and it was compulsory to go out on the welly. Then you were beaten out of the bed at eight in the morning to go to a fitness session.

Ireland started the tour by putting 64 points on Western Australia at the WACA in Perth, then shipped 55 against New South Wales in Sydney. They lost 22-9 to Australian Capital Territory in Canberra and 29-26 to Queensland in Brisbane.

The next stop was a place that even now sends a shiver down the spine of those who went there – Mount Isa.

Victor Costello: Mount Isa was a deep dark shithole.

Keith Wood: It had a claim to fame – the largest Irish club in the southern hemisphere.

Mick Galwey: It was a game against an Australia XV, just before the first Test. But nobody figured out what the Aussies meant by XV. Turned out that it was Australia A.

Neil Francis: It was a fucking hijack.

Mick Galwey: I didn't play in Mount Isa. No, thank God. I was injured. I was there, but I wasn't playing. It was an horrific place. I never experienced anything like that before. I talk to people and they say they've just come back from Australia on their holidays and I say, 'Did you go to Mount Isa?' And they say, 'Where the fuck is Mount Isa?' And I say, 'Exactly!'

Jeremy Davidson: I remember arriving there. The bus pulled up and we were sort of saying, 'Well, we're going to be there soon; shouldn't be too long.' There was nothing other than these wee rectangles of boxes that looked like fuck all else on earth. But there we were in this dodgy motel in Hicksville. And the sun was beating down for 22 hours a day. And you'd get up and say, 'I wonder what it's like today?' And your hand would get frazzled in the window. It was terrible. Fucking awful.

I played that day. It was like a scene from a Quentin Tarantino movie. It was an Irish club and the Irish were everywhere. You couldn't move for all the Irish in this place and everybody was steaming. They worked in copper mines for long periods of time and when they weren't in the mine they let their hair down big-time. Everybody was pissed.

Mick Galwey: Australia A were seriously strong. Savagely strong. Willie Ofahengaue was playing in their back-row – a horse of a man. He was nearly nineteen stone in weight and 6ft 4in in height and hungry as fuck. He was trying to win his place back in the Wallabies team and he was on a mission against us.

Conor O'Shea: I was on the bench that night – it was three days before the first Test – and you'd want to have seen their team: they had Willie O, a young Joe

Roff picked from the ACT Under-19s and Pat Howard in the centre. It was a great rugby side. I was on the bench with Michael Bradley and before kick-off Brads turned to me and said, 'You know what? I've a really, really bad feeling about this.'

Mick Galwey: Ken O'Connell had been flown out from Cork as a replacement. He'd just captained Sunday's Well to win their first Munster Senior Cup in forty-one years and he'd been on the piss for two weeks. Then he got the dreaded phone call. 'Come out, you're needed'. He arrives and he's straight into the team in Mount Isa and who is his opposite number? Only Willie O. He ran over Ken about ten times.

Conor O'Shea: Ken was behind the posts at one stage and said, 'If I had a gun I'd shoot myself.'

Victor Costello: The Aussies are rough as fuck and they were particularly rough in Mount Isa. It finished 57-9. Not nice. The body language in the hotel wouldn't have been great. The Aussies weren't exactly gracious in victory either.

Keith Wood: I was in Mount Isa, but I wasn't playing. I'd had seventeen stitches in my eye so I was spared and then we played Australia in the first Test four days later and that was my Ireland debut. My father had made his debut forty years earlier, so it was nice. Was I emotional about it? I was and I wasn't. It was really nice for my mum, that's for sure. In the match I had Paco Fitzgerald on one side of me in the front-row and the Claw on the other – two Young Munster men and a kid from Garryowen. A cracking fax came in from Clifford Park a few days before the Test, congratulating me on winning my first cap. It said: 'The two boys have been instructed to look after you. However, we must inform you that this only applies on foreign soil.' I thought that was absolutely brilliant.

I was hooking against Phil Kearns. I punched him after ten minutes, just to let him know I was there and he pulled my jersey over my head and beat the crap out of me. They won 33-13 the first week and 32-18 the second week and they were entitled to win because they were a fabulous team. David Campese, Michael Lynagh, Danny Herbert, Garrick Morgan, John Eales. Great, great players. It was a privilege to be on the same field as those guys. And I'd be seeing some of them again soon enough.

TEN

LIKE AN ELEPHANT, CLAW WASN'T FORGETTING

Ireland's form going into the 1995 World Cup in South Africa could hardly have been described as stellar. The Five Nations had been a familiar story; three defeats and one victory, at the Cardiff Arms Park, which for a dozen years had been a strange oasis of positivity for the Irish side. Despite all the hardship in every other stadium they played in, Ireland hadn't lost in Wales in 12 years.

In May, they travelled to Treviso to play an Italian side that had, a year earlier, taken the Wallabies to the wire in Brisbane, eventually losing by just three points. They were fast-improving and too much for the hapless tourists.

The problems started when their transport to the stadium never arrived. 'Kick-off was in the early evening,' wrote Brendan Fanning in *From There To Here*. 'The bus was due to collect them at five. At 5.05 Noel Murphy was already anxious. By 5.20 his blood pressure was rising. By 5.30 the taxis he had called at 5.10 still hadn't showed. So he risked life and limb and set about trying to flag down any passing bus. As it happened, that strip was a haunt for prostitutes, so motorists wouldn't have known what to make of an excited man in a green blazer waving a fistful of cash.'

Italy won 22-12. It was the first time in their history that the Italians had beaten a top-eight nation. It had to be Ireland.

The following morning, as the players boarded the bus to take them to the airport, the hotel manager challenged Murphy about an unpaid bar bill from the night before. An IRFU man tried to blame the media for sticking drink on the union tab. Murphy soon settled the account when the night porter identified the culprit as a member of the team and not the press corp.

There was one last moment of embarrassment when some hotel property was retrieved from the bags of the departing tourists. Next stop: South Africa.

Professionalism was the talk of the rugby world and it was only a matter of months before shamateurism would come to an end and the game would go open accompanied by the sound of screaming from the IRFU.

Some nations had been professional for years, Ireland's first opponent, New Zealand being one of them.

Opposite: Peter Clohessy with Nick Popplewell and France's Fabien Pelous during the 1996 Five Nations encounter in Paris.

Gary Halpin: It was a strange no-man's land to find yourself in, really, because we knew we were absolute amateurs in what was effectively a professional environment. All the chat out there was how much money South Africa Breweries would lob into the Springboks' fund if they won the first match against the Wallabies. Meanwhile, we were listening to speeches from IRFU committee men, actually during the tournament, celebrating the amateur ideal. In truth, we'd no idea the game would go pro in a matter of months. What we did know was that we didn't have the technical back-up of some other teams. Even England were miles ahead of us at this stage, as were the southern hemisphere teams. They were much slicker outfits.

Ireland met the All Blacks at Ellis Park, Johannesburg on May 27. The date is important for it was the night that a twenty year old winger made his debut for the All Blacks.

Richard Wallace: I was walking through reception in the Sunnyside Park hotel in Johannesburg when a journalist comes up to me: 'Richie, have you got a few minutes?'

'Yeah, sure, what do you want to talk about?'

'Well, this fella you're up against on the wing.'

'A typically fast, powerful All Black no doubt.'

'Yeah, yeah, He's 6ft 4.'

I thought, 'Jesus, that's tall.'

'He's more than 18st.'

The colour started draining from my face.

'And he does the 100m in 10.7sec.'

I'm thinking, 'Holy shit! How am I going to keep a straight face here and pretend I know this? My brain was doing somersaults.

'Ah, you know,' I said. 'The bigger they are the harder they fall.' I didn't realise he was going to be falling on top of me.

Neil Francis: It was the night Jonah Lomu said hello to the world.

Gary Halpin: We made a brilliant start which, in hindsight, was maybe not the best idea in the world. We were pretty ferocious. I took a tap penalty from Michael Bradley after eight minutes and I battered my way through Jamie Joseph and Mike Brewer and I scored. Then I turned around and gave them the fingers. It was very much a spur of the moment thing. In those pre-professional days we had a feeling that the New Zealand players were almost God-like. They had that aura of invincibility about them. I was actually quite friendly with Jamie Joseph and

Gary Halpin gives a two fingered salute to the New Zealand fans after scoring his try.

subsequently had a good relationship with Zinzan Brooke, but on previous tours they'd looked on us as second class citizens, in a sporting context and it was very much a reaction to that. It was born out of frustration more than anything else. Sean Fitzpatrick had been winding us up, calling us Paddies. And I couldn't really believe I'd actually scored a try. It was a rather stupid thing to do, being a teacher and all. It's kind of embarrassing, but I dined out on it like a lord. I loved telling the story. You'd embellish it a bit every time, just to get bought another beer

Neil Francis: We were ahead for half an hour, then yer man took off.

Richard Wallace: There was a fifteen metre blindside. There was me and there was him. And I'm going, 'This guy is going to run right over the top of me so I'd better just go for it.' So I went for it. Suddenly there was a hand on my head or shoulder or wherever and I'm going, 'Hang on, this is not going according to the script.'

Brendan Mullin: Lomu scored and then he scored again and it was obvious that this was a pretty significant night in the history of rugby because he was a phenomenal individual. We played well and we still lost 43-19.

Conor O'Shea: We beat Japan in Bloemfontein in our second game and then it was back to Ellis Park for the big one against Wales. Whoever won it was going through to the quarter-final. We scraped it by a point but it goes down as one of the worst games of rugby in the history of mankind. And yet we were all ecstatic to win it. It was no-risk rugby. Nobody was trying to play and we were kicking the thing at every opportunity and I was thinking, 'Is this why I play this game? Just to stand at full-back and leather it?' I almost quit after that match because it was so little fun to play. You wanted to play rugby, not be in a team that just hoofed it all the time.

The destructive power of Jonah Lomu is announced to the world against Ireland.

Neil Francis: We had a week before we played the French in the quarter-final in Durban so Noisy decided we'd go to Sun City and chill out, which was great. We came down from Sun City and we had a fella called Giles Warrington with us. Giles really knew his stuff in terms of physiological conditioning. He was top class. He said, 'Right, we're going to stay in Pretoria for the rest of the week and then we're going fly into Durban on the morning of the match and we'll over-ride the whole altitude thing.' We thought we had a good chance against France. Noisy said, 'No, we have people in Durban who want to see us, Irish fans.' Giles said, 'You don't realise what you're doing. You're bringing the lads down from altitude to sea level a few days before the match. Are you fucking mad?'

That's what happened. Giles was side-lined and we went down to Durban and trained in King's Park and it was super-charged stuff. We were running around like lunatics. Everybody was superman. And then on the Friday before the match our energy levels disappeared and we couldn't walk. It was the worst dressing room beforehand, nobody could say a word. Had we played against France the way we had trained on the Thursday we would have won that match. Instead, we lost 36-12. We were brave but we had nothing in the tank. To be hamstrung by our stupid preparation was hard to take. Giles knew it was going to happen. He was an expert. And he wasn't listened to. I remember sitting in the dressing room afterwards and thinking, 'This is my last World Cup and we've fucked it up again.'

Gary Halpin: The regret I have is that we underperformed as a team and I felt bad about that because we had some very good players: Simon Geoghegan, Brendan Mullin and so on. But there was so much in-fighting in our union at the time, the sort of feudal horseshit that had gone on the previous 100 years. I got over it because those guys' hearts were in the right place.

Just over two months after Ireland were knocked out of the World Cup, the International Rugby Football Board voted in professionalism. A large degree of pay for play was expected but what shocked some in the union was the extent of the transformation – it was total. Lock, stock and barrel.

The IRFU were vehemently opposed to professionalism and now portents of doom came spilling out of HQ. Billy Lavery, the chairman of the amateurism sub-committee, said that it was a 'tragedy for the game.' Ken Reid, the past president, warned that rugby authorities had 'opened up an age of turmoil.'

And Reid was right. While the brains of the IRFU committee were still being fried by the complexity of change, Irish international players started to depart for attractive professional contracts in England.

Keith Wood went to Harlequins. Jonathan Bell went to Northampton. Conor O'Shea, David Humphreys, Jeremy Davidson and Victor Costello went to London Irish. Paul Wallace and Paddy Johns went to Saracens. David Corkery went to Bristol with Paul Burke. Eric Miller went to Leicester.

There was a new reality in one sense but the same old story in another. For the

1996 season, Murray Kidd, a Kiwi who had taken Garryowen to an All Ireland League title, replaced Gerry Murphy and became the fourth Irish coach of the decade.

It was Kidd's misfortune that he took on the job in a spectacularly difficult period.

Nick Popplewell: Murray Kidd. Oh good God, yeah. In fairness, he had a New Zealand passport and if you had one of those at that stage then it was enough. As well as being poor, he was unpleasant. You put that mixture together and it's hard to stomach. You need some element of fun. He had another guy with him, Mike Brewer. I wasn't a fan of him either. It was the New Zealand thing of running through walls. The sessions would finish with a beasting.

Victor Costello: He was a fucking angry coach. He gave me my first cap but he was limited. You didn't learn a lot from him.

Jeremy Davidson: He called everybody Fuck Knuckle. His training sessions would last a long, long time and it would all be horrendous contact work. Basically, we had to beat each other up. After days and days and days of training we'd be injured and he'd say, 'If it ain't fucking broken then get back on the pitch.' That was his attitude.

Victor Costello: I won my first cap against America in Atlanta in January 1996. We went to Atlanta on the Sunday night and it was really all about having a warm weather training camp ahead of the Five Nations. We got caught in a snow storm.

Jeremy Davidson: There must have been six foot of snow when we got there. It was cartoon stuff.

Victor Costello: It was pissing rain on the day of the Test match. If you were at the bottom of a ruck you were close to drowning. The changing room was about 500 yards from the pitch, so we got into our gear and into the back of a mini-bus. We scraped a win; 25-18

The 1996 Six Nations began with the traditional loss to the Scots, the ninth year in a row that Ireland had failed to record a win against Scotland. Next, it was the trip to Paris to face Jean-Claude Skrela's France.

Victor Costello: I was rooming with the Claw. I didn't know what to expect. I was thinking I might have to go to bed with my gum-shield in, but instead he tucked me in and gave me a teddy bear. It was my second cap and there was no better man to room with. He was great; rock steady but nervous like the rest of us. It was all about survival in Paris, for him more than most.

Keith Wood: Peter was an incredibly uncompromising and an extraordinarily skilful rugby player. He could scrummage with his head on the ground, but it was the other sides to his game that he rarely got the credit for. He had an ability to catch a ball off his toes and not break stride that few players had. He could really play, but that tended to get overlooked.

Victor Costello: Pa Whelan was our manager and in the team meeting beforehand he was talking about France's great dangerman, Emile Ntamack of Toulouse, but he kept calling him Natamack. Pa would be incredibly passionate in these situations. He'd almost be crying. He said, 'I don't give a fuck about any of their lads, especially Natamack.' Nobody corrected him. Technically and tactically we were behind them by about three, four or five years, but our psyche was that if we could get stuck in then we might rattle them.

Jeremy Davidson: We were so uneducated, rugby-wise. We couldn't understand why we'd be competing OK for a while and then all of sudden they'd up the gears and Olivier Magne would be flying down the wing. Or it would go the other wing and it would be Abdel Benazzi flying down that side. Or the hooker. We couldn't understand it.

Victor Costello: Kurt McQuilkin played in the centre that day. When France really started to motor he came over to me in a break in the play and said, 'How many balls are on this fucking pitch?'

Jeremy Davidson: They had forwards running like backs. It was crazy stuff. They played with width and that was a word we hadn't heard of in Irish rugby. I was in the back-row and I just ran and ran and ran, chasing shadows the whole day. It was soul-destroying. We lost 45-10.

Victor Costello: None of us knew about the Claw and Olivier Roumat until later that night.

Jeremy Davidson: It was only after the match that we saw what happened – the stamp on Roumat. Normally you'd have gotten away with a bit of that now and again. I'm not condoning it, but it happened an awful lot, especially in France. It was pretty bad, in fairness. You can see him looking down and doing it. Rugby was in the process of change. There was a lot of talk about cleaning up the game now that it was professional.

Peter Clohessy: The match was over and nobody took any notice of it as we were coming off the field. It was actually Neil Francis, who was reporting on the match, who said it to me. 'I think you're in a bit of trouble.' I said, 'Why, what happened?' I had actually forgotten about it. He explained that it had been replayed all the

Peter Clohessy lashes out at Jean Michel Gonzalez.

time on TV. I kind of leaned on his head with my boot. I actually pulled out of it when I was doing it as I realised what I was doing. I didn't put any weight and he wasn't injured. It did look horrific on the TV. Thanks to RTE. They showed it back about fifty times in the forty-eight hours after the game.

Keith Wood: I was out injured and it was my first game working for the BBC. When the Claw thing happened they kept saying in my ear, 'Comment on the incident,' and I said, 'It looks like Olivier Roumat has lost one of his contact lenses there.' It was a big furore and it was part of the change in the sport. Claw was wrong and he almost became the face of the change. In some respects I think he was scapegoated.

Mick Galwey: There was an awful lot said about it, but it was payback. Like an elephant, Claw wasn't forgetting what had happened to him two years earlier. Whatever Claw dished out that day I guarantee you he took the same again and more beforehand. The 1994 game was the backdrop. We got the shit kicked out of us. We didn't give out about it, we just got on with it. But he was caught red-handed with the Roumat thing and he took an awful hiding for it. He knew he was wrong.

Peter Clohessy: After the game there was a committee meeting put together immediately and the meeting was held that night in Paris. I landed in Dublin the following day to find out I had been suspended for six months. It was wrong what I did, but I don't think I deserved six months for it. I had a bad name. I didn't have a great relationship with the French at the time and I think the president of the committee that handed out the suspension was French so that probably didn't stand me in good stead either.

Mick Galwey: Six months of a ban, it was a massive story. The game had gone professional and different rules applied to that kind of thing. I felt very sorry for him because I know it had a big impact on his life. People say, 'Claw is a hard man, he'll get over it.' But it wasn't so easy. That had a very big effect on him. There were a lot of people saying he should get banned for life. But he took his punishment and came back a great player.

Victor Costello: We went on and beat Wales and finished with one win out of four in the Championship, which was about all we ever did. In the November we played Western Samoa in Lansdowne Road in a midweek game.

Rob Henderson: I had the pleasure of playing in that one. My debut. Unforgettable.

Victor Costello: They had Inga Tuigamala and Pat Lam – a half-decent side and a lot better than us. They scored twenty-five points in the first half. I came off the bench and I went to hit a guy and it was like hitting an iron girder.

Rob Henderson: We lost 40-25 – five tries to one. They just blew us away. We disgraced the nation.

Mick Galwey: I played in that one and, as the man says, I didn't see grass again with Ireland for another year.

Keith Wood: I came back into the team after that – and I was made captain. Murray Kidd had been my coach at Garryowen when we won the All Ireland League and he was very enjoyable to work with. His was a very professional way of doing things – in 1991. But by the time we got to 1996 the world had moved on and his gameplan wasn't comprehensive enough. I wouldn't blame him for that. I wouldn't blame anybody really. We just took a long time to get into the idea of professionalism.

Conor O'Shea: Before the start of the 1997 Five Nations we went to Portugal for a warm-weather camp.

Keith Wood: That only goes down to farce. We trained for four hours every day in Portugal and it lashed down with rain. We were at the end of a golf driving range and there was golf balls plopping into the water around us.

Jeremy Davidson: I've been to the same resort on holiday in the years since and it took a while for the penny to drop. 'Oh my God, this is the place where we had that horrific training camp.' We did these bleep tests and Gaillimh [Mick Galwey] and the Claw kicked the cones in about two metres so instead of a bleep test that was twenty metres long we were doing sixteen or seventeen metres. World records were broken that day. We were up to level five and nobody had broken sweat. People like Paco Fitzgerald, Poppy [Nick Popplewell] and the Claw were off the scale. The All Blacks wouldn't have got a look-in. Everybody in the management was jumping for joy. It was only that night that they twigged. The wrath was terrible. Next morning at 8am we were hauled down to do it again. The scores weren't exactly at the same level the second time.

Keith Wood: We did a full battery of fitness tests on the Thursday before we got our flight back. Then we did another two hours on Friday. Now, a week's hard training is absolutely fine, but it was playing Italy on the Saturday that was the problem. I objected to it. I absolutely did, only to be told that the guys had to do the fitness tests because their new contracts were based on them achieving certain scores and Portugal was the time to do it, game or no game.

People said we looked unfit against Italy. But the truth is that we were bloody tired. We look back at it now and we say it's lunacy. But you were talking about an amateur committee who didn't meet all that often and they were trying to keep up with a professional game that was going at 100mph. Every time something like that happened there was a lesson learned from it. And you can say that maybe they shouldn't have had to be learned but the fact was that Ireland wasn't prepared to go into professionalism and this was the legacy. Snap decisions were being made and not fully thought through.

Jeremy Davidson: We lost to Italy. Of course we did. We were mentally and physically shattered and they were very good. That was an excellent Italian team – Paolo Vaccari, Diego Dominquez, Alessandro Troncon, the Cuttittas. Mark 'Small' McCall played in the centre with a broken thumb and he said that was the day he made his opposite number, Cristian Stoica, look like a world class player. Small couldn't tackle him properly and Stoica ran amok on his debut. He got a huge contract with Narbonne on the back of it.

Nick Popplewell: It was ridiculous, no enjoyment whatsoever. You weren't being listened to and you were just being bullied in training. You could see the younger players were being picked on and you didn't need that shite.

Denis Hickie: The whole idea what professionalism meant was different then. Overnight, the game went pro and there was no appreciation of physiology and conditioning. It was a case of yesterday you were working in a job and training twice a week but today you're getting paid so that means you train three times a day for three two-hour sessions and because we're paying you it means that your body is able to do this. That was the logic. You're professional now so that means you should be able to do all this stuff. But it takes years to build up that reservoir of conditioning.

It was strange. The hardest training weeks were the weeks of internationals. The week of a match was brutal. They slaughtered us. We'd go into camp and we'd be training twice a day for four or five days in a row. You couldn't do it. There was no concept of what was possible. The starting point was you are professional and therefore you can do all this training. It wasn't malicious. They weren't saying that we're flogging these guys because we're going to get our money's worth. There just wasn't the understanding. It was a steep learning curve and over-hanging all of it was this massive pressure to win.

ELEVEN

SOMETHING'S AWRY WHEN PA'S THE GOOD COP

Two days after Ireland lost to Italy at Lansdowne Road, Murray Kidd picked up a copy of the *Irish Times* and read a story that said he'd been sacked. He phoned his employers and was told that no decision had been made about his future. Then he received a fax inviting him to a meeting with the committee the following day. At that point he pretty much knew that the story in the newspaper, which contained details of his severance pay, was correct.

Ireland went into the 1997 Five Nations with yet another new coach. In looking for the miracle man to cure all ills they turned to England and Brian Ashton. The little Lancastrian had achieved great things as part of the revolution at Bath. His players at The Rec raved about his coaching; his innovative ideas and his ability to constantly bring new thinking to the table. Jeremy Guscott called him one of the best rugby coaches in the world. Ireland, said Guscott, had pulled off a coup in getting him.

Brian Ashton: You always have reservations about going somewhere that's unknown – and Irish rugby was completely unknown to me. It sounded like a really exciting challenge, so I went across and met Syd Millar, Noel Murphy and Pat Whelan, the team manager, and they offered me the job. If I had my time again I would have asked them, 'Why have we got a five-man selection committee? And why are nearly all the Irish players playing in England? And when are you going to get them back again?' I should probably have taken a lot more time and maybe Ireland should have taken a lot more time as well. They needed to investigate what I'd been doing for seven or eight years at Bath and I needed to investigate what Ireland needed. It was all done very quickly.

My first game in charge was at home to France in the opening round of the 1997 Five Nations. We lost 32-15 and we were applauded back into the hotel by the supporters afterwards. It was very odd given I'd come from a culture at Bath where if you'd lost a game the players would rip the bloody dressing room apart – and the supporters would let you know about it as well. To be applauded into a hotel after losing an international, I just thought it was strange. I mean, fantastic in some ways that the supporters are giving their backing to the players for what

Opposite: Pat Whelan and Brian Ashton.

they'd done, but in terms of building a winning mentality it just seemed a little bit surreal to me.

Denis Hickie: The second game of that season was against Wales in Cardiff and it was my debut. The night before the game the IRFU committee lads set off the fire alarm. It was three in the morning and everybody was evacuated into the street. All the alickadoos were out there going, 'How did that happen?'

Brian Ashton: Oh bloody hell, yeah. They thought it was hilarious. We all trekked outside in our boxer shorts and our dressing gowns and there the boys were, still in their dinner jackets. A laugh a minute, that.

Jim Staples: It was almost like a scene from the Titanic, everybody running around making sure everyone was out of their rooms.

Denis Hickie: I'd been to the Arms Park as a schoolboy, so it was very special to play there. The first five minutes, the pace was incredible. Ieuan Evans scored after about a minute and the noise in the stadium was unlike anything I'd heard before.

Brian Ashton: Denis scored a cracking try down the blindside, linking with Jim Staples, and that was the kind of thing I'd seen on a regular basis at Bath and it was fantastic to see Ireland doing it so soon. But people forget the try that Jonny Bell got that day. We'd talked beforehand about scoring tries, which Ireland had found notoriously difficult to do. I said that there's more than one way to skin a cat. Eric Elwood was playing 10 and I told him that when the opportunity arose he should bang the bloody ball up in the air and actually aim to land it on their crossbar, so when the full-back looks up he's got two posts and a crossbar and a pack of marauding forwards to worry about. Eric executed his kick perfectly and we got a try from it and when I said in the press conference that it had been a training ground move, everybody laughed. And I thought, 'Well, bugger off, you lot.' That try was classic case of thinking and then putting something into practice. And we won the match by a point.

A fortnight later, England came to Dublin and inflicted their heaviest defeat on an Irish team. They scored forty-six points, which was an all-time record for the fixture, and only conceded six. The forty-point winning margin required a swift rewriting of the history books and made for a mortifying afternoon for Ashton against his home country containing some of the players he helped to nurture at Bath in his previous life.

Brian Ashton: For about twenty minutes we were in the game, and then suddenly we lost Eric Elwood and Eric Miller and the confidence seemed to go out of the team because Elwood was a pretty smooth operator and Miller was an outstanding rugby player. England got on a bit of a roll and played probably some of the best rugby they'd played in years. The English subs were sitting about two rows in front of me. Jerry Guscott was one of them. There was about twenty-five minutes to go and the scoreboard was mounting up. I shouted down, 'For fuck sake Guscott, if they ask you to go on, tell them no.'

Paul Wallace: We went to Scotland next and we lost 38-10, so more records were broken.

Conor O'Shea: Brian was too far ahead of where we were. He wanted to push skills, he didn't accept second best, didn't accept people who didn't have the required skill level. He was a brilliant coach, incredibly demanding.

Rob Henderson: He tried to reinvent the wheel. If he'd had a better understanding of the mentality of the players then he would have got a lot more out of us a lot quicker. He was trying to get us to play a certain style of rugby, but we didn't have the skill-set.

Malcolm O'Kelly: In training he'd be constantly screaming, 'Width, width, width!' but the Irish rugby model at that stage meant you could have thrown a blanket over all fifteen of us. We had no concept of playing touchline to touchline. That was his philosophy but we didn't have the ability to pass the ball wide under the pressure of international rugby.

Denis Hickie: He was dumbfounded at the poor level of skill in the team. He had a look of horror on his face from fairly early on.

Rob Henderson: Some of the bollockings he handed out. Fucking hell, he'd cut you down to size.

Reggie Corrigan: He was a grumpy little fucker, no doubt about it. But I got on very well with him.

Brian Ashton: I was pushed forward in my coaching by the sort of provocative, aggressive nature of the players I had at Bath. They never wanted to stand still, were never satisfied with what they were doing, always wanted to be different. It was a great learning environment, but going across to Ireland it was almost like I was going back in time. What I should have done was revert and try to move forward more slowly than I did. But what I tried to do was impose myself and my coaching methods on players who probably had a completely different mind-set as far as wanting to play the game.

I can be pretty stubborn at times so, basically, I thought, 'I'm buggered if I'm going back to what it was like years ago at Bath when we were putting in the foundations.' That is where I made an error. I wanted to do more coaching than organising and I suppose at that time maybe the team needed more organising than coaching. I should have said, 'Oh, hang on a minute, let's sort out our organisation before moving too far too quickly.' It was an environment in Ireland where the coach was king and I wanted to shift it to an environment where the players were king, where the players were given responsibility and freedom to make decisions. But I think a lot of the players were happy to be dictated to. There were mavericks, of course. Keith Wood was an unbelievably talented rugby player. Eric Miller, David Humphreys, Jim Staples, Jeremy Davidson, Denis Hickie. My eyes lit up when I saw that lot. But the majority of players probably wanted a more rigid structure to follow instead of the freedom that I was trying to instigate.

Kevin Maggs: There was a development tour in the summer of 1997 and I was on it.

Anthony Foley: Some day someone will write the book of the tour. It will read a bit like *Alive*, the story of the South American players who crashed in the Andes and ate the bodies of their team-mates to survive.

Brian Ashton: I'm not sure anybody told New Zealand that it was a development tour as opposed to an A team tour. The itinerary they set out for us was challenging, to put it mildly.

Kevin Maggs: I'd waited for my chance for a long time. I was playing for Bristol and I'd sent videos of my games to the IRFU with a letter and I don't think I ever got an acknowledgement from them. I was only noticed because Brian came to Bristol to watch Paul Burke and David Corkery. Somebody said to him that Kevin Maggs' grandfather is from Limerick and he's wanted to play for Ireland for absolutely-ever. He had no idea that I qualified. Nobody told him. He came to Bristol to watch the boys on the Saturday and on the Tuesday I was put on standby for the development tour to New Zealand. I was told I was picked on the Friday and we left on the Sunday. It was a bit mad. A hell of a trip. It was five weeks that seemed like five months.

Brian Ashton: I went to check in for the flight to Auckland and nobody had booked me a ticket. I've no idea how that happened, but I wasn't best pleased when I found out. I was like, 'Jesus Christ, Brian, they're really looking after you well, eh? They get you out the bed at three o'clock in the morning before we play Wales in Cardiff and now they've forgotten to book you on the bloody flight for a development tour that New Zealand think is an A team tour.' We played against sides that, traditionally, play against British & Irish Lions teams. Suddenly we're here with a lot of young players who have never been remotely exposed to anything like that sort of thing and it was pretty tough going. But, again, I thought, 'Bugger it, we're going to have to fight our way through this.' Both on the field and off it.

Malcolm O'Kelly: Brian and Pa Whelan, our manager, really struggled on that tour. Pa would always play bad cop in every relationship but by the end of the tour he was actually the good cop and Brian was the bad cop. People were actually warming to Pa because Brian was so tough. Brian just went more and more into himself and wasn't really communicating with anybody. You know that something has gone seriously awry when Pa Whelan becomes the good cop.

Kevin Maggs: There was a bit of an atmosphere between the two of them, to be fair.

Gary Halpin: When I spoke to Brian, when he asked me to captain the development tour, he spoke to me in terms of, 'I kind of need a guy like you there because I don't know Pat Whelan.' He was very, very sceptical of Pa from the start.

Rob Henderson on the attack against Bay of Plenty during the summer tour of 1997.

Brian Ashton: We had one or two fallouts on tour. I just felt that he was paying lip service to professionalism and it rankled with me and I made the point on a number of occasions that I felt slightly isolated, that I was the only professional on the management side of that tour and all the rest were amateurs. I was thinking, 'Ultimately, to you guys it doesn't matter because you'll go home and go off to work. This is my job, my livelihood.'

Pat Whelan: He was giving out about the training, about the fact that all the gear wasn't there lined up on time and this kind of carry-on, but I was only learning my fucking trade the same as everyone else. I hauled him into my room and I seriously told him, 'Never fucking try and do what you did there again.'

Conor O'Shea: When your coach and manager aren't capable of walking on the same side of the road as each other then it's difficult, but what do you do? You get on with it. By the end of the tour it was very obvious. Did Brian get incredibly frustrated with the players? Yes. Did he get frustrated with me? Yes. I had a great relationship with him even though he was harder on me than most of the others. The more he expected of you the more pressure he put on you. The more he felt you could cope the more he piled it on. He was a tough boy

Malcolm O'Kelly: It was a brutally hard tour. No fun, just training, training, training. And matches – most of which we were hockeyed in. Guys were tired and emotional very quickly on that tour. There was one game, against Bay of Plenty, when Brian made four substitutions after twenty minutes. Savage stuff.

Brian Ashton: I think it was a world record. You'll probably find that my patience was running out. There were probably one or two issues with Pat Whelan at that time. We had completely different philosophies of how the game should be played and so it was going to be quite tricky going forward. Pat was a committed member of the IRFU, an ex-international, a real strong figure. I respected him for what he'd done in the past and, you know, here was this upstart Englishman coming in saying we're changing the way we play the game. I think over a period of time, especially on that tour when the results were as they were, then the relationship became a little bit strained.

Keith Wood: I was on the Lions tour when all that was going on. I'd had nine caps and three surgeries before going to South Africa. And I came back different. I trained very hard on the Lions tour, did a lot of weights, a huge amount of scrummaging and then we all got injured afterwards. I hurt my back at the end of that tour. I went to pick up my shoes and put a disk out. I tore my groin as well. Not a whole lot of fun. Then, first game in the autumn, we had New Zealand at Lansdowne Road.

Rob Henderson: I had one cap plus I was on the development tour and my stats were very consistent. I played against Western Samoa in 1996 and I'd played in seven out of the eight games on the tour and the one I didn't play in was the one that we won. So my record in the green jersey at that stage was played eight, lost eight. And next it was the All Blacks.

Reggie Corrigan: I was in the squad, which was a fair old turnaround. Not long before the Leinster coach, Mike Ruddock, have given me a trial. I was two stone overweight, all over the shop, a mess. But he saw something in me and he liked it. I was working at the time for an air freight company. Not the most glamorous job in the world. Mike gave me a part-time contract of £7,500 and I packed in my job and went full-time. I'd just bought a house, so I took a gamble. It was a three-month deal and those were the hardest three months I ever put in. Ruddock just ran the bollocks off us and got me fit and strong and before I knew where I was I was sitting on the bench for Ireland against New Zealand.

Kevin Maggs: I was sitting with Reggie. I came off the bench for my first cap fairly early in the second half and it was all a bit: 'Jesus Christ, I can't believe this.' It was a daunting prospect because their team had some of the greatest names ever. When you see me coming on it's like I've got no blood left in my body. I was so anxious about it. It was the biggest thing in my life. I came on and I nearly knocked myself out trying to smash Jeff Wilson. I caught his elbow in the side of my head. I was bit dazed to say the least.

Rob Henderson: We were actually doing all right. Woody scored two tries in the first half. We were causing them trouble.

Keith Wood: I scored from a rumble off the back of a maul. Then I got smashed between Zinzan Brooke and Andrew Blowers and I did my ankle ligaments, but I played on. I scored another try after I tore my ankle. I knocked great crack out of the second one because I beat Jeff Wilson to the touch down. The reality is that he had to turn and I didn't but in my mind I ran the length of the field and sped past him. As the half went on my leg started swelling and by half time I had to be helped down the steps.

Brian Ashton: Sean Fitzpatrick didn't play in that game. He was sitting near me

Brian Ashton issues instructions at half-time during one of the tour matches.

in the stand, about six feet away. We played some really good rugby and frightened them to death for a while. When Woody scored his second try Fitzy looked across at me and said, 'Jesus Christ, what's going on? They haven't done this before.' I thought, 'The bloody game lasts eighty minutes, mate.' That New Zealand side was immensely talented.

Malcolm O'Kelly: We got them annoyed and they blew us away in the second half. Absolutely killed us. Zinzan Brooke's command of the troops and his ability to read the game was miles ahead of ours. We were getting battered by forty or fifty points and then they brought on Josh Kronfeld. This guy was a bit of a hero of mine and here he is trotting on as a sub. It was very demoralising to see the level of player they had coming on just as we were out on our feet.

Kevin Maggs: We went to Bologna a month later for a game against Italy. They put thirty-seven points on us. Another sickener.

Victor Costello: Brian brought in a crowd of clowns from England – Dylan O'Grady and David Erskine. You had the likes of Eddie Halvey, Anthony Foley, David Corkery and Alan Quinlan frozen out and these fucking eejits coming in and soaking up caps. It was pathetic. He picked a load of these guys over serious rugby players.

Dylan O'Grady was a flanker with a back story that was straight out of a movie. He left school at sixteen and became a father at seventeen. He supplemented his income as a professional rugby player with Sale by operating as a doorman at a nightclub in Manchester and hung around with gangs of wrestlers and assorted hard cases. 'I have to make it in rugby,' he said at the time of his first cap. 'It's all right for some. They have jobs they could possibly go back to when they're finished in the game, but I've got nothing. I'm not exactly academically minded, so what can I do? Go back working on the door when I'm fifty?'

Malcolm O'Kelly: I was rooming with Dylan O'Grady in Bologna. I've met a few headers in my time but he fairly took the biscuit. He was a great ol' storyteller, you know. He'd given me his life story by the end of that trip. He was a likeable guy but he had a chequered past to say the least. He had all these yarns about organised criminals in Manchester. He was privy to a lot of information. I was loving it. I was all set to go to Manchester with him for a look. I wouldn't slag him or David Erskine over their nationality. O'Grady was passionately Irish and so was Erskine. My parents went over to England around the same time as Dylan's parents and the difference was that my parents came home but his didn't, so I never held that against him. I was born in England so I'd be some hypocrite if I pointed my finger at other people.

Brian Ashton: I suppose looking back, I possibly made a mistake with Dylan. John Mitchell was coaching at Sale. He phoned me up and said, 'We've got this cracking player,' and I went to watch him play and he did really well. And I thought, 'Christ, if I'm going to travel down a new path then maybe this is a guy that can help us.' But what I didn't do was to get to know the player. And, on reflection, it was a mistake doing that.

Denis Hickie: We got bashed by fifteen points. The perception was that we were Ireland and they were Italy and we would win because we were a bigger rugby nation – but they were a better team. They were excellent.

Dylan O'Grady: We should have won. The Italians weren't great, but that's life isn't it? It's all about ifs and buts. If only we'd won. If only I'd got a second chance. No point in tormenting myself about it. It didn't happen and I don't bother about the reasons.

Mick Galwey: The most disappointing thing was that it got to a situation where we felt that you almost had to be playing in England in order to play for Ireland. I got no cap under Brian Ashton and Anthony Foley was the same. We were bitter about it.

Reggie Corrigan: The problem for Brian was that he didn't realise how bad we were when he took the job. It might sound funny, but that's the case. He thought he was coming over to a similar set-up as he had at Bath, but we had no structure, we had no training camp, we trained at ALSAA near Dublin airport on one of the worst pitches you could imagine and other times we were hopping on buses and training at Naas and when Naas was flooded we'd go to King's Hospital and when that was flooded we'd go somewhere else. We were like gypsies travelling around all over the place.

Victor Costello: The relationship between Brian and Pa was getting worse. I got on well with Pa, I knew the shape of the guy; old school, rough as fuck, shy in a lot of ways, deep rooted in the IRFU. And political. He talked out the side of his mouth, but Pa knew what was needed and he wasn't getting it from Ashton.

Reggie Corrigan: It was impossible to read Pa. He had a grumpy head on him at the best of times. You didn't really know what he was thinking but fairly shortly after the loss to Italy you didn't really need to know what he was thinking because you could see it in his body language. The pair of them didn't seem to do too much together and there always seemed to be an edge. There was no upfront confrontation but you could see they were avoiding each other a little bit.

Brian Ashton: We were both fiery characters and neither of us had any intention of backing down. So it probably wasn't what you'd call a match made in heaven. It certainly wasn't doing the players any favours.

Keith Wood: Could we see the problems? We weren't stupid. It's not as if we were a bunch of naive guys not taking everything in. Whether we decided to tell the press about it is another story. There were a few problems, of course there were.

Denis Hickie: I always got on well with Brian. A nice man and a fair guy. He was very progressive. A lot of players thought he was great, but it wasn't going to work out, not with himself and Pa. There was no rapport there. They just had very little in common. You need your coach and manager to have a rapport and it didn't exist between them. I'm not sure we can say that it was Pa's fault or Brian's fault. I'm sure the relationship would have survived years later when the set-up was more professional. There was just so much pressure on them.

Tom English: I was the Irish rugby correspondent for the *Sunday Times* and a few weeks before the 1998 Six Nations I wrote a piece about the relationship between Brian and Pa. I'd spoken to Brian at length about what was going on and numerous players confirmed, off the record, that things had broken down between them and that it was an irretrievable breakdown. They said that Pa had become a negative influence. The headline on the story was 'Time Pa was put out to pasture.' It was very critical of Pa and it caused a stir. The following week the pair of them sat beside each other at a press conference and in an attempt to clear the air they only made things worse. It was obvious that they'd run their course.

Brian Ashton: We lost against Scotland in the opening match of the 1998 Six Nations and I was bitterly disappointed at the way we played in the last twenty minutes. It was there for the taking and we let it slip. I remember getting criticised for some comments I made on TV afterwards. I said something like, 'I don't know whose gameplan that was but it had nothing to do with me.' It was construed as a go at Pat, but it wasn't. It was just my anger manifesting itself. We kicked the ball away for the last twenty minutes and just made it easy for Scotland to eke out the win.

Denis Hickie: People took it that he was trying to absolve himself from blame but that wasn't his personality. He was never abdicating responsibility, that wasn't his thing at all.

Brian Ashton: After the game it was certainly a time to reflect and I went back to England and I developed shingles. One of the triggers is stress. Maybe that's what brought it on. It was bloody painful. I was sitting at home thinking about the whole situation. The relationship between myself and the manager had broken down and I wondered if there was any point in carrying on.

Denis Hickie: I remember going into camp and hearing on the radio that he was gone.

Brian Ashton: It was the right thing to do. The team was full of great guys and we had some very good players. The potential was there but it had just been locked up. It could have been unlocked but maybe I didn't go about it in the right way.

Denis Hickie: We had two weeks before we played France in Paris and they'd just gone to Edinburgh and won 51-16

Victor Costello: People were saying that France would score a hundred points against us.

Keith Wood: We needed a new coach and fast. And from Brian we went in many ways to the opposite – to Warren Gatland.

TWELVE

LENS – I WATCHED IT IN STRANGEWAYS

Warren Gatland: I was thirty-four when I got the job. I'd been on the periphery of it already because I'd been helping Brian a little bit. Brian's philosophy centred around fifteen-man rugby but the unfortunate thing was that Ireland didn't have fifteen players who could play that way. The game was going through a crisis. I got the phone call at home on the Sunday evening from Pa Whelan. He asked me if I'd take the team for the rest of the Five Nations. You don't turn it down, do you? I was young, but I didn't feel young. I'd coached back in New Zealand and I'd coached with Galwegians and I was coaching Connacht at the time and we were going very well. I guess there was a touch of the Kiwi dog about it. No matter what, you'll have a go. You do whatever it takes. That was my background.

Keith Wood: Gatty came in and said, 'I've been in Ireland for a while, I know these guys, I have an idea what makes them tick.' There were problems and he resolved them. He brought in consistency of selection, which we'd been crying out for. He put in a gameplan that was suited to the players he had at his disposal. He was pragmatic and that suited us down to the ground. It wasn't perfect, but we became a difficult team to play against.

Victor Costello: Gatty was a breath of fresh air. He was very young, but he was in tune with the way rugby players thought. He understood us.

Malcolm O'Kelly: I liked him straight away. He gave us a feeling that our input mattered and he wanted more of it. He wanted people to be more vocal whereas prior to that we felt like we were being dictated to. He was keen on defence. He said, 'How do we get a result in Paris? We shore up our defence.' So he brought in a rush defence and as limited as we were in attack we could survive if our defence was OK. He loved putting pressure on teams, upsetting them, annoying them. That's what Gatty was about.

Warren Gatland: Everybody was talking about us being hammered by France in that first game in Paris. There was talk that it might be a record defeat, that France

Opposite: Paul Wallace at the final whistle in Lens.

might score 100 points. The whole week was about trying to stop the negativity from outside influencing us. 'Let's not read papers or watch TV or listen to the radio. Let's have a siege mentality.' I asked the Irish public to send in faxes and letters and cards and we had thousands of them. It was quite emotional, that. We put them up on the walls of the team room and the boys went around reading them. And it had an impact. It was a reminder that even though they weren't successful there were people out there who were on their side. The boys doubted that sometimes.

Conor O'Shea: He told us to forget what the critics were saying and that this is what the people who support us were thinking. What he did was reconnect us with the reason why we were playing the game. We were going around the team room reading cards from all sorts of people from all sorts of places. It was brilliant man management. It was his first week coaching an Ireland team and he did something that made a deep impression on everybody.

Warren Gatland: I said to them that if you put the jersey on then you have a responsibility to it and a responsibility to everyone who wore it before you. Fans don't mind if you lose, but what they want to see is that you tried hard and if you can look yourself in the mirror afterwards and say, 'I gave everything,' then nobody can ask any more of you. The fans wanted to see honesty and effort.

Kevin Maggs: The team run before Paris was terrible. We couldn't string three passes together and you could cut the atmosphere with a knife. There was an eerie silence in the changing room before we went out because everybody knew that if we didn't step up to the mark we could get annihilated. If you'd seen us in training you'd have said, 'These lads are going to get properly hockeyed.' We couldn't do anything right and then Gatty said, 'OK, that's it, everybody back on the bus, let's get out of here.'

Rob Henderson: In the French press that morning they had the top ten heaviest defeats in the history of world rugby. You didn't need to be fluent to figure out what they were getting at.

Paul Wallace: The game started and we were putting it up to them. Our defensive system was working. We were in their faces and they didn't like it one bit.

Kevin Maggs: We just beat the crap out of them. It was pure fear driving us.

Keith Wood: The reason we were competitive was because we didn't doubt what we were doing, because we weren't trying to do a huge amount.

Paul Wallace: Midway through the first half I scored a try which would have been the first Irish try in Paris in donkey's years. The referee had his back turned when I ran in. It was a definite score.

Denis Hickie: Paul's try didn't stand, but mine did. So I was the first Irishman to score in Paris since Freddie McLennan in 1980. I got a call from him afterwards. 'This is Freddie.' It took a few seconds for the penny to drop. He says, 'You're some bollocks. Nobody remembers me apart from that try and now nobody is going to remember me ever again.' Then he hung up, but in a nice way.

Paul Wallace: I got gouged. A real proper one at a scrum, where you feel the finger going in and the eye coming out of your head. You feel your eye being scooped out and the only thing keeping it there is a piece of string. When they resort to that kind of thing then it's proof that you have them rattled, but it's not much consolation if you're going blind because of it. Sometimes, when I think about it, I get a little stressed. I can still feel a tingle in my eye when I cast my mind back to it. It broke up in a scuffle, like it always does. It was pretty nasty.

Warren Gatland: With eight minutes left we were still ahead, 16-13. It was a massive effort. France didn't know what had hit them. Then they scored a poxy try. We lost the lineout on our own line and I still swear they knocked it on. Rafael Ibanez touched it down in the corner and the referee gave it, but we still had a chance to win it.

Victor Costello: At the end of that game I made a gallop and I didn't back myself to go all the way to their line. I was in open space and I should have just pinned my ears back and I probably would have made it. I've always regretted not going for it. I gave the pass to Richie Wallace and it was the wrong thing to do. It's something I've had in my mind for years. I made the wrong decision.

Rob Henderson: Paris gave us a small bit of a boost that what we were doing in training was working and that maybe we weren't as shite as everyone was telling us we were. I was a big fan of Gatty. I just liked his methods. He was a very simple, straight-down-the-line guy.

Paris might have offered a degree of hope for the future but Ireland still finished the championship at the bottom of the table with zero wins and a wooden spoon. Then the manager, Pa Whelan, resigned.

Full time in Paris, the players collapse to the turf in exhaustion.

Tom English: It was a Sunday night in the Brazen Head in Limerick. I was in there with two pals and Pa was at the bar with a few of his mates. I went to the toilet later on and I'm at the cubicle when Pa sidles up beside me. Very cosy. I hadn't spoken to him since writing the article three months earlier but I'd heard that he was livid. I broke the ice by saying something like, 'It was nothing personal, Pa.' When I was washing my hands he gave me a dig in the head. Charming. I grabbed his arms and restrained him, so he started shouting. 'Get out of Limerick!' he said at one point. It was a bit surreal given that I was from Limerick, just like himself. His house and my parents house are about twenty seconds from each other. The news got out the following day. He resigned a day after that. He said it was nothing to do with the incident. Fair enough.

Ireland needed a manager and the choice was obvious. Donal Lenihan, the former captain, had been number three in the management set-up and was a popular appointment as Whelan's replacement. He had time to blink, just about, before the planning started for an unforgiving tour to South Africa. As if things weren't fractious enough the build-up was dogged by the IRFU's continuing difficulty in grasping the concept of professionalism.

Niall Brophy: I was president of the IRFU at that time and the thing that drove me bloody crazy was the change to professionalism and these new contracts and all the players going to England. We were no more geared up for professionalism than the sole of my boot. We weren't ready for it. It was awful. The players were bringing us to the wire on everything. Jeepers, I remember giving instructions for a certain gentleman to be left off the Irish team when it was named the following day just because he wouldn't sign his contract. He was talking about property rights and I was on the phone to solicitors in London and Belfast... holy mother of God, the administration of the IRFU at the time was most difficult.

Keith Wood: I was contracted with Harlequins and most of the other players were contracted to the IRFU and so they were signing over their intellectual property rights to the IRFU as part of their deal. The union had control over their rights. I didn't want that to be the case with me. They were taking control of all my rights for the whole year which I thought was unacceptable. The way it was drafted in the contract they could use my image and assign it to their sponsors in any way they liked, so I said, 'No, I'm not signing the contract.' They said, 'Sure everybody else is signing it,' but everybody else was being paid a full wage for it. I was being paid pretty much nothing for it. They were getting paid £50,000, £60,000, £70,000 for it. I was getting get paid £5,000, which I agreed with, because my main contract was with Harlequins. But I wasn't willing to give away my property rights. All it was, was a lack of knowledge of what constituted professional sport. There was a lot of heartache.

Niall Brophy: I couldn't believe that the game had gone totally professional. I thought it would go semi-professional. I wasn't expecting the whole thing to go pro overnight, lock stock and barrel. Once money gets involved then things go to the dogs altogether. There's a lot of truth in that, you know. Money is the root of all evil. We didn't want it to go pro, but it was inevitable. Professionalism was happening long before it was announced officially. Sure, they were paying players in Wales fifty years before. And New Zealand, Australia and South Africa were at it long before it went professional. Once you start getting big TV money then everybody starts looking for a slice of the cake.

Keith Wood: The dispute with the IRFU was very difficult. It was a stressful time. My mother found it more stressful than I did, but I didn't like it either. I wasn't exactly jumping up and down and saying it was the best thing ever. My mother found it very trying because it was in the papers. There were harsh things written. Most people didn't understand it. It changed my attitude a bit. It reminded me that this career could be very fleeting. I could suddenly find myself in a situation where this could be taken out of my hands and I couldn't play for my country anymore, so it made me more demanding in that you should say what you wanted to say without fear. I was liberated in some respects. I was going to speak my mind and the worst thing they could do was drop me. I stood my ground, they stood their ground, it was at an impasse and it wasn't doing anybody any favours. It got resolved. We signed a contract that both of us could live with and we moved on.

Donal Lenihan was the Ireland manager and even though I argued with Donal about it I have nothing but admiration for the manner in which he treated me afterwards. I made life unbelievably difficult for him at that time. I know I did. He was the manager and he had to make certain the team was doing what was required and I wouldn't sign the contract and I made his life hard. I'm a big fan of Donal's. I thought he treated me with huge respect afterwards. There was never a lingering feeling between us.

Kevin Maggs: We headed for South Africa and it was ridiculously exciting. I used to work for a groundworks firm in Bristol. I laid kerbs for a living and my boss used to let me away early on a Saturday so I could go and play for Bristol in the Courage League. I was doing that until 1996 and here I was two years later heading off to South Africa for my first senior tour. It was dream stuff.

Paddy Johns: The South African media were patronising and dismissive. They saw Ireland as a bit of an irrelevance in international rugby rather than a team to be treated with respect. I resented their attitude right from the start.

Justin Fitzpatrick: Wherever we went, we were like gladiators thrown out to be baited. It's hard to put into words the hostility we encountered.

Reggie Corrigan: I broke my back after half an hour in the first game of the tour, against Boland. Or, should I say, Tommie Laubscher, their tighthead, broke it for me. A knee in the back. Brutal.

Victor Costello: I was standing next to Reggie when it happened and yer man did it deliberately. Did it just for the sake of it. That's the kind of shiteology we had to put up with.

Reggie Corrigan: Years later somebody said to me, 'Do you remember Tommie Laubscher?' I said, 'Remember him? I'll never forget him.' And then they said, 'Do you know he's dead? He was knocked down and killed by a truck.' I got a shock when I heard that.

Dion O'Cuinneagain: I made my Ireland debut on that 1998 tour of South Africa, where I'd been born and raised by my mother and father, who was a dentist from Enniscorthy. My parents went to South Africa on honeymoon and decided to stay. I played for Western Province and the Springbok Sevens and the coach of the Sevens side made me captain because he said he wanted more Irish passion in the team. They always used to refer to me as an Irish player. It was always just accepted that I was as Irish as I was South African. Syd Millar came to South Africa to talk to me and said, 'Listen, we can't guarantee you a contract in Ireland, but you're the type of player we're looking for. You've got a strong Irish heritage through your father and if you get yourself across to the UK to play rugby then we'll look at you closely.'

And they did. And I was lucky because I was accepted very quickly. I'll always be thankful to Paddy Johns, Keith Wood, David Humphreys, Conor O'Shea and all the other senior players for taking me under their wing. Gatty put me straight in the team to play the Boks in Bloemfontein in the first Test.

Kevin Maggs: We'd been given our jerseys in the hotel before the game. I went back to my room and stared at it lovingly for forty-five minutes until it was time to get on the bus and go to the stadium. We got to the ground and the gates were shut. The South African fans were rocking the bus and hitting it with sticks and running their fingers across their throats like they were going to kill us.

Donal Lenihan: I got off the bus and I was fuming. After about five minutes this little fella turns up and lets us in. Turns out that the Springboks had arrived five minutes before us and yer man was away getting autographs.

Kevin Maggs: Everybody was pumped up. We found our way into the changing rooms and I unzipped my bag and my shirt wasn't there. I just looked at this empty bag like it was an unexploded bomb. No jersey! I'd left it on the fucking bed. I could feel all the blood draining out of my body. I was disgusted with myself. Our bagman, Paddy 'Rala' O'Reilly bailed me out. He'd just picked up the kit for the midweek team from the laundry and he slipped me the 13 jersey without anybody noticing. Rala to the rescue. He had everything in that bag of tricks of his.

Dion O'Cuinneagain: In the Springbok team at that time there were quite a few Western Province players and just before the start of the Test all of them shook my hand and wished me good luck. I was standing at the back of the first line-out and their three loose forwards, Johan Erasmus, Gary Teichmann and Andre Venter all shook my hand and wished me good luck. Then Venter punched me in the face and I abused his heritage in Afrikaans and we carried on from there.

The game was memorable for two reasons – Keith Wood hitting Teichmann with a swinging arm – 'This kind of thing will catch up with Wood,' was Teichmann's rather ominous comment afterwards – and the emergence of a new Springbok winger, Stefan Terblanche, who scored four tries against his opposite number, Denis Hickie. It ended 37-13.

The second Test was held at Loftus Versfeld in Pretoria. Hickie had endured a troubled week but he kept his place in the team, a sign of how things had changed under Gatland.

Denis Hickie: Some of my best memories of rugby are from that trip and people will find that hard to believe given Terblanche was on my wing in the first Test. The guy I was marking scored four tries but I don't know how many of those I would have been personally responsible for. In fairness to Gatty he took the view that to drop me at that point might have really damaged me. I remember saying that to him afterwards, when he moved on. I appreciated that he kept me in. If that had happened two years earlier you'd never have heard of me again.

Nobody can say for sure what exactly kicked off the Battle of Loftus Versfeld but the first obvious incident was Joost van der Westhuizen's kick to Malcolm O'Kelly's chest. From then on, it was mayhem. Victor Costello kicked the South African hooker, James Dalton, who in turn had a spat with Paul Wallace. Teichmann and Maggs got stuck into each other. So did Peter Clohessy and his opposite number, Adrian Garvey.

Fights broke out throughout the game but the marquee act was Paddy Johns, the Irish captain. Johns was a man possessed. At one stage he went for Krynauw Otto and thumped him ten metres up the park. 'I hit him so hard that I damaged my thumb,' he said. 'The insults were flying as well. I think a few aspersions were cast about Joost's mother – you know how it is.'

Kevin Maggs: There was loads of off-the-ball stuff. They were putting up bombs and elbowing you in the head. It got out of hand. The hostility was unbelievable.

Victor Costello is upended in a fight during the Battle of Loftus Versfeld.

Dion O'Cuinneagain: South Africa came out to bully us and we weren't in the mood to take a backward step. Mark Andrews and Paddy Johns were having a go at each other. Claw got involved. And Woody. Those guys were never going to back down.

Malcolm O'Kelly: Paddy Johns was our enforcer and there was so much going on it was almost funny. I did a bit of it myself. It was mad and we were knackered long before the end. Punched-out. Trevor Brennan came on in the second half and we might have been losing 27-0 at that stage. We got a penalty in our 22. 'Thank God, take your time lads, a chance to relieve the pressure.' Trevor taps it to himself and runs full pelt at them. 'Oh Jesus, here we go again.'

Donal Lenihan: There was bad blood, definitely. I've never seen so much carnage as there was in the dressing room at half-time. Then, after the game, we were put in a room with some cocktail sausages and left there.

Keith Wood: We lost 33-0. I'd never felt as pulverised after a game in my life.

Denis Hickie: I fractured my cheekbone and broke my jaw and my nose trying to stop Terblanche from scoring. I caught his knee in my face. I was twenty-one and having to deal with the four tries was tough enough because I got a major slagging for that, but then the injury as well was even more difficult. I came back four months later but I lost confidence for quite a while. It was more than a year and a half before I played for Ireland again.

The debacle in Pretoria was Ireland's seventh defeat in a row, a run that came to an end when they played two qualifiers for the World Cup against Georgia and Romania, the former being a seventy-point massacre, the second proving a good deal more challenging. Romania sliced Ireland open and scored thirty-five points. The upside was that Ireland managed fifty-three in reply and booked their place for the tournament the following year.

The 1999 Five Nations began with a second straight agonising loss to the French, this time at home, by one point instead of the two points that had divided them in Paris. It was the fifteenth successive defeat to Les Bleus and it could have been oh so different had David Humphreys' late penalty not missed by the width of a goalpost.

Two weeks later, Wales hosted Ireland at Wembley, where they played their matches while the Millennium Stadium was being built. It was Gatland's first Five Nations victory as a coach. More than that, it was also Keith Wood's first Five Nations victory, four years after making his championship debut.

Two more defeats followed, but the victory at Wembley had done enough to avoid a fourth successive wooden spoon. Euphoria hardly gripped the land, but at least it was a straw to cling to.

Dion O'Cuinneagain: Paddy Johns had been captain and he'd been brilliant. He'd helped me so much. He welcomed me in and taught me about international rugby. In the summer of 1999, in Australia, Gatty decided that Paddy wasn't guaranteed his place anymore so he gave me the captaincy. I remember writing to Paddy to thank him for being so good to me. He was a quality guy.

Paul Wallace: Dion was very popular. He was a good leader and a great bloke.

Malcolm O'Kelly: We went to Australia for a summer tour in 1999 with Dion as captain. Yer man appeared around then.

Conor O'Shea: A frail, scrawny young fella with hands like God.

Kevin Maggs: I'd heard a bit about him, but not much. He was doing well in the All Ireland League. He reported for training and he had his glasses on. Brian O'Driscoll? Fair enough.

Keith Wood: I saw Brian in the team room playing pool and he was wearing glasses with lenses like coke bottles. I didn't know if he was a player or who he was. I knew nothing about him. I was in England and I didn't really care what other clubs were doing. I was just focused on my club. I didn't give him a second glance. And then he trained and he had an incredible eye for a gap and an incredible acceleration through the gap. He was a beautifully balanced and devastating runner, he had an ability to hit a gap and step off both feet. It was phenomenal. His athletic ability and his timing stood out immediately and he was incredibly hard on himself. He wouldn't accept dropping a ball and I really loved that.

Conor O'Shea: That session was in Galway. Warren brought in Brian and Gordon D'Arcy. Warren took four or five of the senior players aside, and said, 'Will you look after these kids? I wouldn't mind you telling me what you think of them.' After the session he came up to us and said, 'What do you reckon?' And we said, 'Can you play them now, please? Because they're miles better than we are.' They were just incredible, the two of them.

Gordon D'Arcy: With Brian you knew that he wouldn't just make the right decision, but he'd excel in the execution of it. Whether it's a well-timed pass, a tackle or poaching a ball, he'd do it phenomenally well.

Warren Gatland: To win games you need some X factor and Brian had it. We needed a guy who would come in with a bit of cockiness, in a positive way. We needed to develop that in the whole team. With young players you have to go through a bit of pain sometimes. They're going to hurt you. They're going to make a few bad decisions. But he didn't make many bad decisions. I saw Drico, with that speed and footwork and skill-set, and I thought, 'I've got to get him in the team regardless of the fact that he hasn't even played for Leinster yet.' I liked that he had no baggage and no fear. I just wanted him to go out and play and enjoy himself. That was the message. It was amazing to see how quickly he developed.

Malcolm O'Kelly: I didn't know him at all. He might have been in training camps that year but I was away with a dislocated shoulder. The thing I noticed about him when he wore the green jersey for the first time against New South Wales was his distribution. He had this ability to let the ball go and suddenly our winger was running down the length of the pitch. We were a team that could defend fairly well and we could battle all day long and our main attacking weapon was the likes of Kevin Maggs blasting through the middle, or the up-and-under. We didn't have the ability to unleash wingers and then suddenly Brian appeared and he opened up a huge new world and gave everybody a lift.

Brian O'Driscoll: I was playing under-21s for Ireland and I remember playing against Wales and I wasn't having the best game and I was subbed off with 20 minutes to go, and I thought afterwards, 'That's my chances of really progressing for the next while gone.'

And then somehow I got called into a national camp and I trained OK. And the next thing, I knew I got a call from one of the admin people at the IRFU saying, 'You're not playing for the As this weekend, you're going to be sitting on the bench for Ireland.' It was the first time that Ireland had played against Italy in a Six Nations game and I just couldn't believe I was there. It was beyond any level of expectation I'd ever had. I'd just really wanted to be capped by the As and the next thing was that I skipped that and went straight to sitting on the bench for the Test team. I didn't get capped that day, but I managed to get capped on the summer tour to Australia – against some of my real heroes, particularly my absolute childhood hero, Tim Horan.

Brian O'Driscoll looks to evade the tackle of Wallaby hooker Jeremy Paul
during the first Test of the summer tour.

Conor O'Shea: To be in the dressing room with him for his first cap against Australia in Brisbane – you knew you were in the presence of somebody special. His competitive instinct was obvious and he had the kind of natural ability that you'd die for.

Brian O'Driscoll: I was pretty calm about it all to begin with, going over there and playing a couple of warm-up games and I played reasonably well, and I got picked for the first Test against Australia. I ran out there for my first Test match and I thought, 'This is OK, it's no biggie.' And then fireworks started going off and I just shat myself. I was like a dog on Halloween night. And I thought, 'Wow, they've got fireworks at a game, this really is a big deal.'

Denis Hickie: The big thing was his ability to throw very long, accurate passes off both sides. That sounds a given now – but things were slower in Ireland as we adapted to professionalism. Brian inspired a new breed of player.

Kevin Maggs: I can tell everybody that I played alongside him in his first two Tests – and I scored in both of them.

Ireland lost both Tests in Australia – 46-10 on O'Driscoll's debut in Brisbane and a respectable 32-26 in Perth a week later. The new centre was the big plus of the tour. Not only had he shown that he had pace and skill he had also proved that he could bring it to table in the heat of a Test match against a side that would soon be crowned as the finest on the planet.

The World Cup began in the autumn of 1999. Ireland were in a pool with the United States, Australia and Romania.

Keith Wood: Against the Wallabies I had about eighteen lineouts and the fact that I lost only three or four of them has to go down as some sort of miracle. I felt I was going to lose every single ball. John Eales was a fingernail away every time. I'm throwing perfectly and next thing this giant launches himself in the air and he's a millimetre away from stealing eighteen out of eighteen. It was one of my best throwing performances because I felt under extraordinary pressure. I was never as mentally shagged after a game in my life.

Conor O'Shea: We beat the United States and Romania and lost to Australia and it was all set-up for a quarter-final against France at Lansdowne Road and we'd a decent record against France. We hadn't beaten them but we'd got to within two points and one point the last two times we'd played them, so we had a real chance of a World Cup semi-final. We had to beat Argentina in Lens first, of course.

Reggie Corrigan: It was the first game I was involved in at that World Cup. It was like Gatty was putting out the second-string against Argentina because he wanted the front-liners ready for France.

Malcolm O'Kelly: We stayed in a town outside Lens in an industrial estate. It was crap. The food was terrible. Fecking depressing.

Kevin Maggs: The hotel was shocking, to be fair.

Reggie Corrigan: It was a dive on a roundabout in some arsehole of a place. We were served up fois gras. The lads were going down to McDonald's to get food into them.

Malcolm O'Kelly: Still, we expected to win – and that mentality is no good for an Irish team.

Dion O'Cuinneagain: Ireland was a professional outfit and some of the Argentinians were playing in France but most of them were amateurs and we'd played them in a warm-up match a few months before the World Cup and we'd beaten them by a substantial margin. The feeling was that this was just going to be a formality. And when you expect a game of rugby to be a formality, you're in trouble.

Rob Henderson: I didn't make the squad, which was one of the biggest disappointments of my career. I do remember Lens, though. I was watching it in a pub in Battersea Rise on an inflatable Guinness chair that I had blown up at a petrol station.

Dylan O'Grady: I watched it in Strangeways prison. I'd been done for conspiracy to supply cannabis and they gave me nine months. The wardens were winding me up that night. Lots of smart-arse comments flying about the place. They were going, 'Oi, Dylan, shouldn't you be playing in this? Weren't you somebody once?' They were decent lads, to be fair. They didn't mean anything by it so I just told them to shut up. I'd got my cap. It might have only been one but somebody thought enough of me at the time to give it and nobody can take it away.

Jeremy Davidson: I got a triple fracture of my finger just a few minutes into the game. An Argie stamped on my hand and smashed it up. Then I got a dead leg. I got shots in the hand at half-time and I got a shot into the leg at half-time as well. I should have come off, but you're a bit stupid, aren't you? You just want to play at all costs. You don't look at the bigger picture.

Conor O'Shea: We were comfortable. Humps [David Humphreys] was kicking the goals and we were going three, six, nine points ahead and we needed one more score to break them. Suddenly, Diego Albanese gets the try. I still have nightmares.

Paul Wallace: We shunted them back in the scrum but they still broke away and scored in the far corner.

Dion O'Cuinneagain: I thought, 'We're in trouble now.' There was plenty of time, but you could sense that the whole momentum had swung against us. I said, 'Let's just get our hands on the ball. Let's get into their half and stay there.' And I remember just after we'd had that discussion we knocked the ball on and twenty seconds after we said we were going to keep the ball we were back on our own line.

Paul Wallace: Argentina were perceived as a very one-dimensional team, but we were even more one-dimensional. It was summed up in the last twenty minutes when we were just hammering away at the line. There was no invention. I remember getting split open. I had to go off and get stitches and I was waiting for five minutes for the doctor to amble down to sort me out. I was going absolutely manic to get back on because they were on our line and there was a scrum siege. The doctor eventually dawdled in, cool as a breeze, and stitched me and then asked me would I give him my jersey after the game. I gave him a look.

Dion O'Cuinneagain: With three or four minutes to go we had a lineout close to their try-line. Gatty had been working on a sort of ten-man lineout and if there was ever a time to call it, it was now. We tried to do a big drive.

Conor O'Shea: It was a twelve-man lineout. I wasn't anywhere near it. I was out on my own on the other side of the pitch. I had half a field in front of me and no Argentina player around. I was waving at Humps for the cross-kick and he couldn't get the ball from the pack. We were just trying to batter our way over. He knew I was there and he knew I was free, but the ball never came. The ball never bloody came.

Virtually the entire team pile into a maul to try to push over for the winning
score – but the Puma's withstand the onslaught.

Dion O'Cuinneagain: We got the lineout maul going, but it was the pressure of
the situation and the lack of patience that made us splinter instead of keeping it all
together. As soon as you splinter the advantage you have as one unit is over.

Paul Wallace: I was sure I was going to score. I got tackled by a fella who was miles
offside and the referee never picked up on it.

Malcolm O'Kelly: The Argies defended like heroes in fairness to them.

Conor O'Shea: The final whistle went and it was painful. I've never, ever been as
upset in a dressing room in my life. World Cup over.

Rob Henderson: Human nature says, 'Jesus Christ, I'm glad I'm not involved in
that,' and anyone that tells you differently is lying.

Keith Wood: We didn't perform and at the time I was embarrassed. I was. I
thought we could have done more.

Jeremy Davidson: It was horrific. Then we had to go and face the Argies knowing
that Mauricio Reggiardo was going to be giving it plenty. He was a team-mate of

mine at Castres and he was a bit of a loudmouth. It was a very low moment. After that, we went back to the hotel in the middle of nowhere, past the tyre factory and straight on for hell.

Paul Wallace: No one was suggesting a few consolation beers. I went to bed. Everybody was just shellshocked.

Kevin Maggs: I was distraught. I went back to Bath and all the England players were taking the piss.

Brian O'Driscoll and Dion O'Cuinneagain after the final whistle in Lens.

Warren Gatland: I remember sitting in the stand and before I even got out of my seat there was a reporter from RTE in my face. You feel so isolated. Guys on the committee were having little chats and you're thinking, 'Here we go'. I went back to Galway and I didn't get out of bed for three days. I was that down about it. I took it really, really hard. The IRFU could have made a change at that stage. The person who really fought for me was Donal Lenihan. I always appreciated that.

Eddie O'Sullivan: Just after the World Cup, I was offered the Eagles job in America. It was a four-year contract and I'd have had to move the whole family to the west coast. I would have preferred to be back in the mainstream, but you have to go where you have to go. I got a call from the IRFU and they asked me would I be interested in coming back. They asked me to be assistant coach. I can't say for sure but I don't think Warren was that comfortable. He might have seen me as a threat.

Warren Gatland: Eddie came in after Lens and everybody says that I was forced to take him, but that wasn't the case at all. I was asked to have a chat with him. A lot of people were saying, 'Don't touch him,' but I said I'd make up my own mind.

Eddie O'Sullivan: There was always a bit of tension. He said he was happy about me being there but I'm not sure that he was. I think I was parachuted in. It's not my fault that I was parachuted in. I was asked to take a job as assistant coach and had I said no to the IRFU I would never have seen the inside of an Ireland changing room again. We had history, you see. Me and Warren. During the All Ireland League days I used to coach the Buccaneers and Warren had coached Galwegians, our big rivals in Connacht. There wasn't any love lost between the clubs at the time. All of that stuff was playing out in the background.

Warren Gatland: Our first game after Lens was against England at Twickenham on the first weekend of the 2000 Six Nations. We shipped fifty points. It was horrendous.

Eddie O'Sullivan: We had our asses handed to us on a plate.

Kevin Maggs: Nobody had a clue what was going on defensively. To lose like we did was sickening, especially when you're playing alongside a few of the England lads week after week. The flak I got, it hurt. It was desperate.

Frankie Sheahan: That was my first time making it into the senior squad. For me it was always all about playing for Ireland, nothing else mattered. It was my dream, my everything in life. I didn't get on the field that day but I was very passionate and very defensive of the boys despite not getting a run. There was a person in the hotel that night calling me out and I took the bait. I should have walked away but I was a young pup and it wasn't in my style to back down from a guy giving me grief. I head-butted him. Stupid. I didn't exactly help the cause.

Conor O'Shea: Twickenham was my last cap and it wasn't the way anybody wants their international career to end. Did I deserve to get dropped? Of course I deserved it. It was a terrible script at the end but I loved my time. To be honest, I needed to be put out of my misery. Not being picked was almost a nice thing. A relief. Something had to give.

Warren Gatland: What I learned from Twickenham was that we'd shown some faith with players who had been involved at the World Cup and we thought then that that it was time to make changes. The next one was at home against Scotland and if we had lost that then I would have resigned and it would have been fair enough. I was getting so much stick after Lens and Twickenham that the only way to stop the negativity at that point would have been for me to go. Scotland was a high stakes day.

THIRTEEN

IN THE CREATION OF BRIAN O'DRISCOLL, I WAS THE BUTTERFLY

The way Eddie O'Sullivan described it, 'all hell was breaking loose' after the butchering at Twickenham. 'There was blood on the walls,' said the assistant coach. Frankie Sheahan was hauled in front of the IRFU and fined £2,500 for headbutting an Irish fan, but the embarrassment that it caused was the least of the problems.

Ireland had to beat Scotland for Gatland to survive, the difficulty being that Ireland hadn't beaten Scotland in twelve years. Even though the Scots had suffered similar humiliation in the opening round of the Six Nations – losing to new boys Italy – they travelled to Dublin as favourites.

Eddie O'Sullivan: I felt we really had to make changes to the team. We had to have a crack. We had the basis of a very good backline. We had Peter Stringer, who was the best passer in the world at that stage. We had Ronan O'Gara, who was just about ready. We had what turned out to be the greatest outside centre in the history of the game in Drico. We had Maggsy who could run down that inside centre channel like a freight train and we had finishers like Denis Hickie and Shane Horgan. We needed to unleash these lads together.

We had a selection meeting below in Cork. I was actually uncomfortable about calling for all these changes because I was only the assistant coach. Eddie Coleman was on the IRFU committee and I rang him before I went to Cork and I said, 'There are things I believe we need to do but I'm reticent to play a strong hand because I don't want to be seen as the guy causing trouble. There's enough friction already.' He said, 'If you believe it's the right thing then you have to say it.' I went to Cork and in fairness to the lads, Warren and the manager, Donal Lenihan, they had both come to the same conclusion. That was a paradigm shift.

Mick Galwey: There were five new caps against Scotland – Ronan O'Gara, Peter Stringer, Shane Horgan, John Hayes and Simon Easterby. It was 'shit or get off the pot' time. All our heads were on the line. It was a big gamble.

Denis Hickie: It was my first international in nearly two years.

Opposite: The players celebrate in Paris.

Mick Galwey: It was my first start in more than three years.

Warren Gatland: We brought back Mick Galwey. You couldn't deny the Munster element. Galwey, Anthony Foley, Peter Clohessy – when those guys put the Irish jersey on they could go to another level and it took me a while to understand that. They weren't the best players but they could get themselves to an emotional pitch that others couldn't. The Munster factor was a turning point and bringing in Mick had a big influence. He was brilliant at getting the best out of other players.

Brian O'Driscoll: For me, the big long-term change that happened for the team was that the self-proclaimed saviours of Irish rugby were the five guys that were capped in that game – Rog [Ronan O'Gara], John Hayes, Peter Stringer, Shane Horgan and Simon Easterby – and you look at the careers that the five of them subsequently went on to have, you have to take your hat off to Gats for going with them. I think that injection of youth – and Hayes – just meant that you were bringing in personnel that had no baggage and, importantly, that were used to winning at underage level. We didn't have the expectation of many Irish teams before us to go hard for fifty or sixty minutes and then capitulate; we were used to winning at underage levels, winning at schools level, we were always in the hunt for winning Five Nations, winning Grand Slams and being very, very nearly there. So we brought a whole new mentality to the senior set-up when we were selected. We brought a positivity that changed the game in Ireland, hopefully, forever.

John Hayes: I don't know why they started calling me the Bull – must have had something to do with my farming background, I suppose. I don't mind it. I've been called a lot worse. Cappamore's a hurling parish. Rugby was unheard of here. I remember saying that when I was growing up, if you'd showed somebody a rugby ball they'd have thought it was a football that had been rolled over by a car. The first game of rugby I was ever at, I played in it. I was nineteen.

Mick Galwey: There's a famous picture from that day of myself standing between Ronan and Peter cuddling them into me. They were like anybody else when they're winning their first cap, they didn't know where to stand. The boys were like little sheep in one sense but they were hard at the same time. Stringer was one of the most mentally tough fellas I've ever come across. The more players who tried to get at him the better he got. And even at that age he wasn't afraid to give you a kick in the hole when you needed it.

Peter Stringer: When I was a boy people would say I was too small to play rugby. I'd get looks from the opposition, fellas saying, 'What's this guy doing here? Is he for real? The size of him!' Comments like that are still in my head. It was only when I was older that I found it was coming from other parents, too. They were saying to my mother and father, 'You're not going to let him play rugby, are you?'

I was much smaller than everyone else. Mum and Dad were worried that I wasn't going to grow at all. Then Mum heard about a relative of hers with a son who was small like me. They took him to hospital and gave him growth hormone injections. He shot up in no time. My parents were looking out for me, they've always had my best interests at heart. They thought if I was to have the treatment I would shoot up too. But I just thought, 'I'm happy the way I am.' I never entertained the idea. There were some arguments. I remember saying to them, 'Look, leave me out of this. I'm happy as me.'

Mick Galwey: We actually went behind very early in that match against Scotland.

Warren Gatland: Kenny Logan scored a try in the opening minutes and I was thinking, 'OK, this is horrendous, I'll be gone before the night is out.'

Mick Galwey: We battered them in the end, thank God. If we'd lost that then we had nowhere else to go. We'd played all our cards with the new lads. If that didn't work we were totally goosed. But it worked great; 44-22. Grand, says he. Then we put sixty points on Italy in the next game. It was the first time in seven years that we'd won back-to-back games in the Championship. And we'd scored a bucket of tries – eleven of them. Shane Horgan had three of them in his first two internationals. That kind of thing was unheard of in Ireland.

Ireland travelled to Paris more in hope than expectation. Nobody expected them to win, but there was optimism that they might perform, maybe run the French close, give them a scare again, like they had done in the previous two meetings.

The French had won two out of three, hammering Wales in Cardiff, then losing in Twickenham before taking care of Scotland pretty comfortably at Murrayfield. Injury had beset them, though. For the Ireland game they were missing their full-back, Thomas Castaignède, their wing, Christophe Dominici, and their first-choice centres, Richard Dourthe and Thomas Lombard. Also out were the half-backs, Christophe Lamaison and Fabien Galthié and the wondrous openside flanker, Olivier Magne.

What they put on the field was still reckoned to be too hot for Ireland, a belief that looked to be justified when France came out of the blocks like a greyhound from the traps. They were 6-0 ahead inside ten minutes but it should have been more. Then things started to get interesting.

Shane Horgan: I didn't play in Paris. I injured my knee in a game against Dungannon – or some other team that really weren't worth me injuring my knee against. I was living in an apartment in Dublin and I was watching the game with a couple of mates of mine and I just saw this thing evolving, this Brian O'Driscoll thing. I knew he was good, but not to that degree.

Mick Galwey: Brian had been on the scene a season. He was a nice fella. You knew there was an honesty and a toughness about him. He had all the skill in the world and that was grand, but there was a hardness about this young lad that you couldn't miss.

Malcolm O'Kelly: I gave him the pass for his first try, which put us ahead 7-6. We were under their posts and in previous years I might have tucked it under my jumper and had a blast myself. I wouldn't have made the line, we'd have had a nice slow ruck and France would have got a penalty. I always said that I created the Butterfly Effect. I read about that once. A butterfly flaps its wings in Japan and sets off a chain of events that leads to a tornado on the other side of the world. I've had a bit of crack with that over the years. In the creation of Brian O'Driscoll, I was the butterfly.

Peter Stringer: I have no doubt they didn't respect us fully. The Ireland team going to France had rarely put in an eighty-minute performance. It was probably only natural for them to think they were going to win the game. From that point of view we caught them by surprise.

David Humphreys: For a long time when Ireland played France there was an aura about their players because we had seen them on TV but not had an opportunity to play against them very much. Because we started playing against them in the Heineken Cup, and with Munster and Leinster in particular winning against their club sides home and away, it stripped away that aura.

Rob Henderson: France got back in control of the match. They scored a try and converted it and Gerard Merceron lobbed over a penalty and fairly early in the second half we were nine points down; 16-7. That was a lights-out lead in every other year.

Brian O'Driscoll slashes through the French defense on his way to a hat-trick in Paris.

Mick Galwey: History told us that you might get on top of France in Paris in the first five or ten minutes but then a wave would usually come and drown you.

Rob Henderson: At 16-7, France broke away and were going to score under the posts. We were hanging on by our fingertips at that stage and Marc dal Maso was about to score. There were 80,000 people in the ground and 80,000 of them would have put their life on Dal Maso. There was only one guy who thought he could be stopped and it was Denis Hickie. He sprinted in from nowhere and carved him down just under the sticks and made him knock the ball on. Whenever I see that moment on TV I still find it unbelievable. Dal Maso is a certainty to score. There's nobody home in our defence. The try and conversion would have taken it to 23-7 and there'd have been no coming back from that. Then Denis appears out of the corner of the screen and catches him. It's incredible.

Peter Stringer: I have no idea how Denis managed to get him because he seemed to come at him from the side and get his head in front of him and threw his body in front of the guy but yet managed to get his arms around him to pull him up short.

Denis Hickie: If I tackled him around the ankles then momentum would have got him over the line, so the only way to stop him was to get in front of him and chop him down and hope that he wouldn't go any further. A conventional tackle wouldn't have stopped the try. As I got closer I knew I was going to have to get my body in front of him. We were under the pump at that stage.

Shane Horgan: I don't know how he stopped yer man. Momentum should have taken him over, but Denis just dropped him. It wasn't pretty and it wasn't safe. It was totally selfless. It personified Denis Hickie.

Brian O'Driscoll: The most impressive and important tackle I've ever seen.

Keith Wood: A guy who never got the credit he deserved. I've big time for Denis.

Rob Henderson: Gérald Merceron put over another penalty and now the gap was twelve points.

John Hayes: I was blowing out of my hole at that stage.

Rob Henderson: We were twenty-eight years without a win in Paris and you wouldn't have found a single person on the planet who would have backed us when we were trailing by twelve. Then Brian scored again. I had a bit of involvement. I broke the line and found him on my inside and away he went. Rog converted it.

Peter Clohessy: Paddy Johns got sin-binned and I remember saying, 'For Jesus' sake, Paddy, don't do this to us.' We got together right away and said that if we didn't win the match, Paddy was going to hang himself.

Rob Henderson: The gap was down to five, then it was eight, then it was five again, then it was eight again. We couldn't get level but they couldn't shake us off either. There was only six minutes left when yer man made it a hat-trick.

Peter Stringer: The French players just seemed to be extremely static and they just didn't seem to be capable to cope with Brian's footwork and pace.

Keith Wood: I was captain that day and I'd experienced all those times when we got hockeyed by France in Paris, and I don't want this to sound like a total Drico lovefest, but I remember that moment, looking over from about thirty yards away, and seeing Brian scooping the ball up with one hand and running in to score his third try, and I remember thinking, 'Anything is possible now. This young kid has got some real magic about him.' He was a very special talent. He was an extraordinary threat on the field. Even without the three tries it was still one of the greatest ever displays by an Irish rugby player. And that was the change for me, but it was also the change for the team because we knew that if things weren't going well we still had somebody who could score tries like that from nothing. It's not an overstatement to say how much changed in that moment.

Johnny Sexton: I was fourteen and I'd been playing golf at Milltown in Dublin that morning. The match had already started by the time I got back to the clubhouse. The place was heaving. I was shocked and excited watching it. In my lifetime, Ireland had never beaten France so that was an amazing moment. I don't remember much from when I was fourteen, but I remember that. When Brian scored his third try the whole place erupted. These were the guys who transformed Irish rugby. I probably didn't even know it at the time but it left a deep impression on me.

Denis Hickie (*left*) and Peter Clohessy (*right*) raise their arms in triumph.

Robbie Henshaw: It was the first rugby match I ever remember watching. I was six. I went into the garden afterwards and beat a rugby ball around the place.

Mick Galwey: I was up in the stand by the time Brian scored his third try. I was sitting beside Donal Lenihan, our manager, who I got my first Munster cap with many years before. We watched Humps land the conversion to put us just one point behind and then we held our breath as Humps stood over a penalty to put us in the lead.

David Humphreys: The year before I had missed the kick to beat France in a wet and windy Lansdowne Road and I still remember standing over the kick I had in Paris and thinking, 'I cannot possibly miss two years in a row.' It would be easy to stand here and say, 'I blocked it out and didn't think about it,' but when I missed the one in Dublin I was desperate to have another chance and to get it a year after was a bit of vindication for me

Mick Galwey: He landed it. When the final whistle went myself and Donal gave each other a big hug. Jesus Christ, we had a lot of hard days between us.

Rob Henderson: The end? I can't describe what that was like. I'd love to bottle that feeling and whenever I feel a bit down I would open it up, take a little sniff and everything would be all right again.

David Humphreys kicks the winning goal as Keith Wood looks on.

Mick Galwey: I went to the Claw and it was hugely emotional.

Rob Henderson: The pair of them were like Walter Matthau and Jack Lemmon. The odd couple.

Mick Galwey: Claw got a right doing in Paris in 1994 and then there was the Roumat thing in 1996 and he couldn't have seen this day ever coming. To be on a winning Ireland team in France? That was the stuff of fantasy. We always gave it our best shot and it wasn't good enough. At last it was.

Peter Clohessy: I knew then that I could die happy.

Denis Hickie: People ask was that the game when I thought Brian was really special but it wasn't. It became apparent before that. It's when you saw him every day at training, the application, the skill level, the execution, day after day, no let-up. That's when you knew. His unique gift was his ability to perform every single time. You have good days and bad days but Brian never had a bad day. And the really weird thing was that his eye sight was comically bad. I mean, it was hilarious. In the days after Paris he was the talk of the rugby world and everybody was going on about his tries and his pace and his incredible vision. He was as blind as a bat. We'd constantly take the piss out of him. When he was driving down the road he

The party in Paris begins.

couldn't see any of the signs. He couldn't see a lot of stuff. He must look back and scratch his head and go, 'How did I do that?' His long vision was dreadful, but somehow he adapted.

Brian O'Driscoll: Yeah, I had really bad eyesight. I ended up getting my eyes lasered after the 2009 Lions tour, but for the first ten years of my career, my eyesight was terrible. Ironically, my eyeballs are shaped like rugby balls, so all I could really see were shapes and colour and none of the detail that I can now see. Scoreboards and the clock and all that – I couldn't see any of it. I remember several times asking Gordon D'Arcy who was in the centre with me what the score was, and he would say, 'Don't be so lazy, have a look yourself.'

One of the most difficult parts was when it got dark and there were bad floodlights, I couldn't see anything. The dark, generally, was terrible. So sometimes you'd hear someone calling from across the street at night time, 'Brian, how are ye?' And I'd be weighing it up going, 'I don't know if I know them or not.' And then you'd cross the street and they'd look a bit alarmed and say, 'Oh… I didn't expect you to come across and say hello…' And I'd just be thinking, 'Oh, I got that one wrong, I was sure it was a friend.' So it's a lot better now. People who knew me knew that I wasn't being ignorant and looking through them – but then again, it was also a good excuse for ignoring people if I didn't want to talk to them.

Shane Horgan: In the 1990s there just wasn't the belief that Ireland could win the big games and then 2000 happened and it recalibrated everybody in Irish rugby. There suddenly was a view that it's not impossible to beat France or England – because we have one of our own as good as anyone in the world. That changed the Irish mindset. We started to believe.

There was a commercial element to it as well because Brian became a superstar. When I played my first game for Leinster in 1998, the year Brian joined us, there were 300 people at the ground – and I knew most of them. Honestly. You'd be running down the sideline and saying, 'Oh, there's mum.' This was against Munster. Now, for a game between Leinster and Munster you get 50,000 people. There was this huge change in Irish rugby and Brian was the figurehead.

Denis Hickie: The meal in Paris is always very lavish and old school – with lots of champagne corks. We went on to Kitty O'Shea's and the Ritz. It was one of those special nights where you're walking through the streets of Paris at four in the morning just hoping it'll never end.

Brian O'Driscoll: Naive me didn't realise that we hadn't won in Paris for thirty-odd years, and I scored a few tries and we won the game, and I thought, 'Ah, this is great, it's very exciting,' but I didn't realise the enormity of it until we got back home. We went out that night to Kitty O'Shea's, and then eventually Mick Galway and his wife said, 'Right, we're going home.'

Rob Henderson: We had a good night out. I came back to the hotel around 1.30am and I saw Brian lying on a couch in the lobby, dribbling. And I thought to myself, 'Hang on, we've just won in Paris for the first time in 28 years and this fella got a hat-trick. It's way too early for bed.' So I picked him up and dragged him down the Champs-Élysées to some shitty karaoke-type bar and we were necking bottles of cheap wine. It was like a scene from Snatch.

Brian O'Driscoll: We went to a club on the Champs-Élysées and went up to the front door – and weren't allowed in. They were having none of it. They didn't care how many tries I'd scored. So we went across the road to an eatery and we had to order some food so that we could get some more wine. We ended up having an omelette and basically a bottle of vinegar – God, the wine was so bad – and when I walked outside and the fresh air hit me, I ended up seeing both the omelette and the wine again, all over the Champs-Élysées. It was classy. Hendo just stood there laughing. 'Jesus,' he said, 'this is some comedown.'

Ireland hadn't won three consecutive games in the Championship since the Triple Crown-winning season of 1982. Brian O'Driscoll was three years old at the time. An air of positivity came over Irish rugby and it continued into 2001 when they won their opening two games of the Six Nations only for the tournament to be halted by the outbreak of foot and mouth disease.

On the face of it, Ireland were going along nicely, but behind the scenes the relationship between coach and assistant coach was getting more tense by the month.

Warren Gatland: Eddie was getting a lot of credit for the way the backs were playing and that's understandable. But, to be honest, it was fractured. I was talking to Donal Lenihan and Brian O'Brien, when he took over from Donal, and I really liked them both. We used to have discussions about things we might try, all sorts of things, and Eddie would say, 'That's a bad decision and I'll tell you why.' I used to say to Brian, 'If he says one more time "That's a bad decision and I'll tell you why" I'm going to smash him.'

Eddie O'Sullivan: Warren had no time for the IRFU guys. He was dismissive of them, to put it kindly. You can't treat people like that. When we started getting some good results he'd be bullish. We were away some place one time and the management went out for some grub and then we went back to the hotel bar for a drink before bed. The committee arrived in and we said, 'Come on, let's call it a night.' But Warren didn't want to leave. Brian O'Brien was the manager and Brian was a very wise man and he said, 'Warren, let's go, nothing good will happen here.' He knew what Warren thought of the committee and that it might get messy. We all went upstairs, but Warren came back down again and had a blazing row with one of the committee.

Warren Gatland: We'd have match reviews and there was Eddie Wigglesworth, Eddie Coleman, Noel Murphy and Syd Millar. It would be up in Dublin on a Wednesday night. You'd have done all your work, all your analysis, all your reviews, you had all your information and you're sitting there discussing the game with guys who didn't have the information. I found that frustrating. Then they'd go: 'In my day, when we played against Wales in the sixties' and blah, blah, blah, and, 'This is what we used to do.' I was talking to a group of guys who didn't understand the modern game. We used to meet with Wigglesworth on the morning of a game and he'd say, 'What are you planning?' I can remember one day he asked me what we were planning to do. 'Will you play a rucking game or a continuity game?' That's a question from somebody who thinks he knows what he's talking about. And I'm sitting there trying to say the right things.

Shane Byrne: The rest of the Six Nations was delayed until the autumn, after the Lions tour to Australia. While Woody and Drico and the boys were away, I finally got my cap against Romania in Bucharest. It was a long time coming. The first time I was in an Ireland squad was 1993, then I went on the tour to Australia in 1994 and to the World Cup in 1995 and I sat on the bench against Wales in 1997. No cap. Mal O'Kelly used to say that I became grumpier and grumpier as the 1990s wore on. A guy in the IRFU told me on one occasion to get my hair cut. I said I wouldn't and I was dropped for the next squad session. Then I went on the infamous development tour in 1997 and it was the worst fucking tour I was ever on. I was drafted in as a late replacement for Ross Nesdale who very smartly pulled out when he saw where the feck we were going.

Brian Ashton said to me, 'I have no idea who you are so unless there's an injury you won't be getting a game.' I'd been playing for Leinster for six years at this point and I'd been in the Irish squad off and on for four years, so that was a bit of a kick in the guts, to tell you the truth. I remember thinking to myself at the end of the 1990s that I was wasting my time. I was pretty self-centred and I had a 'Woe is me' attitude. I told one of the guys at my club, Blackrock, that I was thinking of quitting and said, 'What's the one thing that you want?' I said, 'I just want to play for Ireland. One cap, that's all I want.' He said, 'Well, if you quit now then the one certainty is that you'll never get one. If you stay, you might.'

That focused me and in 2001 the opportunity knocked. I swear to God, I wouldn't change a thing. I'd still wait the eight years. It was my stag weekend. I came on as a sub in Bucharest and it was like an out of body experience. My mates on the stag made up about fifty per cent of the crowd and they were so noisy it was unbelievable. My first lineout happened directly in front of where they were standing and it was the only time in the entire day that they went completely silent. I have thrown lineout balls on my own five-yard line in front of 80,000 people with two points in it on the scoreboard but I haven't felt pressure like I did in that moment in Romania. My hands were sweating. I could almost hear the lads breathing behind me. I threw it to Mick Galwey and he soared like an eagle and caught it and this massive roar went up from the boys. It was terrifying.

Eddie O'Sullivan: We hadn't won in Scotland in sixteen years. Warren had it in his head that he could rotate the team. We got obliterated and he was on his knees again.

Rob Henderson: It was a debacle.

Ronan O'Gara: We were brutal. I was brutal. It's an awful thing to say but for once I wasn't too disappointed to leave the field.

Shane Horgan: It was as if somebody sucked all the energy out of us. We were going over there to kill that Scotland team just like we'd been killing Scottish club teams, putting forty points on them. It was a real eye-opener, the difference between Test rugby and provincial rugby. I started in the centre with Brian and it killed any prospect of us forming a midfield partnership with Ireland the way we had with Leinster. John Leslie cut through the middle of us and I found that really difficult. It was our chance to bring in a new type of rugby and straight away it was a case of, 'Right, that experiment has failed.' I reverted to the wing after that.

Warren Gatland: We changed the way we defended against Scotland that day. Eddie didn't like the way we were defending and we changed it. It didn't work and I was the one who got it in the neck because the buck stopped with the head coach. I did a review on the Wednesday night with the IRFU guys and it was the worst thing I've ever had to do in coaching. I had to sit there in the offices of the IRFU and do a review with four guys who hadn't even watched the game.

I had so many regrets after that match. We changed selection and we changed the way we defended, which was the big change. Five years later, when I was coaching Wasps, my assistant, Shaun Edwards, came to me before we played Leicester in the Premiership final. He thought we should change the way we defended. I said, 'No, I'm not changing. I've done that before and I got burned.' And we won that final by twenty-five points. You can't buy that experience.

Keith Wood: We got carried away. Maybe we made the presumption that we'd carry on where we left off in the spring. We didn't get into the game at all. I carried more ball than I probably ever carried and I got smashed. We had our heads in the sand. It was terrible that we had to learn a lesson that way, but we had to.

Warren Gatland watches as Keith Wood gathers his players for one final talk before they take to the field.

Jeremy Davidson: I was in pain all that week. I was playing too much. I'd played two games in three days for Ulster in the Celtic League, against Bridgend and Pontypridd, then it was into Ireland camp for training and over to Scotland for a Test match that I shouldn't really have been playing in. Three games in ten days, my knee wasn't capable of holding up to that much rugby. I remember walking out of the hotel in Scotland to get on the bus and Liam Hennessy, our fitness coach, looked at me and his face dropped because my gait was awful. I was limping. I wasn't in the right condition to play international rugby.

We were allowed to play with injuries that you wouldn't be allowed to play with now. On two or three occasions I played for Ireland with broken bones in my hands. I wasn't the only one. In the latter days with Ulster I was full of painkillers for my knee. I did it to myself. I just wanted to keep playing, but I regret it now. On the other hand, I'd do it all again tomorrow. That's a contradiction but there you go.

That Scotland game was my last cap. Would I do anything differently? I'd look after myself more, but it's easy to be clear in hindsight. At the time you just want to play for your country or for Ulster. Having been at the highest level I worked like crazy to try to get back there again but you're damaging yourself the whole time.

Gary Longwell: The next game was Wales in Cardiff. At training on the Tuesday my finger got caught in Reggie Corrigan's tackle suit and there was a crack but I thought it would be alright. It was a bit sore afterwards and the doctor sent me to a hospital just outside Dublin for an X-ray. The guy came in and said there was a problem. I said, 'I can still play,' but then he squeezed it and it was agony and he said no way was I playing. So I asked him to amputate it, but he said he wouldn't do it. You hear people saying they would cut off their right arm to play for Ireland and that's the way I felt. It was the first thing my wife said when I told her I couldn't play, 'Would you not just cut it off Gary?' I'd grown up with a guy called Joe Callaghan who was the best player of our generation, and he'd lost his finger in a farming accident, so I didn't see it as a big deal. But they wouldn't let me do it.

Eddie O'Sullivan: We were picking the team for Wales in the Glenview Hotel. That Scottish game had been a trauma for everybody and Rog was caught in the middle of it. He had a shocker. He was very inexperienced and his confidence was shot. Going into Cardiff, the big talking point was who plays 10? Myself and Brian O'Brien, the manager, were adamant that David Humphreys should start, but Warren was belligerent about it and insisted he wanted to start Rog and we went round the block on it. He wouldn't budge. I went back down to my room and said, 'This is a disaster, this is the wrong thing to do.' I rang Brian and we went down and had another run at Warren and we talked him round. Humps played and we won by thirty points. Now, if I was the guy I was purported to be I'd have gone back to my room and sat on my hands. If I was out to get Warren, I'd have said nothing about Humps.

Warren Gatland: I got a knock on my door at about midnight and it's Eddie and he says, 'I think we've made the wrong call at 10'. I said, 'OK.' He said, 'I think we should start Humps.' It was toss-up anyway. I went. 'OK, if that's what you believe.' This was different from changing the way we defended against Scotland. I should have said, 'No,' that time because I went against my better judgement, but Rog v Humps was a very tight call and Eddie felt really strongly about it and made a big case for Humps, so I backed my coach. The team was announced the next day. Rog came up to me and said, 'Can I have a chat?' He said, 'I'm disappointed that I'm not playing but I had a talk with Eddie and Eddie said it was a tight decision and that you made it.' I never said to him that he was in the team to begin with.

Eddie O'Sullivan: We had England at Lansdowne Road next. They were going for a Grand Slam.

Shane Horgan: England were an incredible team and it was one of the times where I was really worried about playing against an opposition player – Jason Robinson. I thought, 'If I get this wrong it could be humiliating.' You have to remember where I was coming from. I hadn't had too much exposure to top-end rugby. I was in the Ireland team quite young and it was an Ireland team that hadn't been successful. You were always doubting yourself. Always waiting for the tap on the shoulder, 'We've figured you out, you shouldn't be here, good luck.' It took me a long time to cop on that I was good enough.

Peter Stringer makes a crucial tap-tackle on Dan Luger just when it seemed that the England winger had breached the Ireland defensive line and was on his way to score.

Keith Wood crashes over from a clever line-out peel to score.

I was a reluctant winger. I wasn't at ease in the role and I thought Robinson could really embarrass me. I never felt comfortable in the match, not for one second. It was at the point in my career where I wasn't really enjoying playing rugby for Ireland. I enjoyed the build-up to games, I enjoyed being part of the squad, I enjoyed training and I loved the crack afterwards, but I hadn't got my head around the game itself. That game was a big psychological step. I survived it and we won.

Keith Wood: They didn't have Martin Johnson or Lawrence Dallalgio and there was something about their lineout calls that was familiar to me. I recognised them during the game but I couldn't figure out where they were from. Mal came over and said, 'Woody, they're using the Lions calls from the summer.' I said, 'Ah, there you go'. So we did a total number on their lineout, and I scored a try off one of our own lineouts. Even then, it all came down to Peter Stringer making a sensational tap-tackle on Dan Luger. I probably left myself down a little after that. We did a half lap of honour, which we shouldn't have done because we hadn't won the Championship, England had. And if I reflect back on that part of the day, it wasn't great.

Kevin Maggs: I arrived back to Bath grinning from ear to ear and didn't say a whole lot. I think my smile got to them more than anything else. Jon Callard, my coach, said I should go to the physio to see if he could ultra-sound the smile off my face. It was sweet, you know?

David Wallace: We had no defensive system. It wasn't until Mike Ford came in a year later that we really started to learn about that stuff. We were miles behind England and whenever I think about that match I wonder how we managed to pull it off.

Eddie O'Sullivan: It was the hurry-up-and-try-harder defensive system and it bit us on the ass when we played New Zealand at the end of 2001. We had a nice lead on them. We played some great stuff, but when they started upping the ante we were all over the place. They tore us to shreds. As a team we were like a bungee jump. Up and down, up and down.

Keith Wood: Just after half-time we were leading 21-7 but we knew they were going to come back at us in a major way. I thought, 'God, if I'm stuck at the bottom of a ruck with Lomu I might whisper into his ear that he's on This Is Your Life on Monday. It might put him off.' I knew because I was a guest. I didn't get a chance and they won the match 40-29. We couldn't live with them and it killed me. That was my chance to beat New Zealand. We had it, not done, but nearly done, and literally it was the harem scarem defensive structure that was the problem. It could work for sixty minutes but it can't work for eighty minutes because it's inefficient. I was just so tired of it.

Eddie O'Sullivan: I got a call to go to Dublin for a meeting with the IRFU at 8pm on a Thursday evening, not long after the New Zealand game. I was coming down Lansdowne Road in the car and I pulled into the Berkeley Court Hotel to go the loo. As I was driving in, Warren was walking out. I rolled down the window and I said, 'Hey Warren, how's it going?' He was the colour of death. He walked on and didn't answer me. I thought, 'What the fuck is going on here?'

Warren Gatland: The decision was made by a small committee – maybe four people. The meeting only lasted a few minutes. 'Thanks for all you have done for Irish rugby but we're not going to renew your contract.' I was shocked and disappointed.

Eddie O'Sullivan: I went to the loo at the Berkeley Court, then across to Lansdowne Road. I was brought into a room and sat in front of the committee and they said to me, 'If we asked you to coach Ireland would you accept the position?' and I said, 'Yes'. What else could I say? They stood up and said, 'You're now the coach of the Irish rugby team'. It was as sudden as a punch in the face.

Warren Gatland: Eddie had an offer from the States and had a contract on the table so that helped with their decision. The IRFU panicked about losing him to America. I think Keith Wood had some input as well.

Keith Wood: Did I support Gatty at the time? The answer is no. Was I involved in getting rid of him? I think he seriously overestimates the power a captain had and I think that probably covers it. Did I support him? No, I thought it was time for a change. We were at a bit of a standstill. I've given Gatty all the credit for what he did. He did really, really well. Back in 1998, after Brian Ashton went, I was asked my opinion about whether it should be Gatty or Mike Ruddock as coach. I really liked Mike Ruddock, but the recommendation I gave was for Gatty. I was a fan. Ireland were in desperate need of Warren when we got him. Eddie couldn't have taken over that Irish team. By the time we got to 2001 we needed something different. Eddie brought a level of detail and expanded the gameplan commensurate with the talent we had. There was no point in playing a forward dominated game when you have backs of the calibre of Rog, Drico, Shane Horgan, Denis Hickie and Geordan Murphy.

I got a phone call from the IRFU to say that Warren was gone and that Eddie was the new coach. I had no idea this was happening. He was up for a review, that's all I knew. I said 'OK,' and I put the phone down and rang my brother because I was flying back from London that day and I said,

'Gordon, will you pick me up at the airport.'

'Ah, well, no, I can't really.'

He was a bit dopey.

I said, 'What's wrong with you?'

'I've taken a couple of valium.'

'Why?'

'I've just had a heart attack.'

'Oh Jesus, who's with you?'

'Just the doctor. I haven't talked to anybody else apart from you.'

I was leaving my phone open so I could get in touch with members of my family and I had members of the press ringing me wanting to talk about Gatty. I said, 'I can't talk,' and they said, 'You have to give us a comment,' and I said, 'No, I don't and I can't.' I got to the hospital and it was horrible. There were tubes coming out of him and he looked awful. I cracked a nervous joke. I said, 'Jesus, Gordon, you wouldn't believe the shit you got me out of today with this Gatty stuff.' He burst out laughing and I burst out laughing and I got a clip around the back of the head from one of the nurses. 'He's not allowed to laugh!'

Warren Gatland: I didn't see it coming. Even after that loss to Scotland we beat Wales and England and we played really well against the All Blacks. We won nine out of eleven that year. Parts of the media accused me of trying to negotiate a new contract through the press but when you are asked about your contract and would you like to continue until the World Cup you just give an honest answer. 'Yes. I'd like to continue.'

When it happened, everybody was looking for conspiracy theories. 'Has he done something he shouldn't have done? What's the real truth?' Looking back, I'm absolutely indebted to Ireland for the opportunities they gave me. I was really disappointed at the time but it was a small group of people who made the decision, so I had to be careful not to be bitter and twisted and let the whole thing eat me up. When I reflect on it, I owe so much to the IRFU and the players and the public and friends we made in Ireland. Without that experience, the highs and the lows, I might not have had success later. We won three Premiership titles, a Heineken Cup and a Parker Pen trophy with Wasps. I went back to New Zealand and we won an Air New Zealand Cup with Waikato. And then Wales, which has worked out very well with two Grand Slams and a Championship. It was also a privilege to coach the Lions in 2013. I was hurt when I lost my job with Ireland, but, in hindsight, it was the best thing that could have happened to me.

Eddie O'Sullivan: I was painted as a Machiavellian character. I get pretty upset when people say that I stabbed Warren in the back. I'll go to my grave being upset about that because it doesn't stand up to any analysis.

Warren Gatland: It's water under the bridge. There was just never enough trust between us.

Denis Hickie: Most of us wouldn't have mourned Warren's loss too much. When he left it felt like a natural progression because Eddie was a better technical coach and he had more ideas for the backline. Gatty was a great stepping stone to progress but it was logical that Eddie would take over. You can look back now at everything he's achieved in the game and think it was a mistake to get rid of him but at that point he hadn't achieved any of that. There was an outcry among the supporters, but it wasn't felt as much in the team.

Shane Horgan: I didn't feel that bad about it. I knew who I wanted to work with and I thought it was to a large degree Eddie's baby at that stage. From a coaching perspective he was miles ahead of Gatty. I can't speak for the forwards. You might hear a different story from them. But a lot of the creative rugby was coming from Eddie and I was happy because that was the kind of rugby that I wanted to play.

Malcolm O'Kelly: The values Warren brought to the squad probably weren't appreciated as much as they could have been. He was important. The lads thought his sacking was a bit harsh but they weren't too upset by it. The relationship wasn't that strong. I felt for him, but what are you going to do?

Frankie Sheahan: I actually wrote Gatty a card and sympathised with him and thanked him for giving me my first cap. I thought he was shrewd and unlucky.

Brian O'Driscoll: He brought a decent edge to the team. Brought us to the next level. He was never afraid to take risks on young, unproven players. Under him we had our highest finish in the Championship in fourteen years, beat France for the first time in seventeen years and won in Paris for the first time in twenty-eight. He raised the bar, but I didn't lose any sleep over him leaving. It's business. Coaches come and go. It's the nature of the game we play. Brutal, at times.

Ronan O'Gara: People always think that players know about these things. That because we're on the inside we can see it coming or that we hear about it first. Most of the time we haven't got a clue. I wasn't aware of any tensions between Warren and the IRFU or that he was making a bad fist of playing politics with them. I was just a player. They only tell us what they think we need to know. Most of the time that means they tell us nothing.

Rob Henderson: You could tell that Eddie was an ambitious person, always chomping at the bit and wanting more responsibility. He was a good coach, full of Americanisms. 'Get the puck on the field.' 'Clusterfuck.' 'In the red zone.' Eh? What game are you playing? Gatty was pragmatic and Eddie had great technical knowledge. There was a problem between them but, in a strange way, they were a good team and they made some great progress. But that's coaching in the professional world, isn't it? Eddie was running the show on his own now.

FOURTEEN

PAULIE – HE JUST HAD THAT DOG IN HIM

Eddie O'Sullivan's first match as Ireland coach could scarcely have gone any better. It was at home to Wales and it ended in a record-breaking pummelling of the visitors, a fifty-point deconstruction that silenced those who felt that Warren Gatland had been treated shamefully and that O'Sullivan was some way involved in his demise.

It was a day to remember for another reason in that it marked the debut of Paul O'Connell, a twenty-two year old lock forward from Young Munster, who had been pulling up trees in Europe with his province.

Paul O'Connell: You'll find it hard to believe but I never went to Lansdowne Road as a young fella. I watched all the Five Nations games because my dad was mad into it and my older brother, Justin, was mad into it, but we never went to Dublin. We went to Young Munster.

We used to go into town for mass above in the Dominicans and we'd come out after mass and dad would be talking rugby to these guys and chatting about what happened in the All Ireland League. There was one particular pal of his who would always have a bag of sweets in his pocket and he'd chat to dad outside mass and we'd stand close by waiting for the sweets. You're not listening to what they're saying, but you're taking it in all the same.

He might have a couple of pints in Austins or the Charlie St George or above in the club and all the chat would be about Munsters – the Claw and Peter Meehan and Ray Ryan and these guys. Peter and Ray were enforcer-type second-rows. If they were around now and did some weights they'd be Bakkies Botha types. Incredible players. Ray Ryan has a bus company and he drove the bus for my stag. He abandoned it and went on the piss with us. He's a lovely man. He's still best friends with the Claw.

Ger Earls was the openside flanker on the senior team and he was the guy for me because my dad thought he was unbelievable. He was one of the main players on the 1993 team that won the All Ireland League. They had an incredible pack of forwards, so hard and so tough. They just ground teams down. They were very aggressive, probably a little bit dirty as well, but those were the stories I grew up

Opposite: Paul O'Connell in action during the 2003 Rugby World Cup.

with. It wasn't about skill or anything like that. It was all about physicality.

Munsters' whole thing was all about the physical challenge and that's all that anybody ever spoke to you about after games. When I started playing they didn't want to talk about your passes or things like that, they wanted to talk about rucks and tackles and mauls and scrums. I was immersed in it through my dad and my brother but rugby wasn't my main focus until I was about 16. I played a bit for Munsters when I was U-10 and U-12, mainly at out-half, but I was heavily involved in swimming and rugby started to get in the way, so I dropped it.

I was about eleven or twelve years of age. I'd do my swimming from six until eight in morning on Tuesdays, Wednesdays and Thursdays and six until seven every evening after school, then it would be nine until eleven on Saturday morning and eight until ten on Sunday morning. I used to love golf as well. We lived in a bungalow in the country on half an acre and I had my own little golf course cut out on the grass with the lawnmower and I used to play pitch and putt. Golf became my thing for a while.

I hit the wall with swimming and then I hit the wall with the golf and around that time my older brother had just won the Munster Senior Cup with Sunday's Well, beating Young Munster in the final. My dad played with Sunday's Well until he was thirty-four. He moved to Limerick and then he was Young Munster. When the 'Well played Munsters in the Senior Cup he didn't know what to do, so he ended up wearing his Young Munster tie and stood in the Sunday's Well crowd with all the friends he grew up with.

I was under a bit of pressure to play at school because I was Justin O'Connell's brother. Justin didn't go to my school, Ardscoil Ris. He was captain of Clement's. He was excellent. Everybody knew him. Dessie Harty, the rugby coach at Ardscoil, applied subtle pressure on me and I got stuck into it big-time at that stage.

Mick Galwey: When Paul came on the scene first he was like a newborn giraffe. He was just all over the place, but he developed quickly. He had that Young Munster hardness.

Paul O'Connell: You might say I'm being modest but I had such a lucky rise. I got on to the Irish Schools team because in the trial my two props were lifting me by the legs and my opposite second-row was being lifted by the shorts and I stole three lineouts and I was in. That's actually true. And then I got on the Munster U-20 team because there were injuries in the senior team so Mick O'Driscoll was called up, so that gave me a chance and I got into the Ireland U-20s on the back of it. And when I came into the full Munster team it was just when Gaillimh was beginning to come to an end and John Langford had just retired, so I managed to get a break there as well. And I was probably too light as a second-row but I went into a pack with the Claw, Frankie Sheahan, John Hayes, Gaillimh, Anthony Foley, Alan Quinlan and David Wallace. It was an armchair ride. I'm not being modest when I say I've had an incredible amount of luck.

Eddie O'Sullivan: He was very, very tough, physically and mentally, an excellent lineout jumper and a good scrummager. He had leadership qualities and was mature beyond his years. He had that healthy disrespect for the opposition. He wouldn't back down. He just had that dog in him.

Frankie Sheahan: Paulie roomed with Claw in the build-up to his debut against Wales in the first match of the 2002 Six Nations. It was the go-to room for the rest of us. We had card schools in there. Myself, Claw, Hendo, Wally, Rog. They went on a lot later than they should have done. It would be midnight and Hendo would say, 'How about some toasties? Who's up for toasties?' Next thing a tray of toasties would be wheeled in and they'd keep us going for another hour. Claw would be puffing away on the fags and leaving the window open and poor old Paul would be trying to get to sleep with five or six guys laughing and smoking and eating sandwiches until all hours.

Paul O'Connell celebrates scoring his debut try.

Ronan O'Gara: Paulie tells a funny story about one night when Claw couldn't sleep. It was the small hours of the morning and Claw put on the television full blast. There weren't even any programmes being shown on the channel he was watching, only those long commercials for mail-order music CDs. Claw took a shine to one of the CDs on offer – The Power of Love. He picked up the phone and rang the number on screen, gave them his credit card details and ordered two copies of the CD – one for himself and one for Paulie. In fairness to Claw, he was always fierce generous. All Paulie wanted at that moment was his sleep but instead he was getting the Power of Love from Claw.

Mick Galwey: I was delighted to be there the day he made his Ireland debut. I was captain. I remember saying to him that these Quinnell boys are playing, so be careful of them, they're big hefty lads.

Paul O'Connell: I went to tackle Craig Quinnell and he elbowed me and knocked me unconscious. I came around and Mick Griffin, our doctor, got me on my feet and put his arms around me and I pushed him away and said, 'Stop, you're making it look worse,' and I ran back into the lineout. I remember Mick Galwey was smiling at me. I suppose he knew that something had happened to me and this was my introduction to it, but I walked into the lineout and I couldn't remember any of the calls. Every time I walked into the lineout John Hayes would have to tell me the calls in layman's terms. 'Straight on you. Straight on Mick Galwey. Lob on you.'

After a while I realised that I didn't know what was going on and I just walked off to the side of the pitch. Mick Griffin was there and he asked me a whole series of questions and I was able to answer them and then he asked if I remembered scoring a try and I said, 'I didn't score, you're only trying to tell me I scored so I won't complain when you tell me to come off. I know I didn't score.' And I looked up at the clock and it was showing two and a half minutes. I thought the clock was counting up but it was actually counting down. I said 'Mick, I'm not coming off after two and a half minutes of my debut,' and he said, 'There's two and a half minutes left in the half and you're fucking definitely coming off.'

I got all emotional after that. I got assessed in the medical room and Chris Wyatt had done his ankle and he was in there drinking a can of Coke and he said, 'Well done on your try.' They showed a replay of it on the telly. I have a cherished photo of me fist-pumping after scoring it, with all the Munster lads and Simon Easterby around me. I wish I could have remembered it because I'd say it was incredible.

Frankie Sheahan: We got hammered by England the next day; 45-11 at Twickenham. We were making progress but we were still miles behind the top teams.

Eddie O'Sullivan: I was afraid going over to England because they were very good and we didn't have a defensive system that could cope with them. I brought in Mike Ford but we were only at an infantile stage of developing our defence and England ripped us to shreds. There were system errors all over the shop. Also, Niall O'Donovan, our forwards coach, was stuck with Warren's lineout calls. Later on, myself and Niallo went down to Woody's house in Killaloe and we spent a whole day putting a new lineout in place. That was after the Six Nations. We had plenty more pain to suffer first, though.

Kevin Maggs, Brian O'Driscoll and an injured Girvan Dempsey in the dressing rooms after defeat against England.

Frankie Sheahan: Then we played Scotland at Lansdowne Road and it was one of the most traumatic times I had on a rugby pitch. The lineout didn't function and I was taken off after half an hour. It took me a couple of years to come to terms with it properly. It was embarrassing. Could Eddie have given it to half-time, just for my sanity? Maybe, yes. It was brutal. I shouldn't have done it, but I picked up a newspaper the next day. Player ratings. Frankie Sheahan: One out of ten. Jesus. It cost me hugely in my international career. Munster's lineout went great guns In Europe afterwards but Eddie didn't really look at me seriously again. Give a dog a bad name.

The team huddle up before taking the field against Scotland

Mick Galwey: I was captain and we won well that day. We put forty points on Scotland and Brian scored another hat-trick. After the hammering in Twickenham it was a good response. But it was my last time playing for Ireland. Every contract I got was a one-year contract. I'd been dropped so often that my Ireland years were always day-to-day and it did me no harm, it kept me honest. I never took a single moment for granted when I was wearing that green jersey but everything has to come to an end sometime. I was substituted with about fifteen minutes to go. The last words I uttered as an Ireland player were, 'Scrum, ref,' and that was probably fitting when you think about it. And we scored off the scrum and I said to myself, when I knew it was all over, 'You captained your country in your final appearance, you won well and the last thing you did was make a good decision that led to a try. That's not a bad way to finish.' I ended on a high, I suppose.

Eddie O'Sullivan's first Six Nations championship ended with three wins and two heavy defeats to England and France. Keith Wood had been injured for all bar the final game in Paris. It was now the autumn of 2002 and Wood was about to hop on to an emotional rollercoaster the like of which nobody could fully understand.

Keith Wood: We were getting ready to play Romania in Limerick and Brian O'Brien took me aside and told me that my brother, Gordon, had suffered another heart attack and had died. Brian's daughter was going out with Gordon at the time. I was at the removal and my phone went. My wife, Nicola, was heavily pregnant and the message came through that things were beginning to happen. I rushed back to London. I missed the funeral and I missed the birth of our son, Alexander, as well. My head was bursting.

Then I got a bad shoulder injury and just after that my mother died. It was as tough as tough can be. I was out injured for eleven months, which was a blessing in one sense because I hadn't really grieved for Gordon because Alexander came along and now I'd lost my mother and I needed time to get my head around it all.

Behind the scenes: A team meeting, 2002.

Brian O'Driscoll: Woody was captain but he was injured and going to be out for the November 2002 internationals, and I remember Eddie decided to send Woody down to my room to offer me the captaincy as opposed to offering it himself. Which was a little weird of Eddie, if you ask me. But I remember Woody coming in and offering it and without any hesitation I said, 'Yes, what a huge honour.' I was 23 at the time. And Woody said, 'Brilliant,' and went back and told Eddie and I was left sitting in my room thinking, 'Oh my God, what have I done? Now actually comes the role of being captain. How am I meant to captain all these guys who have played for so many years? Some of these guys are married!' And I just kind of felt that if I was going to be captain, I had to do it my way.

Keith Wood and Brian O'Driscoll (with Malcolm O'Kelly, left) have
a laugh on the bus on the way to training.

Keith Wood: I asked him how he was going to do it, and he said, 'I'm going to be
a captain that they actually like.' Ha! Very sensitive, you know.

Brian O'Driscoll: I think I was very fortunate to be in a position where the team
I inherited then was full of speakers. In the period before that I remember often
feeling sorry for Woody because he was often just a voice on his own – and if he
didn't speak then nobody else would have. But I had a good core of leaders with
the likes of Anthony Foley and Rog and Humps were vying for the 10 shirt. Denis
Hickie had made his way back into the national set-up and he always had some
very relevant things to say, so I was fortunate in that the side around me was full
of ready-made leaders willing to chip in and I didn't have to be the only voice and
I could lead by the way I played.

Eddie O'Sullivan: Brian O'Driscoll was a warrior. His combination of mental
and physical toughness was very rare. He'd put his head where you wouldn't put a
crowbar. In Woody's absence through injury, I made him captain and I got advice
from every quarter against doing it. I was told I was crazy. He was too young. I
wasn't absolutely sure, but I was sure enough.

Marcus Horan: We began that season with two good wins away to Scotland and
Italy. Then we had France in Dublin. I was given a start that day and I was up

against Sylvain Marconnet, who was a bit of a giant. I look back now and I think, 'How come it didn't faze me?' I was just so confident. I was certain we'd win. I suppose I was still naive. The reaction of people when we beat them 15-12 was huge and I didn't understand it because I didn't have a mental block about France. It just didn't feel like a big deal. My attitude was, 'Look at the team we have. Why wouldn't we beat them?'

Eddie O'Sullivan: We made it four out of four in Cardiff. Rog put over a late drop goal to win it. No better boy.

Frankie Sheahan: Rog was quite slow, he was quite weak, he wasn't good with the ball in hand going into contact and he was targeted on numerous occasions in his tackling, yet I'm not sure I've seen another guy with as much bottle as he had.

Denis Hickie: With Rog there was no unsaid stuff. Everything was said, no matter how raw. We'd constantly wind each other up. There was never a case of, 'Better not say this or that.' Nothing was off limits. He was great at saying, 'Why can't we win these games?' It clicked with him very early. We're playing against these players in different jerseys and we're beating them, so there's nothing to fear just because we're wearing green instead of blue or red. He was very much like that in his battles with his opposite numbers as well. He had great respect for other players, but he had no fear of anybody or anything.

Gary Longwell: We had a showdown with England for the Grand Slam. It was the first time in twenty-one years that we got to the last game with a Slam on the table. The country was going mad. Deccie Kidney, Eddie's assistant, took me for a walk in the car park the day before and just started talking to me, calming me down. He gave me a note – Nelson's Mandela's inaugural speech – and it was brilliant. Whenever you'd have that little bit of self-doubt, Deccie could spot it and get inside your head and you'd feel fantastic after.

Eddie O'Sullivan: On the day of the match I was in the stand and Martin Murphy, our director of operations, sent up a message to me that Martin Johnson had lined up his team on the wrong side of the red carpet and he wouldn't move. I said, 'Tell him to move,' and he said, 'I did and he told me to go fuck myself.' Johnson made that decision as a statement of intent. He knew exactly where he should stand. He was told before he went out. It was disappointing, but I knew what he was up to and there was a bit of me that admired him for doing it. But if it we did that to the Queen at Twickenham there would have been murder.

Geordan Murphy: He was my captain at Leicester and I looked over at him and I knew by the big stubborn head on him that he wasn't going to be moving. At the time, I thought it was gamesmanship but I spoke to him afterwards and he said he couldn't back out of it once he was in position because ten minutes previously in the changing room he was telling his players that we were going to mess them around and they weren't to take a backward step. He said a little grey haired man came up to him and said, 'Could you move please, sir?' 'No!'

Victor Costello: The Irish public took exception to it and I could understand that. A jobsworth wasn't getting Martin Johnson to move just by waving his finger at him. I was standing beside Drico. I said, 'Jaysus, will we stand in front of them?' He said, 'No, we'll stay here.' A lot was made of it, but not within the team. England were wired going into that game. They were phenomenal. We were on a good run but they were on a savage run and there wasn't a team on earth that would have beaten them that day.

Marcus Horan: They put forty points on us and we didn't play that badly. I was up against Jason Leonard. I thought he was on the way out and I could have a cut off him. I thought wrong. He was immense. It was his 101st cap and he'd just won a Grand Slam, but he came into our dressing room afterwards and he sat down for a chat. Old school. A classy guy.

Eddie O'Sullivan: On the famous night I was appointed as coach I was asked by the union if I'd have any problem working with Declan Kidney as my assistant and I said I wouldn't because they'd already made up their minds. Deccie was asked would he be my number two and what was he supposed to say? If you say no you might never be asked again, so you say yes. And it wasn't fair on either of us. Deccie was ambitious and I was ambitious and there was nothing wrong with that. Deccie was a head coach and so was I and it was as difficult for him as it was for me. It was an uncomfortable relationship and it wasn't our fault.

Warren Gatland: I knew what Eddie's relationship with Declan was like, so for him to accept Declan as his assistant showed me how desperate he was for the job, because they were never going to get on.

Frankie Sheahan: You could tell that Eddie didn't really want him there and that Deccie was never really comfortable with a backroom role. Deccie's not a skills coach, he's an overall tactician, but that role was filled by Eddie.

Eddie O'Sullivan talks to the players in the wake of the Grand Slam loss to England.

Malcolm O'Kelly: Eddie wouldn't have been one for small talk. He wasn't the ideal man to be stuck in a lift with. He'd give you this look that would make you feel very uncomfortable. He could look through you. He could see what you were trying to hide.

Reggie Corrigan: We headed off to Australia for the World Cup. We had Romania and Namibia first-up and we took care of them. Then it was the do-or-die game against Argentina, the rematch after Lens. Everybody was talking about Lens. It was like a horrible cloud over us. There was no escape. For those of us who were there four years earlier it was unbelievable pressure. We'd improved a lot since then, but so had they. We were coming down in the lift in our hotel from the eighth floor on the day of the match and all you could hear was noise – singing. The elevator doors opened and the lobby was mobbed with Irish fans. There were millions of them. We were going, 'Holy shit, there's even more pressure on us now.'

Keith Wood: When we got to the World Cup I was fit and flying. It was my last stand. I was retiring after it. My first full game was against Argentina and apart from being a bizarre game it was a very strange atmosphere in the ground. Everybody was nervous because of Lens.

Eddie O'Sullivan: I said beforehand that it would be a dogfight in the trenches and that the tension would be almost unbearable and that was exactly the way it was. Everybody was drained, not just from the day itself – it was the whole build-up. We knew it was the defining game. Had we lost we would have had to have beaten the Wallabies by four tries the following week in order to get out of the pool. It didn't bear thinking about. The pressure was phenomenal, given the history of it. Lens had been hanging over me for two years. People constantly reminding me about it. 'How are you gonna do? Will it be like Lens?' The build-up was intense. It was a game I wanted to win more than any I'd ever been involved in. We had to put Lens to bed. I'm not trying to be Steve Silvermint, but for my own sanity I had to philosophise it somewhat in the days before. I was confident I'd done the best possible job. If I could sit down the night before the game and say, 'Is there anything more you could have done?' and answer, 'No,' then fair enough.

Shane Horgan: Had we lost it was Eddie's job gone and that's what people forget. It's not soccer. It's not like you lose your job and it's OK because you made five million quid last year. There was enormous stress on him. At least we could influence it out there. He couldn't.

Kevin Maggs: The stress Eddie was under was passed on to the players. We flew to Adelaide for the match and we were supposed to have a day off and Eddie cancelled it and we went training instead. For those of us who were in Lens it was a fucking ugly monkey on our shoulder. No matter which way you turned it was looking at you. It still haunted me, that. In training, everybody was tense and biting the head off each other.

Marcus Horan: There was a history between them and us. There wouldn't have been a lot of love there. I wouldn't tar them all with the same brush, but there were a few fellas in their pack who were a bit out of order at times.

Shane Horgan: One of the first penalties in the game was deep in our 22 on the right hand side of the pitch and Humps was playing 10 and Humps throws the ball to Denis and goes, 'Denis you're left-footed, you go for it.' Now Denis hadn't kicked a ball to touch in two years. We'd never planned it beforehand. Fellas were on edge all over the place.

Paul O'Connell: I was only twenty-three so the stress didn't transfer to me but I have no doubt it transferred to Woody and Humps and all the lads who had been in Lens. I wasn't aware of the tension. I was just having a ball.

Keith Wood: I got gouged. I cleared out a ruck and Roberto Grau drew his hand over my eye. He did no damage, but it was pretty frightening.

Reggie Corrigan: I got stamped, punched, gouged. It was an horrendously tough match. I ended up in the dressing room before the end because Mauricio Reggiardo did a job on my eye. We were on the attack outside their 22 and he just went for it. It was terrifying. I completely thought I'd lost my eye. He plunged two fingers straight in and ripped. It happened so quickly that I couldn't defend myself against it. For a few seconds I couldn't see out that side. There was no vision, just blackness. I said, 'He's after ripping out my eye.' Slowly I got my sight back, but it took me out of the match which pissed me off even more. There was stuff going on all the time. They just wanted to bully us. We knew it was coming.

Keith Wood: I thought that Alan Quinlan was going to be the star of the World Cup. I never saw him as focused. He was on fire in training and on fire in matches and then he martyred himself scoring a cracking try in that match against Argentina.

Alan Quinlan: When I was a younger player, breaking into the Munster and Ireland team, I had a negative voice holding me back at times. My personality was probably masking my nervousness about whether I was good enough to play at that level. I was afraid to try things with Ireland. I was OK with Munster but it took me longer to get comfortable in the Ireland set-up. I had a bit of stage fright in the beginning.

By the time of the World Cup I was fitter and stronger than I'd ever been. I was in a good place and I felt like I belonged. I started against Argentina and I thought, 'Yeah, I've earned the right to be here and I've got the respect of the others.'

The try happened pretty quickly. The ball was overthrown at an Argentina lineout and Woody got it. When I got the ball off Woody I thought, 'Jesus, I have a chance here.' I ran as fast as I could. I could see Ignacio Corleto coming at me from the right-hand side, but it didn't matter. I was getting to the line and getting the ball down and that was that. He hit me pretty hard. I smacked off the ground and planted the ball over the try line and then there was a pause and then this incredible pain. I was panicking. I was thinking, 'What the fuck is after happening here?' I could see the bone sticking out of my shoulder. It was murder until the doctor popped my shoulder back in place.

Listen, it was an important try but I paid a fair old price for it. I was out injured for months and then I struggled to get back in the Munster team and it was a couple of years before I had a proper chance with Ireland again. I missed a lot of rugby. I always thought at least I did it scoring a try in a big match in a World Cup rather than in a closed-doors training session. There was some comfort in that.

Paul O'Connell: Quinny knocks a bit of crack out of it. The try that saved Irish rugby.

Alan Quinlan: It was a good line – and I stuck to it.

Alan Quinlan lies injured after scoring against Argentina.

Shane Horgan: Quinny's try put is in the lead, but it was still very early. At half-time we were leading 10-9, then we were losing 12-10. Rog came on and fired over two penalties. We were ahead by four.

Ronan O'Gara: I came on for Humps and I was wound up. I started shouting at everybody. Most of it was the usual stuff that you hear all the time but I said a strange thing to Victor Costello. I told him that his dad was watching, do this for your dad. I'm not sure when his dad had died but I remember reading an interview with Victor when he spoke about what an influence his dad had been and how much he missed him. I don't know how that came into my head but it probably shows how emotional I was. I apologised to him afterwards because I was worried that I had gone too far and caused him offence, but he was cool about it. He said that it was a great thing to hear.

Eddie O'Sullivan: They got a penalty with seven minutes left and it was a one-point game and it was no fun at all. The time passed very slowly. Andre Watson, the referee, was told that the next time the ball went out of play, that's it, over. But instead of calling it, he allowed Argentina a lineout. Argentina put a winger around the corner and my life flashed before my eyes. In fairness to Girvan Dempsey he put the guy into the advertising hoardings and that was it. One of my abiding memories was ringing home afterwards. They'd all been watching the match. I spoke to my wife and daughter and I said put the young lad on for a word and my wife said that he'd gone to bed with a migraine. He was ten years old. At times like that you realise what you're doing to your family.

Keith Wood. I had a meltdown after. I'd a guy who caught me to do a flash interview while I'm standing on the pitch. I said, 'No, I'm going into the changing room first, I'll come out then.' He said, 'You're contractually obliged.' 'Fuck off,' I said, and he followed me all the way down the tunnel, pulling at me. And I said, 'Pull me once more and I'll bust you with whatever energy I have.'

Eddie O'Sullivan: I didn't want to think about what it would have been like had we lost. I didn't want to go there and I didn't want anybody else there with me. It was a strange moment in time. It was like everything converged on one thing and nothing else mattered. We played Australia next and we scared the life out of them. It was a one-point game. Right at the end we set up a drop goal for Humps and it went just wide. He said that when the ball left his foot he would have put his house on it going through the posts, but it just faded at the last second. If that had gone through we'd have been playing Scotland in the quarter-final instead of France.

Frankie Sheahan: I had a lot of personal drama and upset leading up to that World Cup. I was drug-tested after Munster's Heineken Cup semi-final against Toulouse and the sample came up positive for Salbutamol. I'm an asthmatic and there's Salbutamol in my inhaler but what the doping people were saying to me was making no sense. I didn't tick a box on the form to say that I was taking Salbutamol for my asthma. That was my mistake, but they said I was trying to get an advantage from it even though my legal and medical team proved that I'd been asthmatic since I was a young fella and we had experts showing that you cannot enhance your performance by taking eight puffs of an inhaler before a match, which is what I did. In the biggest joke-shop of a hearing they banned me from rugby for two years. I was distraught beyond words. My integrity was blown to bits. I was branded a drugs cheat. I couldn't believe what was happening to me.

We appealed and the committee listened properly to the evidence and they overturned the original decision. I was done for not ticking the box on the form and they gave me a three-month ban for that, which I'd already served. It meant I could go to the World Cup. Fighting the case cost about €150,000, but there was a funny twist to the tale. Anthony Foley was left out of the squad, not to mind the team, to play against France in the quarter-final in Melbourne and he was down in the dumps. A few of us brought him out on the town. We hit the casino and at about 3am I was dealt the equivalent of a Royal Flush in Caribbean Stud. I won AUS$93,000 which was the same as €55,000. At the end of the World Cup the squad had a night out and the bar tab came to four grand. I picked it up and the rest of my winnings went towards the legal bill I ran up to clear my name.

Malcolm O'Kelly: We fancied our chances against France. We'd beaten them in two of the last three years and had almost beaten them two other times, so it was there for us if only we hadn't run into brick walls all day.

Ronan O'Gara: Serge Betsen caught me a beaut early in the game and more or less put me away. I was concussed but I refused to go off and I must have convinced our medical boys that I was only dazed. Playing on was a stupid thing to do but I guess I wasn't in a position to make a wise decision. I've played with concussion a couple of times and it's the weirdest feeling. Everything seems smaller. The pitch was like the size of a matchbox. I half got away with it, but I didn't really. By the time I was taken off nine minutes into the second half we were 37-0 down.

Eddie O'Sullivan: We lost 43-21. Woody was very emotional afterwards. I was crying in the changing room as well. He'd had an horrendous year. His shoulder broke down, his brother died, his mother died. He only made the World Cup by the skin of his teeth and that was him done. He was an incredible rugby player and an incredible leader. He never got a shot at a Triple Crown, which is a terrible shame. Like Gaillimh and the Claw he retired not having won anything with Ireland. That was a sad day.

He went through hell and high water with injury before the World Cup and all the way through the two of us kept saying, 'It's just another setback – the World Cup, the World Cup.' We kept thinking towards the World Cup. And he got there and the great thing was that he had a great tournament. A lesser man would have packed up his tent and said this isn't going to happen. And when he got there he didn't just say, 'I'm here now, isn't it great.' He actually delivered. He was outstanding. So all that emotion was bottled up. You're going into the Melbourne Telstra Dome to play a Test match against France at 8.30pm and at 10.30pm the best career in world rugby, as I saw it, was over. Just like that.

FIFTEEN

CROKE PARK
AND THE CLARE JERSEY IN MY BAG

The most charismatic Irish rugby player of all-time had left the stage, but the show carried on without him – and soon it would carry on without Declan Kidney as well. Eddie O'Sullivan had a brand new contract in his pocket, unlike his assistant. The forced marriage was about to be annulled.

David Wallace: When Quinny got injured against Argentina in Adelaide I got called out as his replacement. I remember speaking to Deccie and he was very disillusioned. He didn't seem to be enjoying it. I'm not sure he was appreciated. Himself and Eddie were very, very different. Deccie would have been more about the players and having a happy camp and getting fellas in the right psychological frame of mind and Eddie would have been more on the technical and less emotional side of it. Who's to say who was right and who was wrong, but I much preferred to play for Deccie.

Victor Costello: Deccie was excellent in that assistant's role even though he didn't like it. He was the kind of guy you could talk to, before he got knifed.

Eddie O'Sullivan: We tried to make it work. After the World Cup I said, 'I don't want to be seen as the bad guy, but this isn't happening, there's too much tension, nobody's happy, nobody's comfortable, this can't go on.' I had my contract extended and he didn't. It was my doing and I did it for the right reasons, but it wasn't an easy thing to do and I didn't feel good doing it. I felt bad. It was a shitty situation that we found ourselves in.

Malcolm O'Kelly: I never had a great relationship with Eddie. Maybe part of it was my own fault. I was a nightmare when it came to punctuality. I was terrible. It's incredible how many times I was late for stuff. Some coaches wouldn't bother so much, but with Eddie, it grated. I'd be two minutes late and he'd give me a right slagging and as the years went on he felt that to get the best out of me he had to give me a kick up the ass. I'd quite often get a lecture. I'd be standing over him and he'd be looking up at me and waving his finger and saying, 'I hope you have your fucking game face on.' I'd say, 'Yeah, yeah, no problem.' It wasn't exactly hugely motivating for me except for the fear factor and the humiliation of being abused in front of everybody. It was embarrassing. The worst one was when we went to La Santa in Lanzarote for a camp at the end of 2003 and we had a great week's training.

On the last night we were allowed a few beers and a few beers turned into a load of beers. Everybody was there. Great crack. I rolled into the nest at an ungodly hour. We had a gym session the next morning so everybody had to be there. Myself and Anthony Horgan were rooming together and we completely slept it out. Liam Hennessy, our fitness man, barged into our room and said, 'Get your asses out of bed.' I jumped out, got the gear on, ran down to the gym and there was nobody there. Empty. 'Where is everybody? Fuck this, back to bed.' Then Liam comes back up to the room and finds the pair of us back in our scratcher and he flips. We missed the session. The lads were in the swimming pool the whole time. At the airport Eddie comes up to us and says, 'I'm suspending you.' There was a post-Christmas training camp and we weren't allowed to go.

Then the papers got hold of it. It was a real mess. It was an unnecessarily severe punishment especially since it was the management who'd plied us with the drink in the first place. My relationship with Eddie went downhill from there.

The 2004 Six Nations brought a renaissance story in the shape of Gordon D'Arcy. It had been almost six years since D'Arcy, still a schoolboy, was invited by Warren Gatland to go on the summer tour to South Africa, the youngster declining the offer because of exams. It had been more than four years since he make his debut off the bench in a World Cup match against Romania.

In the years that followed, D'Arcy had accumulated just four more caps, all of them as a substitute. To say that he lost his way would be putting it mildly. It wasn't until Matt Williams entered the scene at Leinster and told D'Arcy some home truths that he started to turn it around.

Gordon D'Arcy: My head was still a bit up my own arse. I was thinking I was better than I was. I was complacent. I got angry with myself for what I let myself develop into. I was cutting corners. I can still remember one Sunday night going out and meeting a fella for a pint. I literally wanted to go for one and ended up having five or six. Nothing too bad, but reeking of booze the next morning. I can't drink to save my life. If I have anything over one bottle of beer I'll stink of it in the morning. So I arrived into training and Matt Williams tore me apart in front of everybody. Told me to get the fuck off the pitch. He didn't want me anywhere near the Leinster set-up.

When I wasn't getting picked for Ireland, I lost my enjoyment of playing rugby and I lost the things I enjoyed about the game, like beating a man one-on-one and putting in a good tackle. After I wasn't picked for the World Cup squad in 2003 I went home and had a good cry on the phone to my mum.

Ireland began the Six Nations poorly – an 18-point loss in Paris – but they followed it up with a thumping six-try victory over the Welsh, a game that D'Arcy lit up with his footwork and running power.

England's first match back at Twickenham after winning the World Cup was against Ireland in round three of the Six Nations. Clive Woodward's team had already put fifty points on Italy in Rome and thirty-five points on Scotland in Edinburgh and another victory was expected in the homecoming of the all-conquering heroes.

Gordon D'Arcy: All week, everybody was 'locked and loaded' as Eddie liked to put it. Brian made a throwaway comment that he hoped Ireland would make the Twickenham crowd choke on their prawn sandwiches. The English media whipped up a storm about it but we didn't let it faze us.

Shane Horgan: England emptied their tanks at the World Cup and they weren't intimidating any more. They were world champions in name only. Too many big names had gone. They were still a very good side, but they weren't intimidating. They'd lost that aura.

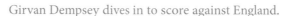

Girvan Dempsey dives in to score against England.

Shane Byrne: They genuinely discussed us clapping them on to the pitch before that match. That was suggested by the powers-that-be, the alickadoos. What they'd achieved was incredible but they were still England and we wanted to kick the shit out of them. It was the shortest discussion ever – 'Fuck off.'

Reggie Corrigan: They were coming home with the World Cup, there was a big party and we completely wrecked it. It was the best moment of my career. We were 8-1 underdogs. I rang all my mates and said, 'Lads, training is going great this week, 8-1's not a bad bet'. They said, 'Go way, you haven't a hope.' I said, 'I think we have.' We said we'll play in ten-minute blocks and try to be ahead or close in every ten-minute block. England weren't expecting the Paddys to put it up to them. They wouldn't have respected us. They thought they were a better team and they probably were. They had a lot of big names and had a right to feel arrogant. They were thinking, 'You're standing up to us but we'll get you eventually,' but we just wouldn't back off. People forget the work that Mike Ford did in sorting out our defence and even when they broke through we always had somebody to make a key tackle. Mal O'Kelly made one. Stringer made another. Girvan Dempsey finished off a great team try and it was meant to be our day.

The players celebrate their famous victory as the final whistle goes at Twickenham.

Shane Horgan: We'd already beaten Wales so now we were going for a Triple Crown against Scotland. My first rugby ball had the words Triple Crown on it. It was in my back yard for about 15 years and in all the years playing with that ball we never won a Triple Crown. When you were a kid in the 1980s in Ireland it had a romance about it.

Reggie Corrigan: We hadn't won it in nineteen years and we were terrified going into the Scottish game, absolutely shitting ourselves. Everybody was talking about the Triple Crown and I was bricking it that we would fail on the day, but we won well in Dublin.

Brian O'Driscol: Darce was on fire again. A glutton for work, a constant menace to the Scots.

Reggie Corggain: Gordon scored two of our five tries. He was unstoppable. The win was great for the players, great for the country, great for Eddie. Listen, he was never pals with any of us and I didn't mind that. Some of the lads found him aloof and he was. He could walk by you in the hotel corridor and not acknowledge your presence. But you respected him.

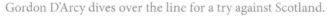

Gordon D'Arcy dives over the line for a try against Scotland.

Paul O'Connell: Eddie was excellent. I'm not the type of person that needs an arm around me, but I think certain people are. And maybe he wasn't good at that. But plenty of other coaches performed that role for him. He gave us a really good environment to train in and be the best we could be.

The players celebrate winning the Triple Crown.

Reggie Corrigan: He took all the responsibility on himself, which was a good thing and a bad thing. He didn't sleep. He'd be up all night studying DVDs and looking for an edge. He didn't delegate as well as he could have to make his life easier and he was always a man who seemed to have a burden on his shoulders. That's probably because the pressure on him to get results was huge. So I was happy for Eddie. We'd won something at long last. We were finally getting a bit of respect.

In the summer of 2004, Ireland went to South Africa for two Tests with the Springboks, who were still coming to terms with the horrors of the World Cup the year before – not so much their limp exit to New Zealand in the quarter-final but their pre-tournament training camp, the details of which caused scandal when they emerged.

Kamp Staaldraad, or Camp Barbed Wire, had created a crisis in South African rugby. Before the World Cup, the Springbok squad had been taken to the Limpopo bush two hours north of Pretoria and subjected to psychological torture and physical threats all, supposedly, in the name of team bonding.

Photographs emerged of the players crammed into foxholes while being doused with ice-cold water. *God Save the Queen* and the New Zealand haka came blaring from loudspeakers around them in some cack-handed attempt to toughen them up ahead of the World Cup.

The coach, Rudolph Straueli, was sacked and replaced by Jake White. The games with Ireland were his first as the new Springbok coach.

Paul O'Connell: I wouldn't say South Africa were in disarray but they'd had a difficult time and we thought we had a genuine chance of beating them. But we lost both Tests pretty convincingly. It was my first time playing against Bakkies Botha and Victor Matfield. I'd been aware that they were very good second-rows but I might not have been as respectful of their ability as I am now. You learn. I grew up watching Keith Wood playing for the Lions against South Africa in 1997 and there was something magical about rugby over there. We had them again in the autumn and there was a small bit of controversy before it.

Eddie O'Sullivan: After the second Test in Cape Town I told the players that we'd beat them in the autumn. I wasn't being cocky, but I knew we had the firepower to get them. I knew we could live with them physically and out-smart them.

Paul O'Connell: Jake White said that based on South Africa's playing population and physical profile they should never lose to Ireland, which might be a fair comment but it's probably not the kind of comment you want to be making the week of a Test match. He said that Drico was the only Irish player who would get on the Springbok team. We used it. Rugby is a physical thing and all those old-fashioned motivational aspects still apply. You use everything you can. And, of course, we won. It was another milestone for the team. It was the first time we'd beaten them in nearly forty years.

Ronan O'Gara: Eddie said after the game in Lansdowne Road that White's comments weren't the source of our motivation. Eddie was being diplomatic. For all the giant strides that have been made in sports science and sports psychology the power of wounded pride is still huge. At his captain's meeting on the night before the game Drico made a big play about White's lack of respect for us. I said my piece too. 'He'll remember our names tomorrow night,' was the gist of it. Malcolm said afterwards that there were fifteen bitter men going out onto the field and that's how it was. We beat them 17-12 and I got all the scores. The try was cheeky, I tapped and went when their backs were turned because the ref had asked John Smit to speak to his players, but he let the try stand and it drove them bananas.

Ronan O'Gara touches down after his quick tap penalty.

Eddie O'Sullivan: It was another great win, but I knew 2005 was going to be a ropey year, I just knew it. We won three out of five in the Six Nations, which wasn't bad given that one of the three was another win over England. But we lost our last two, against France and Wales, and then the autumn was dreadful. We played New Zealand first-up. Some new faces came in and I was warning the media, saying, 'Lads, this is going to be bumpy,' because Brian O'Driscoll and Paul O'Connell were both injured, so that's your two main leaders gone.

The All Blacks demolished us. Then we got hockeyed by Australia. It was traumatic. During the Australia game I took off Rog and put on Humps and Rog took it very personally. I had a row with him over it and it turned into a big furore. I loved Rog's directness. He'd tell me what he thought, good or bad, and that was great. He argued his corner and I respected him for it. He absolutely hated being taken off. We were up in Terenure the following week at training and he was in foul humour over the substitution. We had a discussion and he gave me two barrels about taking him off. I gave it back to him.

Ronan O'Gara: I told Eddie, 'I'm trying to organise the backs and the second things start going wrong you whip me off. I don't intend hanging around for that. I'll gladly go home and play for Munster and be happy for the rest of my career, I think I'm respected down there.' At that point he flipped. 'What's your fucking problem? You're over-reacting here. Don't be throwing the toys out of the pram.' The argument must have lasted twenty minutes.

Eddie O'Sullivan: In fairness to Rog, once he said his piece that was it, but the next thing I know it's in the *Irish Independent*. They made it look like the Irish camp was Guantanamo Bay. The flak was flying and the mood wasn't good.

Jerry Flannery: The third autumn international was against Romania and I was called into the squad. Everything was going pretty shittily when I got into camp. It was a toxic environment. The games hadn't gone well and the lads were getting panned by the media and the majority of them just wanted to get the fuck out of there. The whole vibe in Irish rugby wasn't great. Munster and Leinster both got knocked out in the quarter-finals of the Heineken Cup and Ulster didn't get out of their pool. There wasn't much feelgood. We beat Romania handily and I came off the bench for my debut, so I was thrilled. But there was a tired atmosphere in the squad.

Eddie O'Sullivan: How quickly it turns. I was told by the union that I needed to have a good Six Nations in 2006. It was conveyed informally, but I got the message.

Jerry Flannery: Limerick had a part to play in me making it. You never felt that people from Limerick got anything too easy. That's the way you were brought up. The Munster attitude is that you're better off when you have a bit of bitterness and a chip on your shoulder. I'd been waiting so long to get on the international stage that it couldn't come quickly enough for me. And things improved quickly.

We went from a shithouse atmosphere in the autumn of 2005 to a really good vibe in the Six Nations in 2006. We beat Italy, Wales and Scotland and then we headed off to Twickenham looking for a Triple Crown. I was naive in some of the things I said in the build-up to the game against England. I got asked if I was looking forward to it and I said I couldn't wait to rip into their forwards. I got pulled aside and was told that I didn't need to give them any motivation. I was innocent, but I was desperate to have a cut at these lads.

Eddie O'Sullivan: I've a good memory for these things. We were losing 24-21 and the clock was running down. We were inside our own half and Rog put in this sublime chip-kick, Drico picked it up and put Shaggy [Horgan] away in the corner. In fairness to Shaggy, he knew that Lewis Moody had him, so about 10-fifteen yards out, instead of trying to beat Moody on the outside, he cut infield and Moody tackled him and the first guy to clear out the ruck was Rog. Then Drico arrived and jammed it infield so there was another ruck on the line and Shaggy got up from the first tackle and went to the wing. Stringer went right and threw a floater over the top and Shaggy scored. I've a photographic memory for that stuff.

Shane Horgan reaches out full-stretch to score at Twickenham.

Shane Horgan: That finish was instinctive. As I was getting tackled I thought I was too far away from the line but then I realised I could see it and I felt I could reach out and get it. It all seemed to happen in slow motion. Rog jumped on me but I couldn't allow myself to celebrate because I thought if I did and the referee disallowed it because I had a foot in touch then I'm going to look like an awful eejit.

Eddie O'Sullivan: When the ref went upstairs on the try I checked the clock and there was a minute and ten seconds left. The try was good and it was a two-point lead. Niall O'Donovan was my assistant and he was sitting beside me and I said, 'This is a big kick for Rog.' He said, 'Yeah, we could do with it.' I said, 'I bet you he'll get it.' If I could give somebody a kick to save my house I'd give it to Rog. I wouldn't miss a beat on it. He had that ability. He was uncanny. It made him what he was. I knew he was going to kick that conversion.

Shane Horgan: It was a great win and another Triple Crown and the country was buzzing. For a little time after that match I had a tiny glimpse of what Brian's life was like. I got huge attention but it came and went pretty quickly whereas Brian had it all the time. It was nice for the ego but a bit draining.

Paul O'Connell and Brian O'Driscoll get the Triple Crown celebrations under way.

Jerry Flannery: We were full of confidence going to New Zealand for two Tests in the summer. We lost both of them but they were close. We had our chances. New Zealand were sloppy. I thought, 'If these guys are the benchmark then we're doing OK.'

Rory Best: My first two starts were against South Africa and Australia in the autumn of 2006. We won them both and it was very special. Rugby was in my family from way back. My grandfather played for Banbridge and my dad played for Banbridge and all my Saturday afternoons were spent down in Banbridge rugby club playing minis in the morning and watching my dad playing in the afternoon. Sundays were spent playing rugby in the garden with my brothers knocking lumps out of each other from the age of about four. We would have gone to Lansdowne Road quite a bit as a family. My grandfather used to quiz us on the way down getting us to name every town we went through on the way. It was something like twelve or thirteen different places.

Watching Ireland was a big part of my life from no age, so to be in the team was a very big deal for me. It was intimidating at the start. These guys were heroes. Some guys went into the squad and they had innate confidence and it was as if they had been there all their lives, but I wasn't able to do that.

Marcus Horan: When the bulldozers moved into Lansdowne Road, the GAA allowed us into Croke Park. My dad was from Tipperary and I would have been brought to Croke Park to watch Nicky English and Bobby Ryan and Aidan Ryan and all those fellas. But I'm a Clare man through-and-through and when Clare made the breakthrough in 1995 I was there again. I was GAA as a kid, nothing else really. I was brought up on hurling and my dream would always have been to play in Croke Park with a stick in my hand.

Jerry Flannery: I'd never been to Croke Park before the French game. Of course I hadn't. I'm from Limerick. What would I be doing above in Croke Park?

Marcus Horan: I never thought I'd get there once I turned down the rugby road. I remember talking to Martin Johnson in 2003 after the Grand Slam game and he said he saw Croke Park as they were coming into Dublin and he said it looked amazing. He said, 'Will we ever get to play there?' I said, 'Ah, there's history. We haven't a hope.' For it to happen was unbelievable.

Shane Horgan: There was this undertone among GAA people that their Irish identity was somehow different from ours. I resented this idea that just because we were playing rugby we were less Irish compared to somebody who played Gaelic. I grew up in a Gaelic community. I was first of all a GAA player. It was a big part of my life and I loved it. But there was this pressure on us. It was like, 'Jesus Christ, they've let us into Croke Park so we better not lose.'

Marcus Horan: Before I went up, I got a present from the Clare hurling team, a jersey signed by the panel. I brought it with me that day. I had it in my gear bag. It was a special thing to have.

Donncha O'Callaghan rises to win a lineout against France at Croke Park.

Rory Best: I'd been there a few times watching the Armagh footballers, but to me Croke Park didn't have the same historic appeal or emotion attached to it that Lansdowne Road would have had. I grew up watching games at Lansdowne Road not Croke Park. What was special, though, was seeing what it meant to the other boys to be playing there. You couldn't miss it and seeing what it meant to the Leinster and Munster boys just put the pressure on because on this day of all days you didn't want to let them down.

Geordan Murphy: I was selected on the wing and I missed a bad tackle on Ibanez and he scored early in the game, but we recovered and got ourselves into a winning position. I wasn't on the field at the end when Vincent Clerc went through four or five defenders but the blame was laid squarely on my shoulders, which was a bitter pill to swallow. I knew I'd cocked up with the Ibanez thing. I wasn't hiding from it, but at Leicester I'd been used to coaches taking a bit of heat off their players in tough times. Eddie didn't do that. I missed the tackle and it was a bad error, but Eddie scapegoated me, which led to a couple of verbals. It wasn't a great relationship.

David Wallace: The endgame was sickening, absolutely sickening. And it gets more sickening as the years go by.

Paul O'Connell: I'd have a lot of regrets about that one. We won a lineout just around halfway and we mauled them downfield twenty-five or thirty metres, got the penalty and Rog put it over and that gave us a four point lead. It should have been a nail in the coffin for them. They were going deep with their restarts all day so I set back but I should have known they were going to go short. They had to get the ball back and the only way they were going to do it was by kicking short and it was a poor decision from me. I should have been up more flat. And then I got taken out on the way to the ball which would have been a nice one had the ref given me the penalty, but he didn't. They won the kick-off and two or three phases later Clerc went under the posts. It was devastating.

John Hayes: They threw a long skip pass to Clerc. He had men over, but I'd say his eyes lit up when he saw me in front of him. I thought I had him; I got a hand on him, but he just skinned me on the outside.

Denis Hickie: It was a slow motion thing at the end. I was coming across but couldn't get to Clerc in time. I was closing in on him but there wasn't enough space. It was a horrible feeling.

Marcus Horan: It's amazing how a game can affect you. It wasn't a final and there was no trophy, but it felt like the worst defeat ever. To get our noses ahead with so little time left on the clock, you would have expected us to put it away. That was the hardest thing to deal with, the fact that we had it in our hands and we let it slip through our fingers.

Eddie O'Sullivan: We had England at Croke Park and the one thing we couldn't do was play badly. There was no next day. This was it. It was a game of rugby that we could not lose under any circumstances, which is a lot of pressure. What hit you more and more as the week went on was that there were people invested in this emotionally who had nothing to do with rugby. This was a national historical event and you had responsibility for how it turned out, but you didn't want to think about that too much because it wasn't going to make you feel any better.

I was trying to play it down but once we got to forty-eight hours from kick-off I was losing the battle. Guys just knew the magnitude of it. My worry was that we would end up playing the occasion and not the game. My abiding memory was of the tension on the bus going to the ground. It was extraordinary. I asked myself, 'Why am I doing this? I could be at home with a beer in front of me watching it on TV,' My life was in a grinder.

Paul O'Connell: I get stressed before games sometimes. I get a fear of the feeling that you get when you lose. I get nervous and I don't want to be there anymore.

Rory Best: Sometimes, going to the ground, you'd rather be anywhere else than sitting on the bus and looking out the window.

Paul O'Connell: You'd be looking out the window and you know that if we lose then these people will be very disappointed, but they won't go through what I have to go through. There'd be fellas drinking pints and other fellas walking to the ground with their kids and you'd almost be jealous of them. That feeling passes pretty quickly, but for a few seconds you wish you were out there with them having a sup of that pint.

Brian O'Driscoll: The beauty of our sport, what sets it apart from so many others, is that often it comes down to who has the greater desire on the day, because at Test level there's often very little between two teams. At Croke Park on 24 February 2007, there are no circumstances under which it is possible for England to want it more.

David Wallace: It felt different. At the anthems, Hayes and Fla were crying. I never witnessed an anthem like it. .

Brian O'Driscoll: I was oblivious to it. I didn't know it was going on. Hayes was never one for singing anthems too loud, so I couldn't tell if there was emotion or not. It was only subsequently I saw them, when I saw the tears in the pictures. If

I had known, I don't know if I would have started laughing or whether I'd have started crying myself. You knew how important the game was when that freak was crying.

John Hayes: It was just a bit overwhelming. I felt the weight of responsibility. We were trusted to look after the place and not let the country down. And the missed tackle on Clerc had been haunting me. I took personal responsibility for that and I'd carried it with me for two weeks. I badly wanted to make amends. So the whole day took on an extra bit of meaning for me. I can only say that when the waterworks came I was as surprised as anyone.

Fire and ice: Brian O'Driscoll remains focussed during the national anthems, while the emotion of the occasion is writ large on John Hayes' face.

Jerry Flannery: It was very hard to ignore the history of playing the English at Croke Park. It was difficult to cocoon yourself away from that. I never sang the national anthem before that. I used to get too worked up and I didn't have a clear head for the first five or ten minutes of the match, so I never sang it. But that day I said if I don't sing it at Croke Park against England then I'm never going to sing it. I was very conscious of the English anthem and very proud of the respect it got. Then for our own, I was all over the place. You're standing there thinking about all the people that helped you get to that stage and how proud you want to make them and I was in bits. It was lucky that Rory was starting. I'd have been useless.

Paul O'Connell: We used the emotion of the occasion massively. The anthems that day, I know it's cheesy to say it, but they were incredible. I remember saying to myself that I'd never be part of something like this again.

Shane Horgan: When *God Save the Queen* was so well respected it was almost disarming for the English team. Martin Corry, who's a really nice guy, applauded the crowd after it.

Eddie O'Sullivan: I've got great time for Martin Corry – a real warrior. He didn't have to applaud the crowd after *God Save the Queen*. He had a game to play and he shouldn't be worried about applauding anybody, but that was the magnitude of the guy. It was fantastic that he had the presence of mind to do that as the England captain. But then our anthem was played and fellas were crying all over the place.

Shane Horgan celebrates his try with Denis Hickie and Girvan Dempsey.

I said, 'Jesus, some of the lads are emotional wrecks and they have a game to play now'. I mean, John Hayes was roaring crying. 'Are our heads in the right place?' Against France, it took us twenty minutes to get ourselves together just because of the enormity of the occasion. We watched them for twenty minutes and if we did the same against England we'd be fucked.

Brian O'Driscoll: Luckily it didn't become overwhelmingly emotional for me. I think that I was just so focused on the game that I wasn't going to allow my emotions to boil over. At times I've been teary-eyed singing the national anthem in big games, but I think I was so focused on our performance, the process of that performance, that I wasn't going to allow any external factors put me off. You can see me smiling in the huddle just before kick-off, barely able to contain myself. I was just so excited to get out and play.

Shane Horgan: We had done a lot of homework on England and we knew that Jonny was a great defender in one-on-one tackles but he used to leave space on the inside shoulder, he used to disconnect and we went in there loads of times. It was a smart play by Eddie. Physically and emotionally we were on top but we coped very well technically.

Rory Best: We were 23-3 ahead at half-time. In my memory, all matches of significance seem to end with the rain falling softly with about twenty minutes to go and it was the same that day. The rain drifted in ever-so-slightly and the *Fields of Athenry* filled Croke Park. We had the game won and we cruised through those closing stages. It ended 43-13. It was bliss.

Eddie O'Sullivan: If you'd said to me the night before, 'OK, write your dream script for this game,' I couldn't have written anything different. To deliver such a clinical performance under that pressure was pretty extraordinary. There was magic in it.

Paul O'Connell: We did the occasion justice.

Brian O'Driscoll: Call it a perfect day.

Marcus Horan: The fact that we had lost to France was the driving force. After losing that game there was no way on this earth we were going to lose to England. The elation of beating them, and the manner in which we beat them, was amazing but ten minutes afterwards we were sitting in the dressing room and there was a real sense of deflation and a realisation of what we'd left behind us against France.

That's when it hit home. We had highs and lows that day. A lot of people would have thought that we'd be going mental inside in the dressing room after beating England but we weren't.

Jerry Flannery: What stood out was how humble and how gracious the English players were after the game. Phil Vickery was their captain and he got up to speak at the dinner at the Shelbourne and he was so thoughtful and generous. He said that there was only one team in it and that he knew how much the occasion meant to us and I was sitting there listening to him thinking, 'This is a great guy.' He was hurting massively but all he did was make us feel better about our big day and that was a top class thing to do.

David Wallace: We went on to beat Scotland at Murrayfield and then we went to Rome for our last match. We had Italy, and France were at home to Scotland in the late kick-off, and we knew the Championship was going to come down to points difference.

Denis Hickie: The priority was to win, but we were also very aware of the Championship coming down to points difference. I'm sure we had spoken publicly about focusing on performance and winning the game, but privately we focused on scoring as many points as we could from the start.

Ronan O'Gara: We ripped them apart.

Denis Hickie: At half-time we knew that there was another twenty or thirty points in us. Sometimes you just get a sense. We felt we had another couple of gears in us. We put fifty-one points on them but we conceded a try late on. Initially we thought we might have done enough but then in the changing room we realised we'd put ourselves in danger of not doing enough. Back at the hotel, some of the guys watched it on TV but myself and Shaggy went down to the pool to do a recovery session. We didn't watch the match and we didn't hear any of the roars. Marcus Horan came down to the pool to say that France had scored in the last minute and that was it.

It was disappointing but there was a silver lining. The World Cup was coming up and we were flying. We were in the form of our lives. Everybody was excited about going to France. We couldn't wait.

SIXTEEN

WE PLAYED LIKE A HORSE'S ASS

In the wake of the Six Nations, Ireland were installed as fourth favourite to win the World Cup in France in the autumn, behind New Zealand, South Africa and the host nation, but ahead of Australia and the defending champions, England.

The mood in the camp was one of embracing expectation. Instead of playing it down, some of the Irish players talked it up. 'We have to be one of the top four or five who can actually win it,' said Brian O'Driscoll.

Ireland's preparation involved a whole load of training and not a lot of matches. They played Scotland in Murrayfield – and lost. They had a match with Bayonne in the south of France – and it was a calamity. Bayonne were more interested in looking for scalps than looking for scores.

'That was the filthiest match I ever played in,' wrote Donncha O'Callaghan in *Joking Apart*. 'At the first lineout one of their guys grabbed my balls; later on, one of them head-butted me while I was lying on the ground.' After an hour, O'Driscoll warned referee, Wayne Barnes, that unless he did something about the incessant stamping and biting and gouging then he was taking his players off the pitch. Soon after, the captain got a thump in the face from a Bayonne bruiser that fractured his sinus. 'Two yards away and a split-second later Marcus Horan also hits the floor and another scrap breaks out all around him,' wrote O'Driscoll in his autobiography, *The Test*. 'Our medics burst on to the pitch, like scalded cats.'

The final warm-up game was against Italy in Ravenhill. An understrength Ireland scraped home by three points. They looked undercooked and ill-prepared for a World Cup – a shadow of the team that almost won the Championship five months earlier.

Jerry Flannery: The World Cup. Christ. Let me get into a dark room and have a think about it.

Paul O'Connell: We trained the house down before the World Cup. I think we over-trained. We never really had a down-week during the training phase and it's important to let the body rest. Any time off we were given we were all training on our own. We were a very, very driven group of people and I know when I had time

Opposite. Malcolm O'Kelly hangs his head as Juan Martin Fernandez Lobbe of Argentina celebrates their late drop goal in the 2007 Rugby World Cup pool encounter.

off I rarely took it. I used to train and if I was doing it then Donners was doing it, Rog was doing it, Stringer was doing it, everybody was doing it. We were just flat when we got to France. We couldn't get going.

Eddie O'Sullivan: The catastrophic decision was to play only two warm-up Tests and that ultimately was the problem. I knew we were in trouble the night we played Italy in Ravenhill and Rog got a late try to win the game. Only five months earlier we had gone to Rome and put fifty-one points on them. We did too much training and we should have played more games and then I compounded the problem by not putting the starters out against Scotland. Outside of Drico and Paulie the rest of them were rested. We went to a training camp in the south of France and played against Bayonne and a guy cheap-shotted Drico. That was a mistake, that game. But it was necessary to play it. I knew we were short of match practice.

Denis Hickie: Eddie was calling all the shots and there wasn't anybody there acting as a foil, the way Brian O'Brien had done when he was manager. Eddie was controlling everything and everybody was doing what he wanted them to do. That manifested itself in our preparation, which was awful. He needed somebody to challenge him on that stuff.

Rory Best: He was a brilliant coach but he didn't have coaches around him that were up to the level he was. When things started to crumble and he was looking for support nobody really ventured much of an opinion because that was the culture that had been created. Eddie wanted to keep control of everything himself and everybody else knew their place. That was Eddie's biggest undoing.

David Wallace: It was like there was a big cloud over the team. We had no momentum and it seems a trivial thing to say but the food was awful in the hotel in France. Somebody went in to the kitchen on the first day and showed the chef how to make porridge. We ate Nutella sandwiches. I lost about 10kgs. A lot of guys would have lost weight.

Donncha O'Callaghan: The flavour of Nutella is the bad taste of the 2007 World Cup.

Jerry Flannery: The place was grim.

Andrew Trimble: We were stuck in this hotel in an industrial estate in Bordeaux. Now, Bordeaux is a beautiful place, but we never got to see it.

Denis Hickie: We were supposed to stay in a lovely Radisson in the centre of town but it wasn't finished in time so they put us out in the sticks and it was crap. Nothing to do. Bored out of our minds.

Eddie O'Sullivan: A big fuss was made about the hotel. The hotel in Bordeaux was the best hotel we could get. The other ones were unsuitable, they were out in the country. We tried to bring our own chef and were told by the IRB that that was unacceptable, we had to use the hotel chef. He was supposed to be a Michelin star chef. It wasn't a bad place but because things were going badly, that stuff gets magnified.

Jerry Flannery: We had Namibia first-up. I'm getting horrible flashbacks here.

Ronan O'Gara: Namibia had six professional players in their squad. In their final warm-up match they had lost to South Africa by 105-13. We were expected to beat them by fifty or sixty points at our ease. Instead we got a dodgy late try to win by fifteen. We were brutal. The worst performance any of us could remember.

Eddie O'Sullivan: We were undercooked and went out in the first match and played really badly against Namibia and everybody got a bit panicky and tight. Fellas started to doubt themselves.

Ronan O'Gara: Fellas were saying all the right things afterwards. Disgrace. Unacceptable. Take a look at yourselves. All the things you'd expect. Eddie hammered us. Brian hammered us. We hammered ourselves. But where was it getting us? Nowhere. Attitude wasn't the problem. We couldn't try any harder. We couldn't have been more desperate to make it right. We analysed ourselves to death. We knew what was going wrong, we just didn't know why. Everyone was making two or three errors that they hadn't been making in the Six Nations. Multiply that by fifteen players and you're looking at thirty or forty mistakes. Namibia made twelve unforced errors; we made eighteen. We're the professionals. How do you explain that? We couldn't.

Paul O'Connell: You always think it's going to come right, though. After the Namibia match I wasn't going, 'Oh fuck, I can't wait for this to be over.' You just think that something's going to click.

Ronan O'Gara: Brian stopped me in the corridor at the hotel one night. It was a couple of days after we played Namibia, a few days before the Georgia match.

He was tearing his hair out. Totally bewildered. He asked what the hell was going wrong and I honestly didn't have an answer.

Eddie O'Sullivan: Then Georgia. We played like a horse's ass. Edgy. Dropping balls. Sloppy. Then panicking about it.

Denis Hickie: I didn't play well. I got a really bad clash of heads in the first game against Namibia and I wasn't really right for the rest of the game. I don't know if I was concussed, but didn't play well in that game and I didn't play well in the second game against Georgia and the pressure was mounting. Guys who were performing well for three years in a row suddenly weren't playing well and I was one of those guys and I think Eddie felt let down by that. He had a real go at me after the Georgia game. 'You played shit in the first game and you've played shit in this game.'

Jerry Flannery: It was an absolute fuck-up. After Georgia, we'd reached panic mode. We were spending longer and longer on the training pitch. Everything snowballed.

Denis Hickie: I was finishing after the World Cup and that's what made it worse. I knew this was how it was going to end. Guys who had so many great days and who'd achieved a lot were looking at each other going, 'Why can't we do it?'

Geordan Murphy: The mood was low and the rumour mill was flying. Somebody was having an affair with somebody else's wife. Peter Stringer had punched Ronan O'Gara at training. I'd walked out. It was a circus.

Jerry Flannery: Geordan was supposed to have fucked off to Derry.

David Wallace on the charge against Georgia.

Marcus Horan: There was another one that he'd gone to Mexico.

Jerry Flannery: He was sitting opposite me at the dinner table.

David Wallace: Myself and Hayes were supposed to have had a fight.

Jerry Flannery: People were making shit up.

Eddie O'Sullivan: We used to read the rumours out on the way to training on the bus. There was a rumour that Denis Leamy had diabetes and I wouldn't let him take his insulin. There was a rumour about a player being seen going into a hotel in the afternoon with a woman in Bordeaux. And he did – it was his wife. Frankie Sheahan would read them out on the bus.

The media bought into it. I talked to a journalist and he said, 'What's going on?' and I said, 'On my mother's grave, there's nothing going on, you have to stop believing this nonsense.' He looked at me like, 'I'm not sure.' We realised that this wasn't funny anymore. People were believing this crap. A French journalist did a number on Rog and his supposed gambling debts. I got stuck into the French journalist about what he wrote about Rog and then the journalist did a number on me and painted me as Osama Bin Laden. In fairness to Rog, I knew it was wearing him down. It was vicious stuff.

Ronan O'Gara: How do these things start? Who makes them up? We're a nation of gossipers, that's at the heart of it. When we hear bad news, we can't wait to pass it on. We don't question it. If it's bad news we assume it must be true.

Marcus Horan: It was depressing. We were laughing on the bus and five minutes later we were thinking, 'What the fuck is going on at home?' It had an effect on players. A lot of us became reclusive. When things went wrong there were guys not socialising. We were hitting the laptops more in an attempt to figure out what was going wrong. We were trying to catch up.

Donncha O'Callaghan: I remember looking at the Georgian players as they walked out and thinking they were all the same shape. You couldn't tell the second-rows from the scrum-half. They all seemed to be about 6ft 3in, eighteen or so stone and square. It was the most physical game I'd ever played in. They were like the world's hardest junior team. Every time they got the ball they wanted to run over the top of us. After every hit you were rocked. This was old-fashioned rugby, dog eat dog.

Rory Best: Donners said that the World Cup never existed, we just moved out of the country for a month. The reality is that Georgia probably deserved to beat us when they mauled us over our line towards the end, which would have given them the win, which is a frightening thing to think about.

Donncha O'Callaghan: Georgia were camped on our line, looking for the try that would destroy us and our World Cup. They were picking and jamming, picking and jamming, and we were hanging on for dear life. When they finally got over the line the referee went to the television match official. The replays seemed to show that Denis Leamy got his hand under the ball before it was grounded and the try wasn't given. From what I could see Denis got his hand under the ball after it had been grounded. The TMO didn't have that camera angle. We got away with murder.

Brian O'Driscoll: It was like we'd spent the best part of four years preparing to be tested at the highest level, then some impostors had gone in and sat the examination.

Ronan O'Gara: A couple of months after the World Cup I watched the last few minutes of the Georgia game on DVD. Sitting down, a long way from the battlefield, and watching it on screen it looked even worse. They were within

Brian O'Driscoll cuts a despondent figure in the wake of the loss to France.

inches of beating us. Losing that match would have been the lowest point in the history of Irish rugby. Winning that match seemed the lowest point in the history of Irish rugby.

Eddie O'Sullivan: There was no discord in the camp, the team just played badly. It was down to the fact that we hadn't played enough warm-up matches. I'd swear on a Bible at my mother and father's grave that there was nothing else going on at that World Cup other than guys trying their guts out to overcome a lack of confidence and me being unable to turn it around. We lost to France and Argentina and we came home with our tails between our legs.

Looking back on it now, Ireland was in the throes of the greatest economic boom in its history and the biggest problem people were facing was whether to buy another investment property, take a second holiday or buy a third car – those were the big issues in life. Rugby was the hottest ticket in town and everybody was set-up for a trip to France and 'Ole! Ole!' moments in every bar in Ireland and we came up painfully short. We crashed and burned. The vitriol that was unleashed was like, 'How dare you do this to us?' We had created expectation. With every step forward, expectation goes up. The whole thing was a massive damp squib. And somebody had to pay for it.

Jerry Flannery: We were flying home and wondering if people would be throwing eggs at us at Dublin airport. Myself, Hayes, Horan, Paulie, Tony Buckley, there was a bus that brought us back to Limerick and my mates had stuck up a load of balloons outside the house and they were playing that Coldplay song, *Fix You*.

When you try your best, but you don't succeed
When you get what you want, but not what you need
When you feel so tired, but you can't sleep
Stuck in reverse
Bastards!

I was so used to walking around Limerick with my head held high. People would look at you after games, win or lose, and they'd know that you'd given it everything you had and that was good enough. I remember walking down O'Connell Street after the World Cup and thinking, 'These people must think we're a right bunch of wankers.' It still rankles, that World Cup. One big clusterfuck – that's an Eddie O'Sullivan word.

Rob Kearney: When the Six Nations came around you could sense that there was a little bit of fragility in the environment and we knew that if we didn't have a good Championship then the coach was going to be under pressure.

Tommy Bowe dives in to score despite the efforts of Scotland flanker Ross Rennie.

Eddie O'Sullivan: The union gave me the Six Nations to get my house in order and I didn't get it done. The vitriol was still there from the World Cup. The players were behind me but there was a lot of sulphur in the air. We played badly against Italy but we got a win. Then we went to France and had a poor start but nearly came back and beat them. Against Scotland, we beat the snot out of them at Croke Park. Then the big crunch game against Wales – Wazza rolls into town and we started that game well and we were all over them. They were hanging on by their fingernails. Shaggy got held up over the line and had we got that try then they were in big trouble. As it was, we lost 16-12.

Brian O'Driscoll: Sometimes when you hit a downward spiral it's hard to break the fall.

Donncha O'Callaghan: To a certain extent Eddie changed in front of our eyes. The absolute conviction that he brought to team meetings and the training ground slipped a little. With twenty minutes to go in the Wales game the system was basically thrown out the window by the players and we started playing a different game to the one Eddie had laid out for us. If that had happened at any other time in his reign as coach there would have been blood on the walls at the next video session, but he seemed to accept it. Losing to Wales with Warren Gatland as their coach would have been a bitter pill for Eddie with their personal history. Around that time nothing was easy for Eddie.

Warren Gatland: I loved it. When I came out of the coaches box at Croke Park I made so much noise, I was jumping up and down and fist-pumping so that people could hear me. I did it deliberately.

Eddie O'Sullivan: It was a sore one given all that had gone before, but that night at the dinner at the Shelbourne Hotel I went over to Warren's table and asked him to come up for a pint at the bar. The place almost fell silent when the two of us walked out of the room. I said to him, 'Warren, I think you've been very unfair to me for the last number of years over why things went wrong for you with Ireland. I did my best for you when I was your assistant and I never had anything to do

Alun-Wyn Jones, Gethin Jenkins and Ian Gough celebrate the victory at Croke Park that was one of the last actions of the Eddie O'Sullivan era.

with you getting the chop.' It was a bit awkward but once we cleared the air and started talking about other stuff it was fair enough.

Shane Horgan: We should have won the Wales game but now we had to go to Twickenham for a do-or-die match – and we died.

Donncha O'Callaghan: We caved in that day. It was the first time I had experienced that in a green jersey. There had been other bad beatings, but this was different. The World Cup had been a disaster but every time we took the field at that tournament we believed in what we were doing and we believed we were going to win. At Twickenham we didn't believe in anything.

Shane Horgan: There was nothing in the well. The bad momentum from the World Cup couldn't be arrested. The thing had gone and Eddie knew it.

Donncha O'Callaghan: I felt some players were hiding behind him, blaming Eddie for our performances instead of looking at themselves. I stayed away from

Eddie O'Sullivan at the fulltime whistle at Twickenham.

whatever bitching was going on. He'd been a good coach for us, and I was loyal to him. He could have been leading us into the fires of hell but I was willing to follow him.

Shane Horgan: He came into the changing room afterwards and he went around to every player and thanked them. He didn't say he was going, but you sensed it. It was such a classy thing to do. I have a really fond memory of that. It was very touching as well. We played like shit in that match and he should have been giving out to us, but he wasn't going to have his last interaction with his players ending in screaming and shouting.

Eddie O'Sullivan: I had to admit to myself that I hadn't been able to turn it around. The stick in the media was getting worse and worse, not just towards me but towards the team and it was impacting on the players. To stay on would have been impossible. The pounding was only going to increase if I'd dug in.

The perception of me in Ireland is bad. I know it is. There's a legacy there from when Warren went. The perception is that I'm a narcissistic control freak who bullies people – all that stuff has been written about me. But I've a good relationship with the players I coached. I think there's a respect there. The only one who has said bad things about me is Geordan Murphy, who wrote some appalling stuff about me in his book. I was disappointed in that. His premis was that I didn't pick him because I didn't like him. That's a horrible thing to say about a coach. Your integrity is all you have. He got fifty caps on my watch. How can you say that you got seventy-six caps and the guy who gave you fifty of them didn't pick you enough?

That jars, but it's isolated. For the sake of the team, for the sake of my family and for my own sake I had to walk after the Six Nations. Leaving was the right thing to do. You can only take so many kickings.

SEVENTEEN

DECCIE, WHAT'S GOING ON, MAN?

David Wallace: When a coach comes under the amount of fire that Eddie came under it sends a lot of upheaval into the team. Everybody feels it and there's only one way out. Deccie arrived on the back of Munster winning a second Heineken Cup and he instilled confidence where previously there wasn't any. We had a meeting in Enfield, County Meath, in the autumn which has gone down in folklore as the moment it all came good. This was the kind of thing that Deccie was excellent at. He created the kind of environment which allowed us to talk freely about what the issues were. And Rob Kearney led the charge.

Rob Kearney: It's probably been blown out of proportion. Had we failed that year I probably would have been cast as the villain for causing the downfall of Irish rugby but because we did well people looked at it little bit more deeply. My point was that I always used to look at Thomond Park in awe at what was created down there. I was envious of the intensity and the atmosphere at Munster matches because Lansdowne Road was never like that. I was 100% envious of what Munster had. When you want to become the best you look at the best and you try and figure out what they have and what you don't and Munster had something really special. We were divided into little groups that day in Enfield and in my group I questioned why we didn't have that Munster feeling in an Irish jersey. I wasn't questioning the commitment of the Munster players' commitment to the Ireland cause. That's not what I was doing.

It was something that needed to be aired. Everyone else in the country was talking about it except the players in the team. A lot of the media were talking about it. I hadn't planned on saying it. I almost walked myself into it. I said it to my group of about five or six or seven people and then it got brought up in the wider group so I was put on the spot to back up my comments. I couldn't bottle it at that stage. Rog had said something similar a few weeks before but it's OK for somebody who was such a cornerstone of the team and such a huge personality to question it but when a twenty-two year old from Leinster with five caps talks about it then it's very different.

Opposite: Brian O'Driscoll at fulltime at the Millennium Stadium in Cardiff, 2009.

Jerry Flannery: Marcus Horan spoke up and said he would be quite offended if somebody thought that he was somehow more passionate about wearing the red jersey than he was the green jersey and I'd have been pretty offended as well if that was what Rob meant, but it wasn't.

David Wallace: It was to do with all provincial teams. He said, 'We're passionate for our provinces and sometimes that gets lost with Ireland.'

Marcus Horan: Rog said to me later that he was in the group with Rob and he didn't mean it the way I thought he meant it. What he meant was we all need to have Munster's passion when we play for Ireland. I came in from training and I saw Rob and I went over to him and said, 'Fair play to you for what you said, it took balls for a young lad to say that in a group, it could be just what we need to get guys focused.' Maybe it was the elephant in the room.

David Wallace: Deccie was standing away to the side. He would have loved it. That's the kind of thing he was brilliant at.

Ronan O'Gara: It's hard to describe it, but Deccie had a way of connecting people. From then on, there was a new code of honesty in the team.

Geordan Murphy: I had a lot of warmth for Deccie. Now, he could rub you up the wrong way and some of the lads got pissed off with him at times, but he tried to be honest. He talked to you.

Tommy Bowe: He was excellent at motivating players. He had a way of getting us up for games. When he came in he brought excellent coaches like Les Kiss and Gert Small and Alan Gaffney and they had new ideas. Deccie was an over-seer. He was in the background but he was always there.

Rory Best: To be fair to him, he was brilliant at team talks. We played Canada in the autumn of 2008 and it was phenomenal. I thought, 'If he's like this for Canada then what's he going to be like when we play the All Blacks?' Deccie had a really good knack of making it feel really special, no matter who we were playing against.

Paul O'Connell: We had a poor autumn in 2008 but we dug in and got a very important win against Argentina and we probably weren't given the credit we deserved. It gave us a lift. In the Six Nations we were very much the underdogs. We got a big result in the first game against France and suddenly we had some momentum. We'd dispatched one of the big teams and we were in with a big shout from then on. It was my first time beating France and to do something you haven't done before it gives you some mojo.

A year earlier, in the opening round of the Six Nations against Italy, Gordon D'Arcy had broken his arm in five places. He had three operations and in the months that followed the rumour mill went wild about his long-term prognosis. Some said we'd seen the last of him – at twenty-eight.

Declan Kidney took a leap of faith in selecting D'Arcy for the France game. He'd seen limited action for Leinster and Lansdowne, but Kidney put him on the bench against the French and then put him into the action just after an hour's play. Then he scored.

Luke Fitzgerald: You could see from everyone's reaction, after Darce scored, how much it meant to all the people around him. We were so delighted that he was back and competing at the highest level. It was a year of frustration and I'd say he was anxious, really worried about his injury. We were as well. There were rumours, there were whispers. It didn't look good for him.

Gordon D'Arcy: It was strange. After I scored the try, running back for the kick-off, there was a moment of clarity. I thought, 'It's all finished now, all done, all behind me – the injury is gone.' For your really close mates to be the guys picking you up off the ground is brilliant. Somebody got the photograph, framed it and sent it to me – it was waiting in the hotel when we got back. And if you look at that photograph, Brian is there, Rob is there, Luke is there, Jamie's there – he's the guy that's first in. Looking at it, you can see they're so happy for me – it means as much to them as it does to me.

It's very hard to articulate something like that, it's a very personal moment. The three or four seconds when you're being yanked up off the ground and everyone slapping you on the head and going, 'Well done! Great try!' – that's fantastic but that's not it. It's the ten or so metres when you're running back to the halfway line, when you're on your own and you have a few seconds for your own thoughts – that's when something clicks inside you. I suppose that's when the reality kicks in. The people who sent me that picture, maybe they don't understand just how symbolic the whole gesture of framing that moment was for me. I'm a big believer that what you do in your life makes you who and what you are – and while you'll always remember the good times, you should never forget the bad times either.

Declan Kidney: When Gordon scored the try the whole team was thrilled for him. Two days of meetings in Enfield didn't lead to that warmth, the camaraderie that people saw then – it was always there. And not alone is it a great try, it's a try scored by one of our own, who had fought his way back. Does it get any better in rugby? Not for me.

John Hayes: We played Italy. One of their former props, Massimo Cuttitta, was quoted earlier in the week as saying that Martin Castrogiovanni, their tight-head, was going to give Marcus a hard time in the scrums. Needless to say, Marcus was ready for battle. And Donncha, who was pushing behind Marcus, wasn't going to take a backward step either. Then the first scrum collapsed and Castrogiovanni decided to have a few words with Horan. I heard him saying it, something like, 'It's going to be long day for you.' He was trying to look all menacing. Castrogiovanni is a good player but a bit of a bullshitter. I told him to shut the fuck up and I wasn't the only one. There were fellas queuing up to have their say. The funny thing was that he had to go off injured about twenty minutes later. He got a right volley of abuse in his ear. ''Twas a fairly fuckin' short day for you!'

Donncha O'Callaghan: I'm friends with Marcus, more so than just team-mates. I knew the agony he went through over that. He was hurting, it really upset him. But I saw it as a rallying call for the whole pack. I thought Castrogiovanni was questioning the whole lot of us, not just Marcus, because we were a unit and we stuck together.

Tommy Bowe: We beat Italy and then we ground out a win over England. It wasn't exciting. It was just brutal. I remember Drico taking a serious smack at one stage. Everybody was out on their feet after that game, everybody put their bodies on the line. It was one of the most physical matches I was ever part of. When we won there was no celebration, we just went back into the dressing room and you would think after beating England everybody would be jumping about but guys were lying on the floor, bloodied, knackered, happy but exhausted. Shattered and battered.

Stephen Ferris: I got showered and changed. I was completely punctured, zapped, wrecked. There's a warm-up area in Croke Park and I went in and slept for half an hour. I'd never felt such exhaustion in all my life.

Marcus Horan: When the team to play Scotland was announced there were four changes and I gasped. Jamie Heaslip, Jerry Flannery, Tomas O'Leary and Paddy Wallace – all gone. 'What's Deccie doing? Why is he dropping the boys? How are they going to react?' I was really thinking that it was madness.

Peter Stringer darts off the back of a line-out to set up Jamie Heaslip to score against Scotland in Edinburgh.

Tommy Bowe: That scared the wits out of everybody. We had three wins under our belt and people were getting dropped.

Jerry Flannery: Deccie was messing with my head. I'd seen him do things like that with Munster but I wasn't on the receiving end of it. I was horrified when I was told I wasn't starting against Scotland. I said, 'We've won our first three games here, we've beaten England and France and now you have taken my chance of playing in a Grand Slam out of my hands'. I went into him. I said, 'What's going on, man?' He said, 'Rory has been going well in training and deserves a chance.' It was such a shock. I said, 'Training! He's going well in training!' It was a complete head-fuck.

Marcus Horan: It might have been a stroke of genius. The boys who were dropped reacted brilliantly.

Rory Best: I'd been coming off the bench and doing well and then I started against Scotland and did well and I thought I had a chance of playing in the big one against Wales. Deccie said, 'I'm going with Jerry, I'm sure you have some questions.' I said, 'No,' and I got up and walked out. I said, 'I don't want to hear it,' and that was almost the worst thing you could have said to Deccie. He wanted some comfort from me that it was OK, but it wasn't OK. I had a few of those sorts of meetings with Deccie before. I was used to them. He'd say, 'I don't really know what to tell you, it's a tough call but we're going with Jerry because of the Munster combo with Marcus and Hayes and Donners and Paulie,' and I'd say, 'That's grand, Deccie, but I played my whole Ireland career with those guys so it's not like we're strangers.' Whether he was holding something back, I don't know. I always felt that he wasn't being brutally honest with me.

Jamie Heaslip roars in celebration as he crosses to score at Murrayfield. The Grand Slam showdown with Wales was now on.

Rob Kearney: On the road to Cardiff, the Scotland game was the scariest. We played England and it was incredibly close but the Grand Slam wasn't real at that point. It was only when we went to Scotland that it became tangible. 'Wait a second, this could be on.' If we won in Edinburgh we were going to Wales for a Grand Slam, so from a mental perspective it was the toughest. Youth and naivety probably played in my favour.

Brian O'Driscoll: There's lots of coulds and ifs and maybes in rugby and especially in tournaments like the Six Nations. People look back at the '07 Six Nations when we lost to France in the last minute at Croke Park and they say, 'Oh, we should have had a Slam that year.' But if you win that game it adds different pressures to the subsequent games and you react differently to those stresses, so you can't ever dictate or predict exactly how something is going to work out off the back of result A or result B. It doesn't work that way.

But when we got to '09, we won the first three games then we had Scotland away and then Wales and people were already talking about the Grand Slam decider before we'd even been to Edinburgh – but that was a really tricky one over in Scotland. We managed to win it and then we did have that deciding game in Cardiff, but there are such small margins in these campaigns. It's all about momentum in the Six Nations, and we had it that year, but it could so easily have gone against us. It's a cliché to talk about fine margins, or to cite the Any Given Sunday 'inches' speech, but it really is that fine a margin between the top international teams. It can be the bounce of the ball, one missed tackle, a lapse in concentration, someone just slightly fatigued, someone being nudged off the ball, a penalty decision being the matter of opinion of the officials – any of these things can be the difference. You get some and you lose other ones.

Donncha O'Callaghan: I found the week leading up to matches torturous, the whole preparation, the getting ready for it. As much as you try and do other things, you can't. There's no escape. I chatted to our sports psychologists about it and they asked me, 'How are you not enjoying it? You're living the dream in front of 80,000 people.' The preparation is intense, the pressure of big games. I always want to be on the other side of it. On the Monday before I'd have paid money to be transported to the other side of the Saturday and be sitting in the dressing room with a win, that lovely twenty minutes before somebody goes and ruins it by saying, 'Another big one next week lads.'

Jerry Flannery: I knew Rory would play well against Scotland, I just knew it. He's a class player. Why wouldn't he play well? So I didn't know if I was going to start against Wales. I also had a shoulder injury the early part of the week of the match. I was dosed on painkillers and I couldn't lift my arms above my head and it was Brian Green, the physio, who didn't give up. I was thinking, 'My fucking chance is gone.' But he got me right and then Deccie read out my name and I couldn't believe it. I remember taking my strapping off my wrist and saying to myself, 'I'm back!'

Brian O'Driscoll: Travelling to games, I tended not to switch on mentally to the game until I arrive at the ground and come back in from walking around the pitch. Basically because I didn't have the capacity to concentrate for two-and-a-half hours solid, so I'd try and relax and have a laugh until that point. Over the course of the years you try and test other things and you work out what's best for you. I tried listening to music for a while, but that didn't work for me – I liked to have conversations with people. Everyone else would be listening to music so I had to tell one person they weren't allowed, they had to talk to me. In the latter years Rob Kearney would sit at the back of the bus with me, so it was always him. Likewise he wasn't much into listening to music going to and from the games, so we'd sit and have a laugh about people out in the street, what the atmosphere is like, or talk about the police escorts and how mad it is, or how brutal, depending on where you were. You know, if you were in Italy they're insane, if you're in Scotland they're absolutely terrible and they stop at every red light, so there's no real point in having a police escort. So just those kind of mundane conversations, but it stopped you from really thinking too hard about what's ahead of you.

Rory Best: Deccie spoke really well before we went out on the pitch. Warren Gatland had thrown some mud in the lead-up, saying that every team in the Six Nations wanted to beat Ireland, or something like that. Deccie was always very reserved in terms of showing his emotions but on this day he really let go. He was almost in a rage about what Warren had said. The players fed off that. I was surprised at Gatland because when you start throwing stuff like that out there it generally comes back to bite you. It gives fuel to the other team. It's the type of game where bitterness is often a useful tool.

Donncha O'Callaghan: It was going to be the game that would define a lot of our careers. We knew if we lost it we'd be known forever as bottlers. Nobody in the squad was talking about the sixty-one years since Ireland last won a Grand Slam – we were focused on ourselves. We were all watching the England-France game the day after we beat Scotland and somebody asked Jeremy Guscott, 'Who will win next week?' He half laughed and said, 'Wales – Ireland will choke.' To be fair, when it had come down to it before, we hadn't produced. We had knocked on the door a few times and made a balls of it. And now this was it – nothing less than a must-win game for us. We had to nail it home. It was a game that could scar your career if you lost it.

Rob Kearney: My back went into spasm the night before the game. I was touch-and-go that morning. You have mental challenges every second week in rugby but this was on a different scale. If it wasn't a Grand Slam game I would have pulled out. I remember coming in at half-time and lying down for fifteen minutes and having to get helped off the table by two physios to go back out.

Paul O'Connell: We went in 6-0 down at half time – six disappointing points for us to give away. But I thought we had been playing quite well – we'd spent a lot of time in their territory. I was happy enough.

Ronan O'Gara: The mood was poor. You're thinking, 'One more score for these guys and we're chasing the game big-time.' But at the same time I was impressed with the mental state of fellas. I didn't see any heads going down.

At half-time, Les Kiss, the Ireland assistant coach, took Tommy Bowe aside and told him he had to get on the ball more because Wales were afraid of him with ball in hand. Brian O'Driscoll called his players together and said he believed in them. Paul O'Connell supported him. 'We're unbreakable! We're unbreakable!' he chanted.

Early in the second half, O'Driscoll squeezed his way over for a try from close-range. In his career, for Ireland and the Lions, it was his 37th try – the least spectacular and yet arguably the most important. Then Ireland struck again. Ronan O'Gara put through a speculative kick and Bowe went for it like a rat up a drainpipe.

'I took it with two hands over my head and Gavin Henson hit me an awful smack in the stomach – he totally winded me,' said Bowe in *Grand Slam*, the story of Ireland's season. 'It fell out of my hands but I grabbed it and just went straight

under the posts. The boys jumped on top of me and I couldn't breathe, I had to push them off. I couldn't even celebrate. My mum and brother were right behind the posts and somebody asked her, "What were you thinking when Tommy scored the try?" She said, "I didn't even see it – I had my hands over my eyes."'

Ireland gave away six cheap points and put themselves back under pressure – and the pressure piled ever higher when Stephen Jones landed a drop goal to put Wales ahead 15-14. The most dramatic endgame was set.

Ronan O'Gara: I nearly got a blockdown on Stephen Jones for his

Tommy Bowe flies in for his try.

drop goal – I could see it coming. But when I saw that kick going over, something clicked inside me. I got excited. I started thinking, 'You're going to have a kick to win this. You're going to have one shot at this to win it for Ireland.'

Marcus Horan: Those last few minutes in the lead-up to Rog's drop goal were probably a reflection of the whole season. Everything was in sync. We called a move to get us in front of the posts. It started with a lineout.

Rory Best: I felt under a lot of pressure at that lineout. Paulie called it on himself.

Paul O'Connell: Great throw by Rory, top of the jump. We mauled it. Broke off. Went infield. Picked and went. We made three or four good gains.

John Hayes: Jesus, if you made a mistake at a time like this it would have haunted you for the rest of your life.

Marcus Horan: We rumbled around and Rog said he wanted one more rumble before he had a go. I saw Wally and I remember thinking there was no better man in the world you could give this ball to because he's going to make ground and he's going to lay it back. Fact.

Ronan O'Gara's drop-goal to glory.

David Wallace: I played with Rog from schools rugby to international rugby. We palled around. We went on holiday together. We were tight. He's the player you would least doubt in that situation. He just had incredible balls for it. He never let the occasion come into it. He could stay in the moment better than anybody. When we got the field position I knew he'd do the rest.

Ronan O'Gara: The ball drop was poor. I'm rushing it. It tilts poorly, doesn't sit up. To be honest, it's haunted it's not charged down. It clears Ryan Jones by inches but I have my chest at the target and the ball goes where your chest points – straight through the posts.

Rory Best: We had the lead again, 17–15. Then Paddy Wallace gave away the famous penalty. I was within touching distance of him when he went and gave it away.

Ronan O'Gara: The first person he saw when the penalty was given was me. And he was saying, 'What have I done? No!' I couldn't say anything. I couldn't believe it.

Donncha O'Callaghan: I don't blame Paddy for what happened. He was trying to poach the ball at the breakdown, and to my eyes he was entitled to go for it. The breakdown laws were a mess at the time and it was a real high-wire act. To give yourself the best possible chance you had to play on the edge of the law, but when you put yourself in that position the call can go against you.

Paddy Wallace: I'm numb. It kicks in straight away, the significance. I look at where we are on the pitch. I know it's within his range. I'm in shock. I've been in a car crash before – it was a similar feeling. Your body tenses and numbs up and you're not aware of anything. I walk back on my own. If there's anyone alongside me I don't see them. I'm in my own world. I reach the posts. I look back down the pitch towards Stephen Jones and the clock is behind him. Just as I look up it goes to eighty minutes. That's when I think, 'When he kicks this we have no chance to score again.'

David Wallace: I'm thinking, 'It's all lost, this is the most horrible situation ever, I'm going to be in tears in a minute.' It was a helpless feeling. We became spectators like everybody else. Nothing we could do anymore. Our future was in the hands of somebody else and I felt sick.

Donncha O'Callaghan: Paulie gave me the job of making sure they didn't steal an inch. I was standing there, pointing, telling the ref, 'I know where the mark is.' I looked at the clock and thought, 'This is all over, there's nothing we can do here.' I said a silent prayer as Jones lined it up: 'God grant me the serenity to accept the things I cannot change...'

Paul O'Connell: I just put my head in my hands. All I was thinking was, 'It's over. It's gone. Gone.' Before the game I had believed resolutely – 100 per cent – that we were going to win. So that penalty was a massive shock to my system. I looked at him as he went to strike it. Then I looked away.

Stephen Jones of Wales reacts as his last minute penalty drops short of the post.

Rob Kearney: I was on the touchline beside Stephen Ferris and the two of us had our head in our hands and couldn't watch the kick.

Tommy Bowe: You always think the worst. Jones had kicked one from that sort of distance earlier in the game and you automatically think the game has gone

Marcus Horan: I was facing Jones and when I turned I followed the flight of the ball and it was perfectly on target and I thought, 'Fuck! That's it.'

Rory Best: I was looking at it going, 'Jesus, it's going over. You're joking me, YOU ARE JOKING ME!'

David Wallace: I saw Geordan making a shape to go under the crossbar to catch the ball and I knew that it was falling short. It was one of the happiest moments of my life. Geordan caught it and I said, 'Why is he not kicking this out? Why?' It felt like an eternity. He ran across the in-goal. 'What are you doing?'

Geordan Murphy: I was trying to kill time. The kick was halfway there when I realised it wasn't going to go over. I got it and as I caught it I went running and booted it into the stand.

Marcus Horan: Paulie went bananas.

Paul O'Connell goes wild at fulltime, while Paddy Wallace cuts
a relieved figure in the background.

Paddy Wallace: He was like a demented horse.

Rory Best: Paulie came at me like a wild animal and jumped into my arms.

Paul O'Connell: I had imagined what I would do if we won, thought about how I would react at the moment the whistle sounded. I thought I'd be very calm. But I ran off, I went mad. I don't know what I was doing. I don't know what came over me. But I thought it was gone – and it went from that feeling of total despair to, 'We have a Grand Slam.'

Rob Kearney: I ran on and stopped with a burst of pain and then ran on again.

Marcus Horan: We were delirious. It was mayhem out there. Everybody was

Peter Stringer.

going crazy. Then I saw Rog going over to Stephen Jones. He just calmly walked over while we were all going nuts and consoled him after missing the kick. That was special as well.

Brian O'Driscoll: It felt ... weird. It wasn't the elation that I would have felt had there not been that kick. I was so stressed – massive stress. I couldn't get over the emotion for a while. But I remember feeling … just so grateful. You could name a lot of guys who missed out on that moment but more than anyone I felt for Shaggy. For a guy to have played ten years and not to have been part of a Grand Slam-winning team – I would have loved that moment with him.

Declan Kidney: Every so often you find yourself in a place – a happy place – where you don't have to say anything. Not many people get to a place like that. I suppose my only words for it are that your aim is to be able to sit in the dressing room afterwards and look at one another and just nod. That's all. And I think the players will have that for the rest of their lives.

Brian O'Driscoll: When the whistle went and we had finally done it, the overwhelming feeling was of relief more than anything else. It was, 'Phew,' – and then subsequent joy, several days afterwards. I think that because the country was in such a dip at the time because of the financial crisis, it was great to see the elation that we had created. You know, sixteen, seventeen thousand people came down to see us when we got back to Dublin. It was so great; there was palpable excitement in Dublin and, I'm sure, all around the country when the boys went home.

One of the really special moments from that day happened during the lap of honour when I spoke to Jack Kyle. I was lucky enough to meet him on several occasions and he was, first and foremost, an absolute gentleman. Many people will remember us talking after the Slam game and he was just such a humble, kind man; he was so gracious in the way he passed on his mantle to me – he said the weight was off his shoulders and those of his team-mates, and hopefully we wouldn't have to wait another sixty-one years until it happens again.

John Hayes: We heard that there was going to be a civic reception in Dublin the next evening. I was humming and hawing about going, but getting off the plane in Dublin I had my mind made up. I asked Deccie if I could slip away. He gave me the green light and I appreciated that. I headed for my car. It was a Sunday afternoon and there was no traffic on the road. I was back in Limerick in two hours. RTE showed the open-air reception for the players live on television. While Tommy Bowe was belting out The Black Velvet Band up on the stage in Dublin I was sitting at home on the couch with my feet up, laughing my head off and drinking a mug of tea.

Donncha O'Callaghan: When I noticed he was missing I sent him a text; 'Where are you?' 'I'm at home, watching ye fools on telly.'

Irish Grand Slam legends: O'Driscoll and Kyle at fulltime.

Brian O'Driscoll: There's a photo of me and Hayes holding the Grand Slam trophy and it stands out for me especially because Hayes is in it. Normally he'd be on the edge of the picture; he wouldn't want to be seen milking the moment in any way. But that day, I think the sheer joy of the occasion caught him off guard. It's a serious rarity, a photo like that. I'm glad I have it.

Tommy Bowe: That day was unforgettable and it was a day I thought I'd never see. There was a time when I thought I'd never play for Ireland at all not to mind win a Grand Slam. I didn't make the Irish Schools team and I didn't make the Ireland Academy. I didn't take the route that a lot of other players take. Playing for Ireland was a dream I had written off in a sense. I didn't have a good start. I played a few matches and got dropped. In one of my early international matches a pundit gave me a rating of zero out of ten. Other wings passed me by. I just didn't have the confidence in myself to push on. It came to a head when I didn't make the World Cup squad in 2007. That hit me really hard. It's when I had to reassess. 'What am I doing here? Am I wasting my time or what?'

I was at the crossroads. I signed for the Ospreys when I was 24. A lot of people wrote me off, a lot of people thought I wouldn't be good enough to get into their team. I looked at what I was doing wrong in my game and it was simple. I was standing out on the wing and waiting for the ball to come to me. When it came to me I was able to do something with it, but to play at Ravenhill in the pissing rain and gale force winds and to stand out on the wing waiting for the ball to come to me was crazy. I never got it. The strength in my game is carrying the ball, so to only touch it three or four times in a match wasn't enough. People encouraged me to go in search of it. A simple thing, really, but I needed to be told. I got hungry for the ball and took the hard yards. I didn't want to get involved in the rough side before, but that's what I had to do and it turned my game around. And that's what brought me to the Millennium.

Malcolm O'Kelly: I played five minutes against Italy in the Grand Slam season. The way Deccie put it, he didn't think I was doing enough around the place in a supporting role. Maybe he had a point, I don't know. I was delighted for the lads. Some of them had been around a long time and they'd earned it. They'll go down in history. For my cameo against Italy, I got a medal. It wasn't exactly the Millennium Stadium with 80,000 people screaming their heads off. Deccie gave it to me in the car park of the airport hotel.

EIGHTEEN

A DREAM I DIDN'T WANT TO WAKE UP FROM

In Johnny Sexton's house there was always conversation about the merits of Ronan O'Gara versus David Humphreys as Ireland's starting No 10. As a youngster he remembers his father, a Kerryman, saying that there was no debate required – Rog was ten times better than any other out-half in the country and that's all there was to it.

This was the mantra that was imprinted on him. 'My dad's word was gospel and that's what was bred into me. Rog was better than anybody else and that was that. This was a time when Munster were getting to Heineken Cup semi-finals and finals. They hadn't won it yet but they'd gone very close. I watched most of those games. Rog was at the heart of everything Munster were doing. I had huge respect for him.'

Rob Kearney: Everyone knew that Johnny was the coming man in the November after the Grand Slam. He played against Fiji and played pretty well, so it was a 50-50 call as to who would start against South Africa. In the end, it was Johnny. It caused a bit of a stir.

Johnny Sexton: It was a very uncertain time for me. I was picked ahead of a legend of Irish rugby and you know that half the country, most of the country probably, wanted Ronan to play. Suddenly, I'm picked to play and I'm like, 'No one wants me, not even the guys I'm playing with probably want me to play.' When you're lining up a kick and the big screen is behind the posts and you see your rival for the jersey sitting there, of course I noticed it. I'd stand over a kick knowing that if I missed it I was going off. Having those thoughts, you've missed the kick before you've taken it.

South Africa were world champions and they had just beaten the Lions and it was a huge call from Deccie to leave out Ronan because international rugby doesn't get much bigger than a Test against the Springboks. It was a really misty day in Croke Park. I remember getting into the match with a tackle on Victor Matfield and the crowd cheering. I landed my first few kicks and I looked up at the big screen and it had a picture of me and a statistic underneath that said, '100%

Opposite: Sean O'Brien at the 2011 Rugby World Cup.

goal-kicking success rate in international rugby.' I said to myself, 'Jesus, that's great,' then I missed the next one. I kicked five penalties and we won, a famous victory and I felt like I'd arrived on the stage even though I knew I had plenty to learn. I felt like I could hack it at this level.

Paul O'Connell: Gert Smal was our forwards coach but he worked with South Africa for the previous few years and he noticed while watching videos of their games that they hadn't changed their lineout calls since his time. Before that game I asked him to teach me some words in Afrikaans. I learned numbers one, two, three, four, five, six, seven, eight, nine, ten and then twenty, thirty, forty, fifty, sixty, seventy, eighty, ninety and 100. I was able to watch ten of their games where the microphones were pitch-side so I could hear what they were calling and by the end of it I could tell exactly where the ball was going.

They're a big set-piece team and they get a lot of momentum off their lineout. When you're the lineout guy that's what you have to do. It's the same with any lineout caller in any country. You have to do the work, that's the way it is. I was only doing what any other lineout forward would have done. We robbed a few early in the game and then Matfield copped-on that we knew the calls and he started calling them in a huddle after that, but we still managed to get after a few more of them. Johnny kicked his goals and we beat the Springboks 15-10. A great day.

Johnny Sexton: Ronan played the first two matches of the 2010 Six Nations but I came back in for the game against England at Twickenham. It was my first Championship game and we won. It was bittersweet. I played really well and set up a couple of tries but I missed a few kicks – one from the touchline and the other from fifty-five metres. They were really hard but when you're young and you've got Ronan O'Gara sitting on the bench it can lead to some doubts. I was disappointed, even though we won.

We beat Wales and then we had Scotland at Croke Park for a Triple Crown. Because we'd just come off the back of a Grand Slam I was thinking that a Triple Crown wasn't that big. I was young. I remember the game for one moment. We were awarded a kickable penalty and Declan was getting ready to make a substitution – me off and Rog on. Rog was on the touchline. I nailed the kick and that was a big moment in my career. I'd proven, with Rog standing there, that I had the balls to land a penalty like that. I got a great reception from the crowd as I came off. I got a lot of texts congratulating me even though we lost to Scotland and I was in a dark place. It's funny, isn't it? It's amazing what you remember from different games.

The defeat to Scotland was a wounding one – the first time Ireland had lost to them in a Championship match in nine years. Four of their next six Tests were also lost as the feelgood from the Slam slowly dissipated.

In the 2011 Six Nations, the general air of running to stand still carried on. They won two close matches against Italy and Scotland and lost two by a score to France and Wales. They found themselves against England and dynamited their chances of sealing a Grand Slam and then lost four straight games in the build-up to the World Cup in New Zealand. Declan Kidney was experimenting in those games, but expectations were low when heading for the southern hemisphere.

Johnny Sexton: At that time, myself and Rog stayed out of each other's way quite a lot. The awkwardness came when it came to kicking. Rog and Paddy Wallace would pair-up and I'd go off with Mark Tainton or me and Paddy would pair-up and Rog would go with Mark. It was a bit uneasy but as time went on it was just me and Rog. We began kicking with each other and we developed a relationship. I wouldn't say we were texting each other every day, but we were talking to each other more and more.

I remember him ringing me after we won the Heineken Cup in 2011. He congratulated me and I thought, 'This bugger is only phoning me because he's got a Magners League final against us at the weekend and he's trying to keep his friends close and his enemies closer.' At that stage, I didn't trust him 100 per cent. It was a lovely thing for him to do, but I was still in that phase of being suspicious about his motives.

Jamie Heaslip: I've always said that I like good, clear direction from my nine and ten, and I always like them a little bit narky. You know, Johnny's a lovely guy outside of the pitch, but on the pitch he has his moments. But he's good. As a 10 he's very clear what he wants to do, and that's all you want as a forward. You can argue afterwards whether he's right or wrong, and I think he's been quoted as saying he may be right eighty per cent of the time, and that other twenty per cent he'll argue otherwise.

Johnny Sexton: Someone else said that. But you don't argue unless you think you're right. That's what an argument is, right?

Jamie Heaslip: You should have seen the faces on the guys on the Lions tour in 2013 who didn't know him before. They couldn't believe his bark and his bite.

Marcus Horan: I was battling back from a heart condition and I was trying to get fit in time for the World Cup. That was my focus. I was determined to get there, but there came a day when Deccie brought me in and said he wasn't including me. I'd worked so hard and I was so angry with him. I was furious. When I retired he called to the house and thanked me for everything I'd done, which I really appreciated. One thing about Deccie, he's very much a people person. It's important that you remember the person rather than the job because there were decisions he made in the job that people wouldn't have liked, but he was still a very good man.

Ronan O'Gara and Johnny Sexton at a training session during the 2011 Six Nations.

Jerry Flannery: The last eighteen months of my career were an absolute shit-fight and I became so bitter towards rugby at times. I was trying everything I could to get fit, but I couldn't get back playing. It was my calf. Numerous times I thought, 'This is it, I'm OK now,' and I'd say to the coaches, 'Put me back in, I'm ready to kill somebody.' Then I'd go out and my calf would tear again after twenty minutes and I'd be back at the drawing board. I must have done my calf about eight times. I did it against Biarritz, I did it when warming-up against Leinster, I did it playing for the Barbarians. Then I rehabbed it through the summer and tore it a couple more times pre-season.

Then I went to Arsenal to see their calf specialist and came back and tore it against Toulon, then I went to Liverpool to see their guy. I saw every specialist I could see. All I wanted to do was play. I came back against Ulster and said, 'I'm ready to go, I'm going to fucking dominate.' I came on and played twenty minutes and tore it again. It was breaking my heart.

I had an operation on both my calfs before the World Cup but kept having setbacks and it was killing me. I was watching the lads training and I felt like a tool on the sideline. This is the stuff that nobody sees. The mental torture. For my own sake I needed to get to the end of this thing. I was going bananas. I have such time for Deccie because he knew I was in a world of hurt and he was so encouraging. Before the World Cup we played some warm-up matches. We went to Murrayfield to play Scotland and I said to Hayes and Horan that if I was going out, then I was going out playing for Ireland and not on a training pitch at the University of Limerick. I got through it. Then we played against France and I got through that as well. I was conscious that every time I went into a team meeting that it could be my last. My head was all over the place.

I spoke to Paulie and I said, 'I think I'm back, I think my calf has come right.' His words were so supportive. He said, 'To get you back is huge,' and that meant a lot. To hear that from lads you respect is massive. We went to the World Cup and in the first game against America it started to feel wrong again. I was in pain afterwards and then it tore the following week. I flew home and I knew that was it. It took me a while to come to terms with it, but I look back now and I realise how lucky I was to play with these fantastic players in these big games. When I was a kid, myself and my mates wanted to play for Munster and Ireland and I was the one who got the chance. Everybody misses it when it's gone, but you learn to enjoy what you had.

Conor Murray: My mom's dad, Con Roche, played for Garryowen and Munster. He's passed away now but he played against Australia in 1940-something. That's the only connection I had with rugby when I was growing up. My dad's side were a GAA family. All my aunts and uncles still think it's pretty alien, this rugby carry-on.

A family friend, Dom Kelly, used to bring me into Thomond Park when I was a youngster. We'd go in about three hours early so we could stand by the old tunnel and catch a glimpse of the players running out for the warm-up. I went up to Lansdowne Road a few times but it was mainly Munster games that captured my imagination.

I'd be waiting for Rog – when he came out it was pretty cool. I remember being at one match and dad tapped me on the shoulder and told me to look around and Rog was there right beside me, which was crazy exciting, it was like meeting your hero. Then, when you get into the squad, it's strange. It takes a while to get used to them as a person and a team-mate when you've been watching them as idols on a pedestal for so long.

My first call-up was in 2011 and it was nerve-racking going up to Carton House for the training camp. It was a sunny day in pre-season and all the lads were up on the balcony of the golf club. I drove past and saw them – O'Driscoll and these guys. 'Oh Jesus, is this real?' I went off to the World Cup that autumn and it was all a bit of a whirlwind.

Paul O'Connell: I'd been on the Lions tour in 2009 and while we trained very hard there was also a big emphasis on guys having fun and enjoying themselves and as much as I loved working with Eddie maybe that was overlooked a bit in 2007. Or maybe it was our fault. Maybe we were just too focused on rugby. Maybe we didn't even want to have fun. In 2009, Ian McGeechan and Warren Gatland liked us to go out and have a few beers and a bit of crack and in 2011 that's something we did again. We went down to Queenstown, a beautiful village with some lovely restaurants. We were bungee jumping, we played golf, we went white-water rafting, we did this luge thing, coming down hills in these karts. We were very tight as a team.

Rob Kearney: The boys played America in the first game of the World Cup. They got through it, but it wasn't a great performance.

Johnny Sexton: It was a windy night in New Plymouth. I missed my first two kicks at goal. Banged them straight down the middle and the wind hit them and they went wide. Then I landed a few, then a few more. Ronan was on the bench and I allowed the pressure to get to me.

Rob Kearney: We played Australia next and I was picked for that. I don't really get nervous before games, but it was different that time. I was just coming back from a really long injury. I was out of the game for nine months. I'd played 100 minutes of rugby in ten months and then I went to Eden Park for my first ever game in a World Cup. That was the most nervous I'd ever been. Nervous because I wasn't sure if I could cope physically and mentally. It worked out well. Australia didn't see us coming.

Johnny Sexton: At half-time, I felt I was doing OK. I'd missed a couple of kicks at goal but I'd put over a drop goal and I was playing all right. I was sitting in the changing room with a wet towel on my head and, obviously, Declan didn't see me because he asked the kicking coach, Mark Tainton, if he should make a change at

10. Mark said, 'Let's give him one more,' and I felt, 'Fuck sake, I kicked badly in one game against the USA. Gimme a break.'

Just after half-time I had a penalty thirty-five metres out, fifteen metres in from touch and I remember thinking this could be the biggest kick of my career – and I nailed it and I thought, 'That's the turning point for me.' I got a penalty ten minutes later, wide out on the left, and in my head I absolutely flushed it but it hit the post. Darce went off injured and I got moved to 12 and Rog came on and the instruction was that he was to take over the kicking. He took the next two. If I wasn't so young I might have said, 'No, I'm going to keep going here,' because I would have got the next two, they were easy enough. Rog kicked them and he was the hero and I got dropped. At least we won the match.

Rory Best: It was never in doubt. I knew we'd win that game. The Six Nations hadn't been great but we ended it by walloping England when they were going for the Grand Slam and we knew we would produce big performances. Nobody gave us much of a chance and yet in our own minds we were favourites. Nothing was going to stop us.

Johnny Sexton: It was a short-lived World Cup for me and the lowest point was sitting on the bench against Italy in Dunedin. It was an incredible atmosphere, indoor stadium, 30,000 Irish supporters, which we couldn't believe. It was better than if we'd played at Lansdowne Road. I sat on the bench thinking what could have been. I came on against Italy and nailed a few really good kicks, but it was a disappointing experience. I became thicker-skinned because of it. I became a better kicker as well.

Rory Best: I did my AC joint against Italy and they were going to send me home. I couldn't lift my arm past my waist. Brian Green, our physio, reckoned he could do something. He got the hotel to get two dozen polystyrene cups and filled them with water and stuck in them in the freezer. We set the alarm every couple of hours during the night and we'd meet down in the team room and he'd get the cups out and peel off some of the polystyrene and rub the ice on the joint. By the Monday evening I was able to lift my arm to head height and then by Wednesday it got me to a point where they gave me some painkillers and said, 'Let's see what you can do.' It felt really good. I was all geared up to play the quarter-final against Wales. A chance to make history and all that.

Tommy Bowe: It still haunts me. It's something that's hard to live with. They caught us on the hop and we struggled to come back from it.

Rob Kearney: We got out-played. There is nothing worse than losing a game you should have won, but we got out-played that day. Wales were very strong. I don't think we were in with a shout of winning it. Sometimes those games make it a little bit easier to take. I think they were just playing better rugby. I don't think we were prepared for the physicality that they brought.

Rory Best: The better team won, but we didn't put up a fight. We went out with a whimper and if you have to go out of a World Cup then you don't go out with a whimper. You go out fighting.

Paul O'Connell: We played into their hands a little bit by going round the corner to Dan Lydiate, who was having an incredible tournament. We could have been a lot more clever in what we did. We didn't fully recognise Lydiate's chop-tackling ability and Sam Warburton's ability to poach off those chop tackles. They were a really good side. We might have done it differently and still not won. I don't know. It was disappointing but I've got good memories of that World Cup.

Jamie Heaslip: Everyone's analysis of that result was of them winning because they were a young team and us an ageing one. My view is that we weren't beaten.

Stephen Ferris is upended by the Welsh defense during the
2011 Rugby World Cup quarter-final.

We lost the game. We didn't take our opportunities and they took theirs. The margins in Test rugby are so small that that can happen. So why dwell on it? We dealt with the defeat as we would a victory by having a couple of beers and then moved on to the next one. Why stay stuck in the moment? There's more to life than that.

My dad was a brigadier general in the Irish Army, and we moved around a lot as a result –and that was why I was born in Israel – and as a kid, I saw plenty of things from countries being at war that gave me my sense of perspective and I always knew I was a lucky person. But I never got the sense that I had to give out hell to myself for being a child of a certain class. You are born into what you are born into, so get on with it. Life, and especially rugby, is all about gaining a sense of perspective. Now don't get me wrong, I love my rugby. It's a hobby and if I wasn't playing with Leinster or Ireland, I'd be lining out with my mates on a Saturday afternoon. But it's still only a bloody game. It's not life or death and pundits and fans blow it up out of all proportion.

I just don't see the point of that. Yes, I'm competitive and I want to win. And yes, I'd be selfish about wanting more and more medals. But when the game is over – and it is a win or a loss – I deal with each situation the same, by taking the outcome on the chin and moving on.

Conor Murray: I thought we could beat Wales but we didn't have a Plan B. They deserved it fully. I was twenty-two and I wanted the World Cup to go on forever. I loved it, loved being part of a team. It was a dream I didn't want to wake up from.

Ireland's form fell off a cliff after the heartache against Wales. In the 2012 Six Nations they won only two out of five, then lost three Tests in New Zealand, the last of them by a cringe-making 60-0. The 2013 Six Nations began brilliantly with a first half performance in Cardiff that made the eyes water, a display of such power that Ireland were marked down as possible Grand Slam winners.

Things soon unravelled again. They lost their way so completely that they got beaten by Italy for the first time in the Six Nations and only avoided the wooden spoon because the French were just that tiny bit worse.

Declan Kidney's time was up.

Andrew Trimble: Declan tried very hard to have relationships with guys but it never really worked because you never really knew where you stood with him. He spoke in riddles sometimes. It was very frustrating trying to get any sort of clarity, especially when you were in my position. More often than not the conversation was about how I was being dropped and those are the times when you're looking for an explanation and I always felt there was no logic to his explanation. I would rather somebody sat me down and said, 'This is why you are not playing,' but I never got that and it was very, very frustrating.

Johnny Sexton: I owe a lot to Declan, but his best strength is also maybe his weakness. He's such a good person and at times he wouldn't tell you the truth. I said it to him. I said, 'I need to know why I'm dropped so I can improve it. I don't want to hear that I've done nothing wrong or I'm going great. That's not the case if I'm not playing.' At times, I wish he was harsher with me and told me how it was, but he was a good person and that's what made him successful.

Andrew Trimble: I think he wanted to be well-thought of and he thought if he gave somebody some hard truth that it would reflect badly on him. I would have been tough enough to take hard truths. Every time I didn't get picked I got told that there was nothing I was doing wrong and that I was just to keep doing what I was doing, but that's not being honest with somebody. I studied maths and science in school so I'd be quite logical. A+B=C, that's the way I think. Declan said to me, and I remember having this conversation with him, 'You're not doing anything wrong, keep doing what you're doing,' and I said, 'OK, keep doing what I'm doing? I'm doing that and I'm 100 per cent doing something wrong because you're not picking me. That makes no sense. I must be doing something not well enough.' He said, 'No, keep doing what you're doing.' It made no sense. It took me two or three conversations and then I switched off a little bit. There was no point in having a conversation, you only end up getting wound-up and frustrated.

Rob Kearney: He was a difficult man to figure out, but he was a lovely man. You have to see the good things in people. Deccie was a good coach and he wanted the best for his players. He had a good heart and when a guy has a good heart and is looking out for your best interests then it's hard to look negatively at him.

Jerry Flannery: Deccie is a very, very good man. A guy I have a huge amount of time for. A very loyal coach. People will pan him but show me a coach who has two Heineken Cups and a Grand Slam. The lads who pan him need to pay a bit of respect to that.

I know Rog has criticised Deccie. Rog was looking for a guy with a bunch of fresh ideas and somebody who was going to add to his armoury on the field. But Rog had Deccie as a coach all the way from school. It's like listening to your parents. They have a load of good advice but because you've been listening to it forever you might ignore it. If somebody comes in with a different accent then you might listen. Rog is going to have a degree of resentment over the way his Ireland career ended, but how many fucking caps does Rog have? He can't complain that he didn't get enough. The guy was a hero playing for us. When he looked at Deccie he probably thought, 'What am I going to learn from this guy that I haven't learned before?' I never felt that Deccie was going to make me a better lineout thrower or a better scrummager but I felt he made me feel big and I would go out on Saturday and play big for him. He used to say that just because we're Irish it doesn't mean we should underestimate how good we can be. If you make players feel confident then they'll fill that jersey for you and give you everything they have. That was Deccie's strength. He helped you fill the jersey.

Paul O'Connell: Deccie called it a day after the Six Nations. He was an incredibly dedicated person and all he wanted was for us to be successful and he worked night and day and probably made a lot of sacrifices along the way. When a coach goes you almost feel responsible for letting him down, but it's part and parcel of the game. Everybody has a shelf life. Deccie coached Ireland to a Grand Slam and we've only ever won two in our history. That's what he'll be remembered for. It's a fantastic legacy.

NINETEEN

I JUST WENT WALKING, AIMLESSLY

Cian Healy: I always had loads of energy when I was a kid and didn't ever like sitting still for long. That's why I started rugby, because I was allowed pick up the ball and run, as opposed to kicking it along the ground . . . That's pretty much why I went up to Clontarf and started. I played there for four seasons and then went to Belvedere College, where we won the Leinster Schools Senior Cup in 2005. I think Clontarf toughened me up a bit and Belvedere kind of polished it off.

I remember when I was really young telling my Clontarf coaches, Colm Carmichael and Aidan Murray, that I wanted to be the strongest player on the team. They told me to get two sandbags and carry them up stairs. My dad took me down to an Early Learning Centre and we bought a couple of sandbags, each with a handle. I put them at the bottom of the stairs and every time I went up, I'd bring them with me. Coming down, I'd carry them back. Each bag was eight kilos. I was eight going on nine and I did that for two years. I don't know if it made me stronger but it made me tired.

Then, when I was thirteen I got my dad to drive the car down to the beach and then I'd rope the car up to a weightlifting belt and would pull across the sand. It was difficult to get the car moving. Dad steered. Eventually I got it going, did thirty or forty metres, took a break and went again. People were walking on the beach, giving us very strange looks. We spent an hour there. That stuff appealed to me. Being stronger, being bigger than all my mates, being the one they looked to. I liked it.

My dad was always such a support. If I'd said to my dad, I want to hike up a mountain and need you to take me there, he would have said, 'When do we go?' I remember going to a gym with him when I was fifteen to use the weights but I was too young, so we switched my birthdate by two years.

From under-16s to under-20s, I played in the centre. Deadly, I loved it. Drop goals and everything. I really embraced it. I was given carte blanche to do what I wanted. It was enjoyable. Then I became a hooker and only after that did I move to prop. At first I didn't have much technique and just used my strength, but when I played for Leinster I would be found out by technically smarter guys, so I really had to start focusing on what I was doing. Greg Feek was brilliant at Leinster for helping me with that – although the most important thing he taught me was that

Opposite: Cian Healy sends All Black captain Richie McCaw tumbling backwards during the epic 2013 encounter at the Aviva Stadium.

scrummaging is about attitude. If you're thrown into a scrum against the best in the world and you want to survive, you will. You're not going to throw in the towel and take a hiding.

I made my debut in the draw against Australia in the autumn of 2009. It was 15 November at Croke Park. That was very special.

But it was strange, I remember when I was at school thinking that it was all well and good that Ireland were winning Triple Crowns, but it was disappointing that they weren't winning Championships. Then I got into the team and I remember it suddenly dawning on me after a few seasons, 'I used to complain about them only winning the Triple Crown but I've not won anything with this team'. Four years and nothing. I thought this had to change and the coming of Joe Schmidt made a big difference. He brought the 'Joe Show' and the lads moved on to a different level.

Joe Schmidt talks to the players during training at Carton House in Co. Kildare in March 2015.

Johnny Sexton: When Deccie went, there was only one guy I wanted to replace him – Joe Schmidt. All of us at Leinster knew how brilliant he was. We won two Heineken Cups under Joe at Leinster. I'd go in sometimes on the morning after a game and do a bit of recovery and more often than not he'd be in the office. I'd go up and chat to him and I'd say, 'Did you watch the game again?' and he'd say, 'Yeah, I watched it a couple of times during the night.' I'd say, 'During the night?'

And he'd say, 'Yeah.' Like it was normal.

I was almost hassling him into taking the Ireland job. Some of the Leinster boys were sitting on the fence, not sure whether they wanted him to do it or not, because as much as they wanted him as their Ireland coach they didn't want to lose him from Leinster. I was leaving for Racing Metro so that wasn't my concern anymore. I was telling him, 'You have to go for it, Joe.'

Paul O'Connell: We played Samoa in our first game under Joe and we were doing a video session a few days before the match. All these Samoans with all these incredibly long and hard to pronounce names but Joe pronounced every single name immaculately. It might be an NPC game in New Zealand or a Currie Cup game in South Africa involving guys who are below Super 15 rugby and he'll know all about every player in the video. I suppose it's his way of saying, 'I've done my job, I know these guys inside-out and now it's your turn to do your job with the same level of detail.'

Rob Kearney: There's no rugby player in the world that he doesn't know something about.

Conor Murray: No matter who we're playing against when he starts analysing the opposition he almost sounds like he's from that country. He must know every player in the world and what arm they carry the ball in. He just knows things. Ask him any law in the world of rugby and he'll know it. We were discussing something about defending off a scrum and how far the scrum-half can go and I was full-sure that I was able to go the No 8's feet and Joe said, 'No, it's two metres'. I said, 'I'm sure I asked a ref about that, Joe, and he said I could go to his feet.' I thought I had a bit of ammo to back up my point. Joe said, 'No, two metres.' I said I thought I was right and then he repeated the law as it would appear in the manual, as close to word for word as made no difference. I said, 'Fair enough, I'll back down so.'

Tommy Bowe: There's no hiding place. When you step out there, if you drop off for two seconds you will expect to be pulled up on it and likewise when you do something good that ninety-nine people out of a hundred wouldn't see he'll be the one person who will have spotted it and he'll congratulate you on it. It might be the tiniest thing, but he'll see it.

Johnny Sexton: He'll show it on the television in front of everybody and you feel like a million dollars.

Cian Healy: But if you make a mistake, even if it's a small one, all you can think is, 'Shit, that's gonna come out on the Monday video.'

Rory Best: Rugby players, like a lot of people, tend to take a shortcut if they think they'll get away with it. He creates an environment where you're nearly afraid to be the guy who takes the short cut.

Paul O'Connell: It's not just about attention to detail it's being able to communicate it to the players in a way that's easy to understand. Rugby is a tough game, there's a lot going on. It's about making things easy and imparting information in a way that makes it easy to do under pressure and he's really good at that. He's open to ideas but they'd want to be very, very good ideas. Well-thought out and easy to communicate and easy to execute.

Rob Kearney: Joe drills those gameplans into guys so that when the big moment comes you are rattling off your plays like they're second nature, like it's instinctive.

Paul O'Connell: I suppose he's intimidating if you don't know your stuff or you're hiding. There's nothing to be afraid of if you're doing your work and you know your stuff.

Andrew Trimble: It's tough and unpleasant at times. It's not the kind of environment you're there to enjoy. You're there to work. Some of the training sessions and even some of the meetings we had were so stressful. Every ruck you're going into you're going, 'Please, please get this right otherwise Joe will see it.' It's really impressive how he changed the culture to the point where if we're doing things that are not quite up to the level of accuracy or intensity or physicality then it's completely unacceptable. It's embarrassing whenever you get something wrong. And it should be embarrassing. When you make a mistake or forget a play or switch off at a crucial moment in defence or you're inaccurate at the breakdown, that should be embarrassing. It's not the way we want to play.

Brian O'Driscoll: He can be Mr Nice Guy, but he can be ruthlessly honest when he needs to be. He rarely shouts, but his words can be lethal. He can cut you down in an instant and the pitch of his voice doesn't need to rise or fall. He expects high standards, all the time, complete understanding of the game-plan and what it means for every player, whether you're on the ball or twenty metres away. New ideas, new plays, subtleties that demand absolute attention to detail. 'What's your role in this?' 'What exactly are you doing and why are you doing it?' He makes little tweaks in a backline play and all of a sudden an opposition defence opens up in front of you. And you look over at him and he's smiling.

Tommy Bowe: In the second match under Joe we played Australia at the Aviva and we lost 32-15. They scored four tries and we scored none and we were beaten long before the end. We were really hurt by it. We had all the fine detail about what we needed to do to break them down, but we didn't turn up with what Irish teams are renowned for and that's aggression and never-say-die. We almost lay down and let them beat us and we were angry with ourselves.

Rory Best: We had New Zealand next. The only good thing about that performance against Australia was that we felt we showed the All Blacks a lot of things that weren't really true. We were better than that. In a weird way, we'd set a trap for them.

Tommy Bowe: I went into my local butchers on the Wednesday afternoon and he said, 'Jesus, what's the score going to be this week?' and I told him that we were going to win. He wouldn't believe me. He said, 'Honestly? It's the All Blacks, like.' I said, 'Yeah, we're going to win.' I just don't know what it was, but Australia hurt us a lot and I knew there was a big reaction coming.

Michael Hooper and Will Genia do their best to halt a rampaging Rory Best.

Paul O'Connell: There was a little bit of fear heading into New Zealand. We were very, very worried that if we didn't perform to the best of our ability it could be a very long day.

Johnny Sexton: You have doubts. You always have doubts. It's the doubts that drive you.

Tommy Bowe: Paulie said, 'Look, the detail is great, but if we don't go in with passion and physicality then there's no point in us turning up.'

Below: The Irish team face the Haka.
Right: Rob Kearney scorches away to score.

Devin Toner: The atmosphere was ridiculous and then we made the perfect start to the game. We started to believe from there. Our line speed in defence was good and we missed hardly any tackles. Cian Healy was like a wrecking ball.

Against the All Blacks, Ireland scored their first try after four minutes when Sean O'Brien and Jamie Heaslip repeatedly punched holes in the New Zealand defence before Conor Murray blasted his way over despite the attentions of the All Blacks' loosehead, Wyatt Crockett, their hooker, Andrew Hore, and their second-row, Brodie Rettalick.

Six minutes later, O'Brien and Heaslip got on the ball again and this time it was Rory Best who drove over. Seven minutes after that, Israel Dagg spilled a pass into Rob Kearney's hands near the left touchline and the full-back galloped away to score Ireland's third.

To the amazement of the Aviva Stadium – and the wider rugby world – Ireland were 19-0 ahead after seventeen minutes.

It was the 28th meeting of the sides. In twenty-one of the twenty-eight Ireland failed to register nineteen points in eighty minutes not to mind seventeen. In fifteen of them they scored less than ten in the entire match. This was unchartered territory and an opportunity like no other to finally beat the All Blacks for the first time after 108 years.

Rob Kearney: After I scored my try there was part of me that said, 'We're going to do it,' and the other part of me said, 'You do know who you're playing against, don't you?'

Les Kiss, Ireland defence coach: At half-time we were leading 22-7. There was a controlled energy more than anything else. There wasn't any disbelief or backslapping. It was important the players had their two or three minutes to suck it in because we'd made seventy-eight tackles in the first half, and we did a fair bit with the ball in hand. The message was, 'This isn't about shutting up shop.' We wanted to encourage them to stay in the space they were in, to keep trusting and building and growing on those things they'd been doing. We also stressed it was important to score again, preferably early in the half. We dropped a few balls and that meant they spent more time in our 22. We made 152 tackles in the second half – 230 in the game – which is massive and that meant an accumulation in fatigue. We didn't manage things as we would have liked, right through the half.

The All Blacks hunted Ireland down. Aaron Cruden's penalty and a converted Ben Franks try made it a five-point game with sixteen minutes to play.

Johnny Sexton: I damaged my hamstring the week before against Australia and resigned myself to the fact that I wasn't going to be fit to face New Zealand. I re-hurt it with about fifteen minutes to go. The doc said, 'Come off,' and I said 'No.' Then I had a penalty that would have put us two scores clear and I didn't get it done. I was pissed off I missed the kick. I missed one in the first half when I hit the left post from the other side of the pitch. I pulled it ever so slightly. The way to fix a pull is to take a little extra step to your left and I probably over-compensated. It doesn't help when you've got a sore hamstring, but the kick should have gone over.

I thought I'd nailed it, but when I looked up, the ball was on the right post and once I saw it on the right post I knew it was going to fade slightly because there's a little breeze that comes in from that side of the stadium. I knew it was going to drift past. I wish I could have it again, but you can't. We should still have put the game to bed.

Paul O'Connell: We were only hanging on at the end and trying to get the game over rather than continuing to go at them, whether that was in attack or defence. We had to be more aggressive in what we were doing. We had to be more proactive and treating it as the twentieth minute rather than the eighteenth minute. When we had the ball we were negatively playing out the clock and we got a bit sloppy in our breakdown stuff. Nigel Owens was reffing and he looked at one or two breakdowns where he could have penalised us and he didn't. The one he did us for

Sean O'Brien offloads out of the tackle of New Zealand hooker Andrew Hore.

that sparked the All Blacks into scoring the try, you could say it was harsh but it was probably coming.

Sean O'Brien: We should have trusted each other in the last couple of minutes. They're only a team at the end of the day.

Ryan Crotty, New Zealand centre: I just remember believing that we were going to win. That might sound arrogant or silly, but I remember with around thirty-five minutes to go and we had our work cut out for us, but we never doubted it. Even when Johnny Sexton was taking that shot at goal, which would have taken it to eight points, I remember thinking that even if he gets it I still didn't think that they would win even though looking back now I think, 'You were brave there, Ryan.'

I was just absolutely knackered to be honest. I was hiding out on the wing because I was tired and having a breather. I remember the few moments before that, just realising where the space was for us to exploit outside of Dane Cole so. It was one heck of an off-load, I didn't have a whole lot to do but go over the line from five metres and touch down. I got the credit for it, but it was a heck of a team try. It's a personal highlight, an important try and something I'm really proud of even if I have to apologise to everyone for scoring it.

Ryan Crotty goes over to break Irish hearts and end hopes of a
first ever victory over New Zealand.

Tommy Bowe: I thought we'd hold on but they just kept coming and coming and coming. Everything fell apart. I was knackered. I couldn't run anymore. Or I thought I couldn't. If you'd told me what it was going to feel like to lose that match could I have found an extra five per cent in the last few minutes? I probably could have. To avoid the heartbreak, I'd have found five per cent. Since that performance any time I feel I'm struggling, any time I feel there's nothing left in the tank, I think back to that game and I find something. If it's the difference between winning and losing you pull an extra bit out from somewhere.

Rory Best: Johnny put his hand up and apologised for missing the kick and we said, 'No, that's not on.' A team doesn't live or die by one kick. It was heartbreaking that a player of his ability was carrying a lot of the loss on himself. It was fairly depressing.

Rob Kearney: It was horrific at the end. I wasn't right for a week afterwards. On the following Tuesday night, I put on a coat and threw on a pair of runners and I just went walking aimlessly for an hour around Dublin. I'd never done that before. I didn't know where I was going or what I was doing. I've always been able to control my thoughts and emotions after a game but that was one that hit me unbelievably hard.

Conor Murray: We put in a seventy-nine-and-a-half minute performance. If we'd beaten them, would we have fallen in love with ourselves? It's hard to know. When we recovered from the disappointment, though, we could start looking at the positives going into the Six Nations. We knew we were close to being a very good team, but we needed to keep pushing.

TWENTY

IT'S BEEN A PRIVILEGE

Andrew Trimble was twenty-nine years old going into the 2014 Six Nations. He'd been around the team for nine years and the previous summer he had won his fiftieth cap against Canada in Toronto.

And yet he felt like he never belonged. For Ulster, he was a lethal wing with pace and aggression and fantastic finishing power, but he rarely carried that same threat when wearing the green jersey instead of the white. It was down to confidence. He had it in abundance with his province and he lacked it when playing for Ireland.

Johnny Sexton: With Joe, there's been times when some guys have gone, 'I can't do anything right with this guy.' Somebody like Andrew Trimble. Joe gave him a hard time at the start and Trimbs was a bit down about it. I said to him, 'Trimbs, he's not on your case because he doesn't like you, he's on your case because he sees something in you and he wants to bring it out.' Pretty soon, Trimbs started playing phenomenal rugby.

Trimble scored a try in the 28-6 defeat of the Scots in the first weekend of the 2014 Six Nations, but if the narrative of his season was interesting, there was another sub-plot that was utterly compelling – Brian O'Driscoll's imminent retirement. The nation wanted a fairytale finish for the great man. They wanted a Grand Slam. When Ireland despatched Wales 26-3 everything was looking good, but the dream died at Twickenham in week three when England won narrowly. It was now all about the Championship.

O'Driscoll's farewell tour had many stops, but none were as emotional as his final home game in a green jersey, against Italy. Had he suddenly announced that he had found the answer to world peace then the tributes could not have been any more fulsome. They came from all corners of Ireland and from all over the rugby world. It was a tour-de-force of nostalgia and accolades followed by a game which Ireland won in a landslide.

Brian O'Driscoll: I remember several years ago sitting in an ice bath alongside

Opposite: Brian O'Driscoll and Paul O'Connell line up together for Ireland for the last time.

Victor Costello and saying, 'You're thirty-two years old, are you mad? What are you doing in an ice bath at thirty-two?'

I was thirty-five years of age and still playing Test rugby. What was wrong with me? Ah, you know, there was a recession out there.

I wasn't sure if I would play that final year but I considered a number of different things, including how the body felt, talking to my wife Amy, and then obviously a big aspect was seeing Joe Schmidt taking up the reigns with Ireland. That was a big incentive to stay on for another campaign because I'm a big believer that any team that he's involved with he'll make things happen. He has this infectious persona and he's definitely the best coach I was ever coached by. When he came into Leinster it was so exciting because the level of coaching was such that I just felt like I was learning something every single day. It was so refreshing and it made you want to go in every day because you knew you were going to learn something new or hear something that you'd never heard before during the previous ten years of your career. I loved it. Like anyone, you have the odd brutal Monday, but on the whole I loved it – and I never saw it as work. I loved the crack, but I also loved the competitiveness of all our training sessions; I loved seeing how guys could switch in and out from having a laugh in the dressing room, then you had some caffeine chewing gum and got yourself fired up, then you started lifting weights and so on. You were still able to have a laugh in between sets and things, but the competitiveness of 'What's he lifting? He plays in the centre as well. Damn, he's lifting more than me. I've got to lift heavier.' Just small wins, that's what it's about, about getting the edge, the psychological edge on some people.

Ireland blew Italy away scoring seven tries in a 46-7 win. O'Driscoll was named man of the match. The rugby Gods fixed it for his final Test match to be played in the same stadium in Paris where he launched himself into the consciousness of the global game thirteen years earlier by scoring his hat-trick.

Conor Murray: I'd played France twice and drawn with them twice and for a number of us young players we'd never lost to France, so it wasn't daunting to go over there. We didn't have a fear factor going into it. There was a bite in the week. We knew how hard it was going to be and that dictates your mood and our mood was very different to twelve months before. I mean, a year earlier we were playing the last game of the Championship in Rome and wondering if we were going to get the wooden spoon. And we lost that game to Italy and we got lucky because France finished below us. It was a big turnaround in a year.

Rory Best: Everybody asks you about Joe expecting that he's got some sort of magic cauldron that he throws things into and we all drink from it the night before a game. No. He has a phrase – you are what you repeatedly do – and he has us trying to be the best we can be on the training pitch every day and so when the pressure comes on you revert back to what you know and if what you know is good habits then you'll be all right.

Johnny Sexton: We didn't speak much about France being Brian's last game, but we didn't need to. Everyone knew. Everyone wanted him to finish on a high. We wanted to send him away with a title. Just before we left the hotel to go to the stadium the very last point that Joe made was Brian. It was the first time he'd gone there all week.

And you could see him getting . . . not emotional, but you could see it meant a lot to him, coaching Brian in his last game. I could see Brian welling-up a little bit and getting that pale look you get. Joe spoke really well. 'This guy has done it 132 times for his country and every single time he put his body on the line. He did it for you for that long and you're going to do it for him today.' It increased the pressure, but that's exactly what we were thinking anyway.

Victory for Ireland in Paris would give them the Championship on O'Driscoll's 133rd and final cap – and they made a blistering start. Johnny Sexton and Andrew Trimble scored tries within five minutes of each other midway through the first half, giving the visitors a 12-6 lead.

Even when Brice Dulin went over for a converted try on the hour to put France ahead 13-12, the advantage didn't last long. Sexton went over for his second score just after half-time and with the conversion Ireland had a six-point lead.

In the fifty-second minute, Sexton had a kick to make it a two-score game, just like he had at the Aviva against New Zealand four months earlier.

Johnny Sexton: It was from more or less the spot as the one I missed against the All Blacks. It was weird. I kicked from that exact spot in all the other games in the Championship except Italy. It was like there was no escaping New Zealand. I kept on getting dragged back to a kick that reminded me of what happened. In my head, I thought about the miss in Dublin as I prepared for the one in Paris. I nailed it and it put us eight points clear.

Andrew Trimble: France kept coming at us. They picked the last day of the Championship to produce their best stuff and, of course, it had to be against us. They scored to make it 20-22 with eighteen minutes to go and we were under the cosh at that stage. And then we lost Johnny

Johnny Sexton: I went to tackle Mathieu Bastareaud and got knocked out. I was stretchered off.

Conor Murray: I was off the pitch by then. I was watching with my heart in my mouth trying not to think about the last few minutes of the New Zealand game. The defence was unreal. Unreal.

Rob Kearney: With no time left they caught us on the far side. Pascal Pape threw a pass to Damien Chouly on the right touchline.

Brian O'Driscoll: He's on the touchline with nobody near him. Dreamboat [Dave Kearney] is the last line of defence: it's all on him now. In the end, these games come down to the tiniest, most imperceptible margins. It's often a guy making a right decision or a wrong one, under the most severe pressure possible. It's about still being mentally and physically sharp enough after eighty punishing minutes, which is what all the training and all the sacrifice are for. And it's about trust – trust in the guy alongside you, so that your first instinct is to back him up when it's all on the line.

Rob Kearney: Under pressure from Dave, the pass from Pape to Chouly goes forward before Chouly touches down for the try. Or, at least, it looked like a forward pass to me but I wasn't sure whether I was seeing things that I wanted to see because the alternative was horrific. It got referred up the TMO. I was thinking, 'Surely this can't happen to us twice in a few months.'

Rory Best: Everybody was thinking the same. Nobody wanted to be the Grim Reaper by saying it, but we were thinking it.

Rob Kearney: When the pass was ruled forward and the game ended with us as champions it was fairytale stuff, for Brian more than anybody.

Brian O'Driscoll: The realisation that it's all over, the incredible satisfaction over what we've achieved, the stresses of the game I've just played – it all combines and comes rushing up on me.

Rob Kearney: I was very lucky to be exposed to Brian's skills from my very first day at Leinster. I was nineteen and I had the pleasure of training with him every

Opposite: The Ireland number 13 jersey will be forever associated with Brian O'Driscoll.

day for nine years. I'm privileged to say I played alongside him. I learned about his professionalism, his work-rate, his mental toughness, all those little things as opposed to the obvious things you might see on a Saturday.

You can be the most talented player in the world but without mental strength you won't succeed. It's too tough an environment and it's too full of ups and downs. If you're not able to cope with the disappointments then you're not going to make it. Every player goes through phases where they start to doubt themselves, doubt their ability, ask themselves those questions – 'Am I cut out for this? Am I able for this level?' That's why mental resolve is vital because you need faith in your ability. That's probably the biggest thing I learned from Brian. He went through times when he was picking up a lot of flak and people said he was finished and he should retire and he'd come out the next week and have a monster game. He had a few years when he was going in and out of that, but he finished exactly how he wanted to finish – on a high.

Johnny Sexton: After scoring two tries and winning the Championship, the France game should have been one of the great highlights of my career, but I didn't enjoy the celebrations. I wasn't on the pitch at the final whistle and I didn't have the euphoria the other lads had. I was concussed and I was in my own little world.

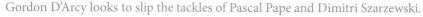

Gordon D'Arcy looks to slip the tackles of Pascal Pape and Dimitri Szarzewski.

Savouring his final few minutes in an Ireland dressing room as a player, Brian
O'Driscoll reads some texts and enjoys a beer with the Six Nations trophy.

That crazy joy that you have with your team-mates, I didn't have that. I was there
on the pedestal when we got the trophy, but I wasn't really there.

I had headaches and I went straight to bed when we got back to the hotel. It
feels like it never really happened. I went into Racing Metro a few days later and
I wasn't sure what kind of reception I was going to get because there was talk in
the newspaper that I might be going back to Leinster. I thought about going in
wearing my Ireland jersey but I ditched that plan.

The boss called me in and he was incredible. He presented me with a scroll with
the Ireland crest on it and this very French quote about rugby being a game of men,
but even when you take away the ball, the man remains. That's probably a terrible
translation, but I knew what they were getting at and it meant an awful lot to me.

Brian O'Driscoll: The thing you miss most when you retire is the camaraderie.
You miss the fun of the dressing room – and this is indescribable at times. It's just
a laugh and it gives you a reason to go in every day because you know you're going
to have good fun.

I miss the night before the game when we'd go to Rala's room to clean our boots. He had a special penknife that he gave me to use. And you'd clean your boots like you'd never clean them otherwise because you'd just want to spend time there. It was fun and you'd have a laugh, and the whole thing was just relaxing. I think that was the best thing about it – if you were a bit stressed about the game, it would just take your mind off it and it gave you a chance to unwind.

I think, outside the Lions, playing for your country is the ultimate honour. I played 133 times for Ireland and I think I could play for another 1033 times and I would never bore of pulling the jersey on, experiencing the feeling of the dressing room before you go out, standing for your national anthem, knowing at times that you really have to dig in when things aren't going well. There are lots of different aspects to the game, but great friendships and camaraderie and the great times you share are the most important ones. I think back to some incredibly magical moments like Paris in 2000, beating Australia in the 2011 World Cup, the Slam, going out with a Six Nations Championship win, they're all memories and links to friends that will remain with me for a long, long time. I don't see much of John Hayes these days, but we fought some hard days alongside one another and I know that you have a chemistry that means that the next time I see him we'll just pick up where we left off. You've lived that moment with him, you've fought hard alongside him and you just know one another, the effort that's gone into achieving the things that we did. That's what stays with you.

Conor Murray looks to snipe between Tendai Mtawarira and
Tebo Mohoje of South Africa.

Joe Schmidt's quest to replace the seemingly irreplaceable was now a live issue. Against South Africa in November 2014, Schmidt picked a new cap to wear the dead weight of the No 13 jersey – the New-Zealand-born Jared Payne who qualified to play for Ireland on the residency rule.

Alongside Payne, in Gordon D'Arcy's No 12 jersey, was the twenty-one-year-old Connacht centre, Robbie Henshaw, who was only six years old when D'Arcy first broke into the Ireland team.

In six months, Ireland had gone from a midfield combination with more than 200 caps to a pairing with just three – and a game with the Springboks to come.

Simon Zebo goes over for Ireland's opening try against Australia.

Schmidt had a long injury list, but you wouldn't have noticed. They blew the South Africans off the park, winning 29-15, the scoreline looking closer than it actually was because of a Springbok try in the last minute.

Joe Schmidt: When I was a kid the South Africans were almost that impenetrable force. I watched All Blacks teams, listened to the radio while All Black teams got beaten in South Africa. Growing up you had this respect and a little bit of awe about them so that game for me was a little bit special. To be 29-10 up with time almost up on the clock and the disappointment of players when they walked off because they had conceded the last try, that was encouraging as well because they could afford to leak it – they weren't going to lose a Test match – but they felt they had set a benchmark during the game that they should have done better with.

The following week we played Australia. I was in pain from appendicitis. I didn't know it was appendicitis. Arthur Tanner, a retired abdominal surgeon, diagnosed it in about thirty seconds after the match. Until then I thought all I had was a bit of gut ache. Probably the toughest thing was that I hadn't slept. It hurt more to lie down. I wandered around my room the night before and it made for a very long day. I hadn't eaten, but you're distracted by the job at hand and adrenaline is a great masker of pain. I have to admit I don't have the highest pain threshold. By the end of the day I was in a fair bit of discomfort but that was tempered by the result against Australia.

Rory Best: We got off to a flier in that match. I wouldn't compare it to the New Zealand game the previous autumn but we scored early and heavily and were leading 17-0 after fifteen minutes. Fifteen minutes after that, it was 17-17 and by half-time it was 20-20. A weird game. Then it went to 23-23 and Johnny had a penalty to put us ahead and he landed it.

Johnny Sexton: The minute the ref signals, the clock starts and you've only got ninety seconds. Straightaway you're switching into an individual sport, not a team sport, and then it's about getting your routine – the steps you take back, the steps you take to the side, getting into that thing that you have practised hundreds of times throughout the week. It's about making sure you do it exactly the same every time and that's where it's hard. The smallest thing can put you off. I missed a kick in the Australia game. There was a baby crying in the crowd. I'm standing there about to take the kick and I'm thinking about my little fella at home and I missed the kick and I'd missed it before I'd taken it. You think of your family in the crowd tearing their hair out, you think, 'Oh my God, you've let the whole country down.' They're the distractions where you have to refocus. It's amazing the stuff can come into your head when you're taking a kick.

Tommy Bowe: There was a massive physical effort involved in holding on to that lead. They were coming at us in waves.

Conor Murray: You have to dig really deep to keep going.

Paul O'Connell: When you're in that situation when the pain is coming on, in the back of your head you're saying to yourself, 'I'm getting better here. This is horrible, but I'm getting better.' When you're on the pitch, when you go to that place where your lungs are struggling and your legs are struggling, you know you've done the work, you know you can work through it.

Robbie Henshaw: You have to stay strong to push yourself through the pain barrier. There's a voice in your head saying, 'Give up now,' but you have to keep fighting.

Joe Schmidt: Some of the leadership, some of the things that were visible, particularly that last two minutes of Australian possession, guys like Paul O'Connell just leading from the front, I thought it was pretty impressive.

Ireland had taken two huge scalps, only adding to the aura surrounding the coach, who was not just proving himself to be an outrageously astute operator but also one who was increasingly beloved by his adopted country. Rob Kearney joked at the time that if Schmidt ran for president then he'd be a certainty to win.

The 2015 Six Nations was a slow-burner. Ireland took more than an hour to see-off Italy in Rome and then won an uncomfortably attritional match against France. They made it three from three when Robbie Henshaw's try was the stand-out in the win over England in Dublin.

All the time, there were gripes in the media about the lack of adventure in Ireland's play, a level of criticism that permeated the bubble that the team and the management normally house themselves in.

Tommy Bowe: There was some flak about our gameplan. Any time we did media stuff there were always one or two questions about us kicking the ball too much and not being exciting to watch. We were never told we weren't allowed to pass or run the ball. Against England, for instance, we went out there to play some rugby but we put two balls up in the air early in the game and they dropped both of them and when we realised that was something that was going to work for us then why would we bother changing it? We wanted to throw the ball about but when you hit on something that works then you do it.

Conor Murray: There was a little bit of flak flying. No player can completely black it out. You can't avoid it in this day and age. If something is being talked about a lot then it'll get to you somehow. There are so many opinions out there and it's guaranteed that somebody isn't going to like what you're doing, that's just the way it is. People got obsessed about our kicking game and it snowballed. Some players got picked on. Some unfair things were said about Jared Payne. I get on well with Jared and he didn't pay attention to it. Most players are well able to deal with it, but it's annoying because sometimes your family, while they say they don't read the newspapers, they probably do and they look for your name and what is being said about you.

Joe Schmidt: One of the things I would say in modern rugby is that there are a lot of big men on the pitch that isn't quite as big. It may look quite big depending on how far up in the stand you are, but there's not a heck of a lot of room out there. Therefore I believe you've got to be three-dimensional in attack. If you play a two-dimensional game, you can only pass the ball backwards, so if you want to go forwards you have to pass it backwards and then carry it forward. The only other way to progress the ball is to use the boot so you have got to be proficient in using all three aspects of the game.

Ireland's kicking game was once again deployed in their fourth match against the Welsh – but Warren Gatland's team were ready for it. Leigh Halfpenny gobbled up every high kick as his team established an early lead that they would not relinquish. Again, the criticism came for Schmidt's tactics.

Joe Schmidt: I was incredibly disappointed with one of the so-called RTE pundits slating one of our midfield [Jared Payne] when I thought he'd played a good game and I thought he actually opened them up. He made a couple of line breaks and was dead solid defensively. That sort of thing, when we're trying to build confidence in players, filters back to players through family and friends and I don't think it helps. I don't think it's accurate, it's one of those unfortunate by-products of having people for entertainment value as opposed to people who are a little bit more in-depth in their analysis.

Tommy Bowe: Wales went 12-0 ahead and they won the 50-50 battles in the air. We came back but we couldn't catch them and it was devastating. Everybody was very deflated afterwards. Training on Monday and Tuesday was very down. I thought it was just me, but it wasn't. Even the coaches were feeling a bit down as well. We had a day off on the Wednesday and it took until Thursday before we had a proper training session and Thursday was decent but still not great. We had a walk-through on Friday. We didn't even have a captain's run on Friday. We just walked around the pitch and had a chat.

Going into the final weekend, Ireland, Wales and England were all in with a shout of winning the title. The one certainty about that famous Saturday was that the title was going to be won on points difference, so tries were key. On that front, Ireland had its doubters.

They had scored just four tries in four games, two from lineout mauls and one a penalty try, against Wales. The defending champions had the fewest tries and the fewest clean breaks of all six nations. 'Gloom seems to be spreading like oil slick,' wrote one correspondent. 'Schmidt's teams have always been defined by intelligence in possession but, against Wales, Ireland resembled bulls charging against a red gable wall.'

Compared to the thoroughbreds of 2014, the 2015 version, it was written, was a dray horse, a bunch of plodders. Schmidt countered by reminding people that the loss to the Welsh was Ireland's first in eleven Tests, but the mood music was set ahead of the final day in the Championship.

Few expected Ireland to win the points race.

Joe Schmidt: After the disappointment of Wales, Paul picked the team up by the scruff of the neck and carried it forward.

Johnny Sexton: He was our captain, our leader. When Paulie spoke to the squad

Sean O'Brien barrels over the try line during a stellar performance against Scotland at Murrayfield.

the hairs on the back of your neck stood up. I don't know if he knew how important his words were.

Robbie Henshaw: Paulie led and everyone else followed. He was just an unbelievable leader. The charisma oozed out of him. He's just an inspirational guy.

Sean Cronin: Whenever Paulie played he made you play better. It was the passion and the physicality he brought and he instilled in the players around him. He set the standard and you had to get up there with him. He demanded it of you one way or another. And his team talks could be very emotional. I've nipped to the toilet a couple of times to dry the eyes. But he scared me more than made me cry, to be honest with you.

Conor Murray: People were saying we wouldn't be able to change the points difference because we weren't playing an expansive game. We had no worries.

Tommy Bowe: When we were driving into Murrayfield we saw everybody sitting outside watching Italy versus Wales on the big screen. Italy had just scored and Wales were only 14-13 ahead at half-time and we were thinking, 'Yes! Game on.' They needed to score a hatful in the second half or else it would be down to just us and England.

Devin Toner: Relaxed is where you want to be. I don't really get hyped up at all. I just kind of get on with it. I don't read the newspapers or see much that goes on. Obviously people want to talk about it but I think I'm just naturally kind of relaxed about it. It doesn't really faze me. It's where you want to be.

Conor Murray: We got to Murrayfield and I went out for the warm-up thinking, 'Nice one, Wales are in a dogfight in Rome.' I came back in, put my jersey on, went to the toilet and I was last in the queue going out for the anthems and I saw Greg Feek, our scrum coach, and I asked him if there was any update on Wales and he said, '61-20', and I asked him to repeat it. 'Sixty-one,' he says. I said, 'Thanks,' but inside my head I was going, 'Oh Jesus, we need to win by something like twenty points now. We have to play seriously well today.'

Tommy Bowe: It was a complete contrast of emotions, from Wales not being a factor to us going, 'Oh my God, they're putting the pressure on here big time.' We had to get a big score, but it was nearly always a one-score game at Murrayfield – three points, five points, seven points. We were confident we could win but winning by the margin we thought we had to win by was going to be difficult. We managed to open them up in the first few minutes and from then on it was the most running we had done in the whole tournament. It was free-flowing.

Conor Murray: Seanie O'Brien scored off a lineout. We hadn't used that move in a good few years. It was an old one. Lukey Fitzgerald came around the tail with me and Seanie went through. That got us going.

Tommy Bowe: We threw the ball around and played some fantastic rugby. We won 40-10, which was a record. It was a weird feeling, though. We should have been delighted, but there wasn't even a cheer. We got changed and went to a massive function room with all the alickadoos and just watched England versus France on the telly and I've never known torture like it.

Conor Murray: We were hopeful. England had to beat France by twenty-six points to catch us. Twenty-six points is a lot. And then we saw France going ahead. Brilliant! They were eight points up after twenty minutes. We were in the dinner room and an SRU man said, 'Look, we won't do any formalities until after the game, so work away at the buffet and good luck.' I went up and got a plate of food and I couldn't touch it because England started scoring all over the place. Then France would score, then England would score again. With five minutes left on the clock England were on twenty points. They only needed one more converted try. I looked over at Pete O'Mahony at one stage and he was just staring at the wall. We were barely able to speak.

Paul O'Connell: Some guys couldn't watch it. Some went in to the reception and just walked around. I was sitting with Dev Toner and Rob Kearney and we were glued to it.

Joe Schmidt: The team was scattered among five or six tables. There were screams at the dinner. We tried to keep an eye on it and not get too involved, but it was pretty inevitable we would be watching it at the end.

Tommy Bowe: I got phone calls from two of my friends who were telling me we were safe and I just had to hang up on them.

Paul O'Connell: When you're in the heat of battle, those nerves don't come into it, but when you're sitting there at a table with a few of the lads and a beer in front of you and you're watching it on TV you're completely powerless.

Paul O'Connell enjoys the conclusion to his final
Six Nations game for Ireland with his son.

Joe Schmidt: It was tumultuous. Exhausting. It builds coronaries for coaches but it also builds character.

Conor Murray: In the last five minutes I was thinking of leaving. I couldn't handle it. I felt ill. Every time England got into the French twenty-two they scored and it looked so easy for them. I was sure they were going to get over and I was sure that George Ford was going to kick the conversion. I thought we were gone. They were banging on France's line, but then France got the penalty and I jumped up with Tommy Bowe and we were hugging each other.

Tommy Bowe: Yes! You beauty!

Conor Murray: And then a Scottish lady from another table tapped me on the shoulder and she said, 'Look!' And Yoann Huget had tapped the penalty and I can't repeat what was said. We probably didn't impress the Scottish people with our language. It was awful. The final whistle was the sweetest sound ever.

Joe Schmidt: The players played one game physically and then they played another game mentally.

Paul O'Connell: God, it was such a tough game to watch. Fair play to England. I thought it was gone at times in the second half. It was absolutely crazy stuff that was going on. Fair play to them, they were incredible.

Tommy Bowe: For once, I could understand how my parents and girlfriend feel when they watch me playing. We were emotionally invested but we had no control over what was going on and it was agony and it's like that for them all the time. My mum is always telling me that I don't have a clue about the angst they go through. That really showed me what it was like to be a supporter on the other side of the fence. But the torture made it that bit more special. To go back out on to the pitch with 15,000 Irish supporters still there, chanting and singing, was surreal and amazing.

Paul O'Connell: Even the crowd afterwards and the music. It was like Robbie Henshaw's twenty-first birthday – the eighties hits coming out.

Conor Murray: My family were there and it was a party atmosphere. I'd never felt elation like that before. Out on the pitch, I was jigging about the place. I got a load of texts from friends about it. 'Look at the state of you – dancing!' I lost all sense of reason. It was magic.

The celebrations begin in a darkened Murrayfield as the
2015 Six Nations champions lift the trophy.

Johnny Sexton: I'm not a great one for looking back and basking in the enjoyment of an achievement, but I know when the time comes for me to start reminiscing I'll think about Murrayfield and I'll break into a great big smile because that was one brilliant day.

Tommy Bowe: We all know how privileged we are to play for our country, but days like that bring it home to you all the more.

Rory Best: It was an honour to be out there, not just that day but every day. Playing rugby for Ireland is not something that I'm going to look back on in five or ten or twenty years and think, 'Wow, wasn't that a special time.' I appreciate it in the here and now. There's a great sense of responsibility and a great sense of pride when it all comes good. That was always there before us and it will always be there after us.

Paul O'Connell: You do your best by the jersey and you pass it on to the next guy. Woody, the Claw and Gaillimh; Rog, Brian and Hayes. We all have our time and then our time is up and everyone gets a little bit sad because it's over, but we're the lucky ones to have had that time in the first place. Rugby has changed so much over the years, but some things haven't changed and never will. The pride in the jersey will always, always be the same.

Paul O'Connell had 101 caps when he let it be known, in June 2015, that he was going to retire from international rugby after the 2015 World Cup, the fourth of his illustrious career. This was his last chance to do something special on the biggest stage of all, the final opportunity to get Ireland into the semi-final for the first time in their history..

Ireland's campaign began without fuss, a 50-7 victory over Canada at the Millennium followed by a 44-10 beating of Romania at Wembley. Their third game was less straightforward, a scratchy 16-9 win over Italy at the Olympic Stadium, which cleared the stage for the big one: the group decider against the French.

The winner would play Argentina in the quarter-final, the loser would have to face the All Blacks. 'Paul spoke really well before the game, he had everyone in tears,' said Chris Henry, who was on the bench that day. 'We talked about being clinical and taking our chances, all these buzzwords, but we knew it was going to take more from us and we'd be going somewhere deeper.'

They went to a place where nobody could have imagined, a place that people scarcely knew existed. In the opening minutes, Sean O'Brien got aggravated by

Pascal Pape and smashed his fist into the solar plexus of the second-row. In that moment, Joe Schmidt knew that he could lose his openside flanker for the quarter-final through citing and suspension.

As the game wore on, Ireland's go-to men started dropping like flies. Jared Payne, one of their most important defensive players, was already out of the World Cup with a fractured foot sustained earlier in the tournament and now they lost Johnny Sexton, their most creative force. Sexton exited with a groin injury and Ian Madigan, in Sexton's shadow for the longest time, came on to replace him. Having lost their leader in the backline they then entered a doomsday scenario when they lost O'Connell.

The captain was going for a poach off Guilhem Guirado, the French hooker, when Pascal Pape and Wesley Fofana drove him off the ball, a clear-out that resulted in O'Connell tearing the tendon from the bone on his hamstring.

Iain Henderson: Coming in to start training with Paul, I learnt a massive amount about how professional he was. He drove you around the pitch. His work-rate inspired you and pushed you harder and further than you thought you could go. I looked at him and learned about his professionalism, not only on the field but off it. His diet, his sleep, the way he looked after himself, his preparation for meetings, walk-throughs, training. The extra few percent. It's only small things but they all add up. I was on the bench when he went down. I was sure he was going to get back up again.

Conor Murray: It looked bad, but I didn't think he was gone, I didn't think that was it. He wasn't getting up, but he always gets up. I went off the field at half-time thinking he was going to get up.

Keith Earls: I was actually next to him when it happened on the pitch and I knew by the sounds of him that it wasn't good. Words can't describe what he has done for his country, for me.

Iain Henderson: After a little while I realised the significance of it because Paul isn't the kind to be rolling around on the ground. How often did you see him go down like that? It's not often you see a man like him roll over.

Paul O'Connell: France were on our line, or close to it, just after I got injured and I was thinking that if they scored without me in the defensive line, it wouldn't be my fault but it wasn't going to help the lads the fact that I was down. It was the worst pain I'd ever had. The pain was going all the way down my leg and into my heel. Apparently when you pull the tendon off the bone you get a lot of bleeding and a lot of bruising, a lot of swelling straight away. I was thinking at the time that I'd only pulled my hamstring, so I'd better get up. But it was too sore. And when the physio and the doctor came on, I was thinking the same thing again – 'It's only my hamstring so I don't need to be stretchered off, just carry me off.' I'd never been stretchered off in my career so I got up again, but I went back down. I got stretchered off and I was on the gas after that. I knew I was out of the World Cup, I knew my international career was over. I got a bit emotional for a little while. It was a just a bit of emptiness.

Conor Murray: Did I see him at half-time? I can't remember. That's terrible, isn't it? I just presumed he was there, I suppose. We went back out and I thought he'd just jog in and join us in the team huddle, but there was no sign of him. I just saw Hendy [Iain Henderson] in the circle. It registered then. Johnny had gone and Paulie had gone. Mads and Hendy are brilliant players, but those were two substantial players to be losing.

Paul O'Connell cries out in pain as the Irish medical team attempt to move him after sustaining his career-ending injury against France.

Iain Henderson: How do you fill Paul O'Connell's boots? You don't. You can't. You just try to do your own thing and hope it's good enough.

Henderson filled the void magnificently, as did Madigan. In as attritional game as you would care to watch, Ireland led 9-6 at the break and 14-9 early in the second half after Rob Kearney's try. Then another leader fell and failed to get up. Peter O'Mahony's knee went in the fifty-fourth minute and on came Henry. Against all odds, Ireland kicked-on. Conor Murray scored a second try and Madigan booted them home from there. A memorable victory had been won, but at a murderously high price.

Conor Murray: Elation was the immediate feeling, then we went in under the stand and Paulie was there. He was in a lot of pain. He was shaking our hand as we walked past. He looked in agony.

Paul O'Connell: I was delighted for the lads. I knew how much pressure they were under, I knew how much they wanted it. I wanted to see their faces and shake their hands and have the crack. The happiness you get from winning is very fleeting. I read a thing a while ago that said the best part of winning is not losing and that rang a bell with me. The ten minutes after the final whistle is the best part. That

The emotion of helping guide Ireland past France is writ large on both Keith Earls' Ian Madigan's faces at fulltime.

ten minutes in the dressing room is the best time and I just wanted to be in there congratulating them. Then I went to hospital to try to straighten the leg. I was given morphine and I don't remember much about the next twenty-four hours.

Conor Murray: I saw Paulie and I was going, 'Oh Jesus, this doesn't look good.' It was a strange and eerie feeling that he might have played his last game. It was one of my best days in an Ireland jersey and also one of my worst.

Sean O'Brien: I had my disciplinary hearing the following week and I got banned for the quarter-final against Argentina. If the shoe was on the other foot I certainly wouldn't have been whingeing or crying about what happened but that's the decision that was made and I think the coach [French coach Philippe Saint-Andre] had a big part to play in it with the way he reacted. Look, it shouldn't have happened. I shouldn't have done it, but they made a good song and dance about it when they had an opportunity. There's a part of me that regrets it and a part of me that doesn't. I think it [the punch] put a statement out to a few of their bully boys that we weren't going to be messed around.

Of the team that won the Six Nations Championship at Murrayfield the previous spring, five players were missing for the Argentina quarter-final – Jared Payne, Johnny Sexton, Paul O'Connell, Peter O'Mahony and Sean O'Brien.

Joe Schmidt: We lost 250-odd caps in the space of eighty minutes against France.

Conor Murray: Did it make a difference in the Argentina game? I'd have to say yes. Are we disrespecting the players who came in? No, because they played unbelievably well, but in terms of a settled team and a well-oiled machine to have that many changes so late, it was disruptive. You'd be foolish to say you could lose players like that and think you could be as good as you were – you can't be. You're missing a lot of quality and experience.

Sean O'Brien: You couldn't have written the script for that quarter-final. A third of the team missing.

Joe Schmidt: Paul was a voice of calm, but it wasn't a voice that was used often; it was his presence. He had a calming presence, an ability to lead men without saying too much, an ability to lead men by doing. Between him and Johnny, they tended to run the team. It's a very player-driven environment and it's hard to keep driving it when you lose the real hub that the wheel turns on and Paul was the axel the hub turned on.

Rory Best: If you look at the senior player group that we had, we got decimated. The boys who came in were very, very good players but when you build your team around a core and you lose your captain, Paulie, one of your main lineout forwards, Pete, you lose your main ball-carrier, Seanie, you lose your main playmaker, Johnny, and somebody who has been really important to us defensively in Jared – they were all key cogs.

Sean O'Brien: It was a huge disappointment to miss it. Huge. I was frustrated because I was fit and the other lads weren't. They couldn't play because they were hurt. I couldn't play because I'd done something silly.

Luke Fitzgerald: I wasn't picked for the Argentina game. I thought I was playing really good rugby at the World Cup and was really disappointed to not get picked. That was a real bugbear. If you actually just pick me here, I'm going to do something. I'm going to do something special. I actually just said to Joe that I completely disagreed. 'I think I'm the right man for the job. From a defensive point of view and from an attack point of view, I think you're making a mistake' and it proved to be right. Without cutting anyone, you can take from that what you will. I told him after he selected the team for Argentina that I thought it was a mistake. He was saying that he obviously didn't think it was a mistake . . . 'Hard luck mate, I make the last call.'

Paul O'Connell: It was horrible. I was looking down at the lads during the anthems and thinking, 'Oh my God, what must they be going through?' When you're in it, it's easier to deal with than when you're watching in the stand. It was such a strange feeling to be that connected to it and yet to be so far away from it. When you're out there on the field you're just playing moment by moment and the bigger picture doesn't distract you. When you're in the stand the bigger picture is the only thing in your head.

Iain Henderson: Argentina came out all guns blazing and we just didn't start the way we usually would. Rory had spoken about it during the week, when we play well we come out firing immediately and try to earn a penalty in the first few minutes. Argentina did to us what we had planned to do to them, which we had done successfully against France.

Argentina did more than that. They'd been impressive in the group stages, running the All Blacks to within 10 points and putting a combined 163 points, and twenty-one tries, on their opponents, Georgia, Tonga and Namibia. They'd played with élan. If Ireland had been at their strongest it would still have been close to a 50-50 game. But Ireland were drastically weakened – and vulnerable.

They were destroyed in the opening dozen minutes, the Pumas scoring through centre Matias Moroni after only two minutes and then scoring again after twelve when the wing Juan Imhoff went through. Ireland were cut to ribbons out wide. They trailed 17-0 before the first quarter was up.

There was a fight-back. Luke Fitzgerald came on to the field and scored a try, then Jordi Murphy scored early in the second half. Along with Madigan's success with the placed ball, Ireland had gone from losing 17-0 to losing 20-17. Then the wheels came off again. The rest of it was brutal. Argentina scored again and again to win 43-20. Ireland had failed to make the semi-final once more.

Sean O'Brien: In games like that you need people to go out there and lead, to step up. We were just off the beat by a yard that day and we got done. Afterwards you're looking around at lads who have given everything on the field knowing that you could have done something to help. That wasn't a nice feeling.

Rory Best: When we lost to Wales in New Zealand at the 2011 World Cup it was easier to deal with because we just didn't play well on the day. We had every opportunity and we didn't take it. This time around it was harder because there's always going to be this 'if only' thing in our heads. If only we'd played Argentina with a full team. We were really happy with the team we went in with, but the thing I struggle with is the thought that if we had had all of our missing players, or even a couple of them, would that little bit of experience been enough to stop us conceding 17 unanswered points at the start of that game?

Paul O'Connell: One of the great regrets for me is not making a semi-final or a final of the World Cup. It was a chance to change how rugby is perceived in Ireland. We talk about New Zealand and their skill level but the fact is that New Zealand are the equivalent of Kilkenny in hurling. They have the best brains, the best athletes, the most skilful and clever footballers playing rugby in New Zealand. Brian Cody would be involved in rugby if he was in New Zealand. Henry Shefflin would be playing first centre or out-half. I'm a rugby man and it's a pity that we missed that opportunity to put rugby further up in the minds of kids in Ireland.

Rory Best: Against Wales in 2011, we had no excuses. We took the field with everybody fit, in form and ready to go. We just took our eye off the ball. We'd beaten them a lot in previous years and we just underestimated them. Whereas this time around we didn't underestimate Argentina, we just got rocked at the start with the speed they played at and made a few fundamental errors and a lot of that was down to missing a spine of experience. What an opportunity it might have been. I feel we would have had enough firepower to overcome them had we had everybody fit.

Tommy Bowe: We didn't do it and in a way we did everything for nothing. The great games are the ones that stay in your mind but the bad ones linger too. That game is one that will last in my memory for a long time.

Conor Murray: I'll tell you a story about coming home from the World Cup. We knew how poor we'd been and we were very low. I spent one night at home. I went to the shop to get some groceries and there was a woman in there doing her shopping and she turned around and said to me, 'It must be difficult to be home, is it?' Irish people can be very blunt. She was right, though. It was really difficult. The next day I went to New York. I'd pre-booked it months before and I was so glad because I missed all the flak flying. I didn't go on Twitter, I turned my phone off, I left it all behind me. I pretended it never happened.

Already the destroyer of two previous Irish World Cup campaigns, Argentina once again deny the men in green a shot at a World Cup semi-final.

Paul O'Connell: That was it for me. Your time comes to an end and you have to move on. That's just the way it is.

Iain Henderson: I look back on the World Cup now and it was massively frustrating, but I had to put it into some sort of context. I'd come a long way. It didn't seem that long since I was messing about in my student house. We had two microwaves in the house – and who needs two microwaves? It was myself and a couple of my mates. We decided one of them could be experimental. We put a massive array of things in there just to see what would happen. Aerosols, eggs, metal, batteries. Now, I wouldn't like to encourage anybody to do this at home. The eggs were the funny one because they exploded. We use to put whole boxes in there and have bets to see whose would last the longest. We'd have them all marked. It all stemmed from one of my brothers. We were always doing all sorts of stupid stuff around the house. My mum got one of those blowtorch things for doing the top of crème brules, but mum disassembled it into three different pieces and hid them in three different places in the house so I couldn't get hold of it. She was worried we were going to start blowtorching things.

That's where I came from, not that long before playing in a World Cup. Some of the boys said that the noise in the Millennium on the day we played France was the loudest they'd ever heard, so it was great to be part of that. Argentina was a soul-destroyer. You let it get to you for a while afterwards, but you have to drive on. You can't mope. There are too many games to play

Joe Schmidt: I know and fully accept the criticism of the World Cup. I'm not sure what people expected, losing our five most influential players the week before and one of them two days before the quarter-final. I take nothing away from an outstanding Argentinian performance but I don't want to go there again.

Ireland came home to a kicking and the mood hadn't lifted any by the time the Six Nations came around. Jared Payne was fit again and took his place in the midfield to face Wales at the Aviva on the opening weekend, but a host of other names were still absent.

Paul O'Connell was in retirement and his replacement, Iain Henderson, was injured. Rob Kearney and Tommy Bowe were also missing. So, too, Peter O'Mahony, Sean O'Brien and Chris Henry. Ireland were decimated to such an extent that Joe Schmidt discounted the notion that his team could become the first in history to win three consecutive outright titles in a row. The coach said he'd be content with a mid-table position.

Schmidt had a big decision about who would take on the captaincy from

O'Connell. Jamie Heaslip and Johnny Sexton were mentioned by many, but the favourite won. Rory Best was named as Ireland's new leader.

Rory Best: Speaking to Paul before he took over from Brian, it was a big challenge stepping into those shoes. Brian, before that, taking over from Woody. Every time there's a bit of change in the captaincy you're filling big shoes because they've been pivotal parts of Irish rugby. It's a challenge but I think the one thing that Paul certainly did really well was that he didn't change how he went about things. He got put in there because of how he was around the place. You don't have to reinvent things just because you're captain. You just keep trying to lead by example.

In the opening game of the campaign, Ireland built a 13-0 lead against the Welsh at the Aviva, only to be pegged back to draw 16-16. It was a point that many thought they wouldn't get given the number of important players they were missing.

There was a first cap for CJ Stander, a twenty-six-year-old farmer from George in South Africa's Western Cape. Stander had played for the Bulls in Super Rugby and had moved to Munster in the summer of 2012. He qualified for Ireland on the residency rule. Stander was immense on his debut and was voted man of the match.

CJ Stander: At the age of twelve everything for me was farming. It was just farm, farm, farm. I didn't really know what rugby could provide. Then I got selected for this U-12 provincial team and that just opened my eyes. The whole group of people were passing the ball left and right. I was getting my hands the wrong way and people were laughing at me. I was a centre at that stage and I couldn't really pass. I started working with my mates on skills.

For sure, when I was a youngster I wanted to play for the Springboks. That's your team, that's your country. Then, when I moved up and became professional, that's where I saw what was going on; who was getting picked and how it was all about size. I started pulling back and not enjoying watching them any more.

When I went to Munster I knew it was on the table to play for Ireland one day and seeing how big rugby is in Ireland, the supporters, the culture, I was getting this feeling that I wanted to play for Ireland that I can't really describe. It was a bigger feeling than I'd had for the Springboks, because when I was a youngster you think you want to play for that team but not really knowing how to get there.

We have the old quote, 'Home is where the heart is', written on the wall at home in Limerick. I would love to say the farm in George is home, but it's not. The last eight years, I've been there for a week or two weeks at a time and that's not enough. When I'm on vacation in South Africa, Limerick is home. My life is here, my wife is here, my dogs, my family is here. Limerick and my house is my home. I've only been here for four years, but that's just the way I live. I remember getting my jersey in the team meeting before the Wales game, going down through the hotel and the support that was there; I was so emotional getting to the bus that I was one more clap away from crying.

Ireland lost their next two games in the Championship, consecutive defeats that hadn't happened since the end of Declan Kidney's time as coach. In Paris, they led from the thirty-eighth minute to the sixty-ninth, but Maxime Medard's try won it 10-9.

Against England at Twickenham they led until the fiftieth minute but the home team, and soon-to-be Grand Slam winners, were too good, winning 21-10. Schmidt deepened his pool of players by giving a first cap to three new talents: the Ulster centre Stuart McCloskey, the Connacht second-row Ultan Dillane and the Leinster back-row Josh van der Flier. In the 58-15 hammering of Italy, another new cap appeared on the scene – the Connacht prop Finlay Bealham. Ireland finished off their campaign with a 35-25 victory over the Scots at the Aviva. In the post-O'Connell age they had finished where Schmidt had thought they would finish – mid-table.

In the summer of 2016, Ireland went to South Africa for a daunting three-Test series, the first in Cape Town, the second in Johannesburg and the third in Port Elizabeth. They went there yet again dogged by injuries. One withdrawal followed another – Rob Kearney, Dave Kearney, Simon Zebo, Tommy Bowe, Luke Fitzgerald, Johnny Sexton, Cian Healy, Nathan White, Sean O'Brien, Peter O'Mahoney and Josh van der Flier.

Between them, more than 420 caps. The Springboks were also much-changed. They were missing seven of the team from the two-point loss to the All Blacks in the World Cup semi-final, among them some of the most iconic names in South African rugby. Victor Matfield, Fourie du Preez, Bryan Habana, Schalk Burger and the du Plessis brothers, Bismarck and Jannie, were all absent for reasons of retirement, injury and through the decision-making of the new coach, Allister Coetzee. For that opening Test in Newlands, Cape Town, Schmidt gave a first cap in two years to the Ulster centre Luke Marshall and only the second start in two and a half years to the Ulster fly-half Paddy Jackson. He used Tadhg Furlong, the prop, off the bench. Furlong had only played eighty-five minutes of international rugby. Craig Gilroy was also used. It was his first time wearing the green jersey in eighteen months.

Ireland weren't given much, if any, chance of winning a Test. They'd gone to South Africa first in 1961 – and lost. In all, they had played the Springboks on their own turf seven times, losing all seven in a combined score of 186-80 and on an aggregate try-count of 24-8.

Devin Toner: My father passed away the week before we were due to leave and the whole family were saying, 'You're definitely going on tour', so I didn't really have an option to be honest. They were telling me I was going. Then, it was hard for me to get my head around it at the start, getting back into things and then at the start of the week I wasn't feeling great but as we started getting closer to the Test match it kind of clicked that this was obviously a massive Test match with history to be made. All the lads were so supportive. They were all down at the funeral as well.

Conor Murray: The hope was that we'd catch them. That's always the hope when you go to the southern hemisphere in the summer. The first Test is your biggest chance. They had a new coach and lots of pressure to win. I thought we had a very decent chance.

Andrew Trimble: We began well. Jared started at full-back for the first time and he scored early. We were 10-3 ahead when it happened.

Ian Henderson: CJ was competing for a ball in the air with Pat Lambie and Lambie hit the ground. I didn't think much of it, then the referee gets out his red card.

CJ Stander runs past the Springboks as he leaves the field after receiving his red card.

Mike Ross: A red card for that? It was incredible.

Conor Murray: None of us could believe it.

Joe Schmidt: The red card was very, very harsh. CJ had both hands extended. Once you're in the air you cannot change your trajectory. I know CJ and Patrick are friends. CJ was upset that Patrick was hurt as much as he was upset that he had to leave the field. Sometimes I think when there is an injury like that, the consequence is that a card comes out.

Within nine minutes of Stander leaving the field, the South Africans had scored 10 points to make it 13-10 to the home team. In the build-up to their try, Robbie Henshaw was done for a late and high hit on Elton Jantjies and was sin-binned. Ireland were now down to thirteen men for ten minutes.

Mike Ross: I remember Rory turned to us underneath the posts after they scored the try and said, 'If you want a challenge lads, here it is. Just think of the reward if we manage to pull this off.'

Joe Schmidt: Those minutes before half-time when we were down to thirteen players – to scramble and work as hard as they did to survive, they can be incredibly proud.

They did more than survive. They drew level. Paddy Jackson's drop goal made it 13-13 at the break, but even still, nobody would have given tuppence for their chances. Then it got interesting again. Two minutes after the restart, Conor Murray went over for his fifth try in eight Tests, a scoring rate that any winger in the world would have been happy with not to mind any scrum-half.

Ireland dug in heroically. Jackson's boot put them further ahead at 23-13 before South Africa struck back with a converted try from Pieter-Steph du Toit. There were twelve minutes left and only three points in it.

The fourteen men secured a momentous, history-making victory when Jackson put over another penalty four minutes from time. Nothing that the Springboks threw at Ireland in those closing stages was good enough to break the visitors' resistance.

Rory Best: We knew we had to keep going at them and at them because if you sit back against the Springboks and try to soak them, it's just not going to work; they're too big, too good a rugby team.

Andrew Trimble: I went into the scrums. Believe it or not, we did actually look at

Jared Payne crosses to score in the first Test.

the forward roles in training. I'm not sure if Joe meant it seriously but even if he meant it as a little bit of a joke, there's a little bit of seriousness there. There was one or two times on our scrum when I was torturing Jamie, trying to find out what I needed to do, but it all fell into place.

Mike Ross: It was pretty tough, especially when they got that du Toit try. I was like, 'Please, let's hang on for five minutes, another five minutes.'

Conor Murray: Right at the end they came on a serious wave and moved it wide. JP Pietersen was bearing down on the try line.

Jared Payne: I made the tackle and was just lucky enough to get a bit of help from a few boys because he's a tough competitor is JP. There was nothing going through my head except to try and stop this big guy running at me as best I could.

Mike Ross: There's like two or three lads coming across, fighting with each other to get to him. That was really heartening to see.

Rory Best: We dug really, really deep to get that win. It was really tough. There's a reason no Irish team has ever done it and to do it for just short of sixty minutes with fourteen men took a lot of character. You tell a lot about the individuals you have at your disposal by what they do when they're faced with adversity. What a way to make history

Luke Marshall: It was special, extra-special because I felt a long way from the Test scene for a long time. A year earlier I felt a long way from the Ulster team and to be honest at the start of the season I was thinking about moving on elsewhere. A couple of decisions in that match we couldn't believe, but we needed to come together as a team. We knew we could get through it. We just sort of embraced the challenge. The experienced players stepped up. Rory talked to us, Jamie was incredible at No 8, Jared at full-back was a really calming influence. Those guys stepped up and calmed us younger guys down a bit. Conor was massive, too. There's a lot of leaders in this team.

Andrew Trimble: We were clever. Streetwise.

Iain Henderson: An incredible feeling. Indescribable actually.

Mike Ross: South Africa? Foaming at the mouth.

Joe Schmidt knew that he couldn't send the same team out again to play the Springboks, not after the physical toil of the first Test and the knowledge of what awaited them in the third one. He shuffled his deck. Quinn Roux, the twenty-five-year-old Connacht lock from Pretoria, was parachuted into the Test team for his debut.

Given that Roux had been a bit-part player in Connacht's Pro12 success, his inclusion in Schmidt's squad was a surprise. The fact that he was now in the starting line-up was a shock. Stuart Olding, the twenty-three-year-old Ulster centre, was named in the midfield for just his third cap. There was more new blood on the bench. Sean Reidy, the New Zealand-born back-row, made his debut as a substitute. So, too, Tiernan O'Halloran, the Connacht full-back. Finlay Bealham, the Connacht prop, ran on for just his second cap. It was a day of drama, an afternoon that promised history but that ended in despair.

Ireland began thunderously. Paddy Jackson booted them ahead and then Devin Toner scored a try that put the visitors into a 19-3 lead approaching half-time. Just short of the hour-mark, Jamie Heaslip crashed over for another try. Ireland now led 26-10. Having rewritten the record books with their first Test triumph in South Africa the previous weekend, they now looked certain to clinch the series.

Conor Murray: It was painful. Sickening, actually.

Devin Toner: They brought on their subs and the game changed. They threw everything at us. In fairness to them, they hit us with a lot.

Jamie Heaslip crosses to score in the second Test, but momentum
in the series was soon to turn, irresistibly, South Africa's way.

Joe Schmidt: They delivered an onslaught that we didn't quite match up to.

Rory Best: They got around the corner, they carried and we started to soak tackles
which is something that even before we left Dublin we talked about. If we got
physically beaten up by South Africa around the fringes we were going to be on
the back foot and if you go on the back foot against a team like that you're going
to be struggling.

Andrew Trimble: They scored a try and then another. It was a fierce battering.
They scored 23 points in the last eleven minutes. We'd no answer to it.

Joe Schmidt: How often do you get that opportunity to create a bit of history?
Very few teams win a Test series in South Africa and we had the chance that day.

Andrew Trimble: We just couldn't get over the line. We did everything but score.
If they'd given us a hiding it would have been easier to take. We lost 32-26. Then
we were ahead again in the third Test. Luke Marshall scored a try and we were 10-3

after twenty minutes. They pegged us back. Six points we lost by. Six points. Three Tests and a single score in each of them at the end. Nobody would have thought that before we left. Not that it was much consolation to us.

Conor Murray: It wasn't any consolation. That hurt, big-time. It's a cruel sport sometimes. The loss to New Zealand in Dublin, to loss to Argentina in the World Cup and the loss of the series in South Africa when it was there for us to win. These things torment you for a while. The what-might-have-beens can eat you up, but you have to move on. Once you stood back from the South Africa tour, you could see the positives, you could see all these new players that were coming into the mix, you could see that the squad had expanded and Joe's options had become greater. A new generation was beginning to appear over the horizon. That's exciting.

It was a galling loss in that third Test given the fact that Ireland had sixty-eight per cent possession and seventy-three per cent territory. They beat twenty-five defenders to South Africa's five. They had nine line breaks to South Africa's one. They carried for 405 metres. The Springboks carried for 154. The bottom line was defeat, though. So close and yet so far.

Eoin Reddan retired in the wake of that loss in Port Elizabeth. It was always his intention. He'd won seventy-one caps over ten years and exited with a good memories. 'For the lads going forward it was a brilliant tour,' he said. 'Look at the players we have now. A bit of bravery, a bit of dreaming will do them all good. If they aim high enough, there's no stopping them.'

Luke Fitzgerald was next to go. Gone before his time at the age of twenty-eight. He retired with a neck injury and with thirty-four caps. He would have had many more had the game been kinder to him.

Fitzgerald was another broken link to the Grand Slam winners of 2009. O'Driscoll and Gordon D'Arcy; Fitzgerald, Ronan O'Gara and Tomas O'Leary; Marcus Horan, Jerry Flannery and John Hayes; Paul O'Connell and Donncha O'Callaghan; Stephen Ferris and David Wallace. All have left the Test stage. So, too, the subs who came into battle on that famous day at the Millennium – Denis Leamy, Peter Stringer, Paddy Wallace, Geordan Murphy.

It's as Jack Kyle said all those years ago, though. It's as Willie John McBride and Keith Wood and Paul O'Connell repeated in his wake. You have your day and you're lucky to have it. Then along come others – and that's the way it should be.